CULTURAL DIVERSITY
AND THE
U.S. MEDIA

SUNY Series, Human Communication Processes
Donald P. Cushman and Ted J. Smith III, Editors

CULTURAL DIVERSITY AND THE U.S. MEDIA

Edited by

YAHYA R. KAMALIPOUR
THERESA CARILLI

Foreword by

GEORGE GERBNER

State University
of New York
Press

Published by
State University of New York Press, Albany

© 1998 State University of New York

Production by Susan Geraghty
Marketing by Patrick Durocher

Printed in the United States of America

For information, address State University of New York
Press, State University Plaza, Albany, N.Y., 12246

Library of Congress Cataloging-in-Publication Data

Cultural diversity and U.S. media / [edited by] Yahya R. Kamalipour,
    Theresa Carilli.
        p.   cm. — (SUNY series, human communication processes)
    Includes bibliographical references and index.
    ISBN 0-7914-3929-1 (alk. paper). — ISBN 0-7914-3930-5 (pbk. :
alk. paper)
    1. Mass media and minorities—United States. 2. Mass media and
ethnic relations—United States. 3. Mass media and race relations-
-United States. 4. Pluralism (Social sciences)—United States.
5. United States—Ethnic relations. I. Kamalipour, Yahya R.
II. Carilli, Theresa. III. Series: SUNY series in human
communication processes.
P94.5.M552U628 1998
302.23'089'00973—dc21   97-43215
                                                            CIP

10 9 8 7 6 5 4 3 2 1

To my family: Mah, Niki, Shirin, and Daria

—YRK

For my sisters Angie and Gigi, whom I cherish

—TC

CONTENTS

Part III. MASS MEDIA AND CONFLICTS

ILLUSTRATIONS

TABLES

FOREWORD

For the first time in human history, most of the stories about people, life, and values are told not by parents, schools, churches, or others in the community who have their own stories to tell but by a group of distant media conglomerates that have something to sell. This is a radical change in the way we employ creative talent, the way we cast the symbolic environment, and the way we learn our roles in life.

The roles we grow into and the ways others see us are no longer homemade, handcrafted, community-inspired. They are products of a complex image manufacturing and marketing process. The cast of characters and their fate we see every day in the media shape our images of the roles we try to seek or to avoid. The issue of cultural diversity in the U.S. media is at the very core of that process.

Channels multiply but communication technologies converge, media merge, staffs shrink, and creative opportunities diminish. Fewer sources fill more outlets more of the time with ever more standardized fare. Global marketing streamlines production, homogenizes content, sweeps alternative imagery from the mainstream, and moves cultural policy beyond democratic or even national reach.

There is no historical precedent, constitutional provision, or legislative blueprint to confront the new consolidated controls over the design, production, promotion, and distribution of media content and the iniquitous portrayals embedded in it. Informed opinion leading to independent citizen action offer our best hope for meeting that challenge. A movement toward a free, diverse, and fair cultural environment has become a necessity for democracy in the telecommunication age.

This book is a guide to such judgment and action. It maps the territory where stereotypes of women and men, young and old, rich and poor, people of color, various racial and ethnic groups, natives and foreigners, and so-called majorities and minorities compete and conflict and occasionally find ways to speak for themselves in the cultural mainstream.

The focus is on what large communities absorb over long periods of time. It is on recurrent and inescapable images of the cultural environment in which we all live. These images cultivate conceptions of majority and minority status and the corresponding calculus of visibility, power, and risk.

The lessons of the chapters that follow are essential for readers concerned with communication, culture, and community. They can be useful also for the media industry—the people who sponsor it, run it, write, produce, and direct its content. Understanding the cultural territory is the first requirement for successful intervention. This book will help move us toward such understanding.

George Gerbner
Professor and Dean Emeritus
Annenberg School of Communication
University of Pennsylvania

ACKNOWLEDGMENTS

Foremost, we would like to offer our deepest gratitude to the contributing authors of this book, for without their genuine support and interest, this project could not have materialized. Also, many thanks go to the authors' colleges/universities and organizations for providing financial, research, administrative, and secretarial support to them during the course of this project.

Furthermore, we are indebted to Michael R. Moore, Dean of the School of Liberal Arts, and William L. Robinson, Head of the Department of Communication and Creative Arts, Purdue University Calumet, for their valuable support and encouragement in terms of granting us research release time, financial, and secretarial support throughout this project.

We are grateful to Dennis H. Barbour, Head of the English and Philosophy Department at Purdue University Calumet for his conscientious reviews, comments, and editorial assistance. We would also like to extend our gratitude to Professors Jane Campbell and Thomas Roach for their insights, advice, and editorial perspicacity. Also, thanks to Sue Roach and Adrienne Viramontes for their assistance. Elizabeth Paschen, the secretary of the Department of Communication and Creative Arts, also deserves to be mentioned for her assistance in typing/retyping some of the articles.

We are, of course, indebted to our families and friends for their love, emotional support, and understanding throughout this project.

INTRODUCTION

Culture is the medium evolved by humans to survive. Nothing in our lives is free from cultural influences. It is the keystone in civilization's arch and is the medium through which all of life's events flow. We are culture.

—Edward T. Hall

In contemporary global society, culture, media, and communication are inextricably bound together. We no longer learn about our cultures merely through the elderly or through printed materials. Today, the multinational conglomerates, employing the modern electronic media, have permeated practically every aspect of our daily lives. They have succeeded not only in marketing and selling their products worldwide, but, in the process, have promoted a "culture of consumption" that is slowly eroding the traditional or indigenous cultures of the world. In other words, indigenous cultures have been overshadowed by the culture of consumption.

We now live in a mass-mediated cultural environment in which the mass media play a crucial and often decisive role in the enhancement or destruction of images of other people, places, religions, and nations of the world. For instance, much of what we know (or think we know) about other peoples and places comes to us primarily in an array of prepackaged programs such as news, soap operas, sitcoms, features, commercials, talk shows, and so on. Consequently, we often focus our attention on daily events and other matters in tandem with what the media choose to report or portray. In other words, "we are not born knowing what clothes to wear, what toys to play with, what foods to eat, which gods to worship, or how to spend our money or our time" (Samovar, L. A., & Porter, R. E., *Communication Between Cultures*, 1995, p. 45).

A quick survey of the global cultural environment indicates that in terms of foods McDonald's,™ Pizza Hut,™ Kentucky Fried Chicken,™ and Burger King™ have tantalized the taste buds of people, especially the youth, throughout the world. In terms of music, American celebrities such as Michael Jackson, Madonna, and others have gathered followers, especially among the youth, in countries such as Iran, Botswana, Saudi Arabia, Nigeria, Chile, Russia, Poland, England, and elsewhere. In terms of fashion, Western clothing, makeup, and even hairstyles are used to symbolize modernity and civility. In terms of news and information, four major wire services (Associated Press, United Press International, Reuters, Agence France Presse) provide most of what people see, hear, or read, via the media, throughout the world.

Clearly, the 1990s have ushered in a multiplicity of questions about cultural awareness and sensitivity while engendering appreciation for various racial and ethnic groups. Ironically, as journalists have debated issues ranging from political correctness to affirmative action, the mass media themselves have been scrutinized for unfair depictions of marginalized groups. *Cultural Diversity in the U.S. Media* presents provocative forays into the depictions of various racial and ethnic groups who reside in the United States, challenges media portrayals, and critiques the prevailing American culture.

Some of the common themes presented in this book include the following:

- *Stereotyping*: Stereotyping, based on historical, political, or social information (or misinformation) is insidious, very much alive though sometimes covert, and continues to damage the target group. As negative constructs, media stereotypes produce at least two tangibly deleterious effects. For cultural nonmembers, stereotypes can contain and limit the potential of a specific cultural group. For cultural members, stereotypes can become internalized components of identity that insidiously affect members' views of their opportunities or choices.

- *Self-identity*: The second emerging theme is about identity and the process of negotiating identity when cultural nonmembers look through a stereotyped lens. For instance, the phrase "people of color" used to replace the inaccurate "minority" represents one such reconfiguration of identity. As an empowering term, "people of color" mandates a richer, more positive construction of identity. This phrase asserts place and value in White hegemonic society, while "minority" indicated a sublevel or even subhuman group. With this new labeling comes the request for the media to embrace and give richer, more positive depictions of people of color.

  Simultaneously, "White" ethnics, challenged by this dichotomy between White people and people of color, are reclaiming their place in American history. Ethnic groups such as African-Americans, Arab-Americans, Asian-Americans, Euro-Americans, Greek-Americans, Italian-Americans, Iranian-Americans, Latinos, Native-Americans, Polish-Americans, and other ethnic groups are evaluating their place and value in a White Anglo-Saxon society and are calling for accurate media depictions as well. This awareness of identity brings a request for the media to represent the experiences of all racial and ethnic groups with greater authenticity and frequency.

- *Status quo:* While the experiences of people of color and ethnic groups might be represented in the media with more frequency than ever before, this representation evokes the status quo. For instance, American media can show images of people of color and other ethnic groups as long as the white Anglo-Saxon character emerges as the victor. Instead of allowing the cultural groups to resolve their conflicts in a manner that is culturally appropriate to them, the great Anglo-Saxon way often intervenes to demonstrate truly appropriate behavior. Such status quo depictions acknowledge America's true indifference to difference.

- *Media responsibility:* The papers in this book point to the responsibility the mass media have to facilitate cultural awareness and understanding. Having the economic resources to address social issues that are critical to harmony in America, the media must lead the way in the 21st century and beyond. The media must take a stand, promoting cultural awareness and teaching people to recognize and embrace difference, or else the media will be viewed as divisive and destructive communication channels.

Cultural Diversity in the U. S. Media is a wake-up call to the American mass media to reevaluate their social responsibilities, to realize their crucial role in American society, and to balance their portrayals of cultural groups. It asks the media to take actions that are motivated by humanistic principles rather than by primarily capitalistic principles.

This book is divided into four parts: Introductory Perspectives, Mass Media and Ethnicity, Mass Media and Conflicts, and Mass Media and Education.

Part I, "Introductory Perspectives," lays the groundwork for the book by illustrating, through numerous examples of institutionalized discrimination, how ethnic depictions or depictions of people of color/minorities have changed only slightly, if at all. Whether it be through newsprint cartoons or the Disney empire, subtle forms of racism are prevalent in the American media. These introductory perspectives cast a critical eye on media organizations which pride themselves on fairness and objectivity, yet are unwilling to examine their own treatment of ethnic groups.

Part II, "Mass Media and Ethnicity," demonstrates the insidiousness of stereotyping and the resulting consequences. By taking a closer look at the themes outlined in Part I, namely those of subtle racism and institutionalized discrimination, this section challenges issues of fairness to particular ethnic groups based on negative stereotypes which continue to feed American consciousness. Some stereotypes have even subsumed the ethnic group, rendering its members as a caricature. These articles, some authored by members of the ethnic groups under study, identify some of the difficult and painful trials of understanding oneself being viewed only as a stereotype.

The essays in part III, "Mass Media and Conflicts," provocatively demonstrate the ways that the media create division between cultural groups. Through these articles, we see just how media can create a consciousness about an ethnic group, whether that be a "raced" consciousness or the consciousness of being "enemy." This development of an "otherness" consciousness, inherent through the descriptions of conflict between ethnic groups, promotes ill will toward specific groups, and further marginalizes those groups.

Part IV, "Mass Media and Education," describes some of the ways in which the media attempt to educate students, as well as the masses, about cultural matters. Often, instead of educating and explaining ethnic difference, the media tend to reinforce the consciousness of "otherness." These papers raise issues about what it means to understand the message behind being "culturally diverse."

Our intention for this anthology has been to contribute to the existing literature on media effects, intercultural communication, and cultural awareness, while encouraging a dialogue about the U.S. media and their depictions of ethnic groups through papers that are descriptive and, at times, personal. We hope that *Cultural Diversity in the U.S. Media* will encourage interested readers, scholars, students, media professionals, media conglomerates, and other groups to examine and reexamine some of the consequences of mass media's depictions of racial and ethnic groups, and to envision racial and ethnic identity as a component of American identity that should be understood and appreciated, not simply dismissed.

In short, this book is intended to mitigate the relationships between the mass media and ethnic communities in the United States, to promote a constructive dialogue, and to foster an understanding of the ways in which individuals come to know and perceive various racial and ethnic groups. Of course, studies relative to the issues raised in this book, including scholarship that would reflect and critique the ways in which the electronic media (radio, television, movies, music) and print media (newspaper, magazines, books) represent and portray images of cultural groups, should become routine and integrated into the educational system in the United States and elsewhere. In the final analysis, there is no "them"—it's only "us."

PART I

Introductory Perspectives

CHAPTER 1

U.S. Minorities and the News

Bradley S. Greenberg
and Jeffrey E. Brand

Social science research on specific media behaviors and orientations of U.S. minorities to general mass media is sparse; extant literature focuses on minority portrayals in entertainment and is confined largely to Black Americans, with rare additional studies of Hispanic Americans (Greenberg & Brand, 1994), let alone other ethnic groups. A social science focus on minorities and news is even more rare.

News and minority studies derive from a single question: How are they portrayed? Surely, this is an important query, but it begs other important questions: How are minorities represented in the news industry workforce? What use is made of the news? What are the attitudes of minorities toward the news? What effects does news have on minority and majority groups? The pastiche assembled here integrates the best research entries for such questions. But the skeletal character of this research quickly becomes clear. Conclusive findings in the social sciences generally are difficult to produce; here, they suffer further from lack of replication and lack of theory if not lack of interest.

With these caveats, we advance five propositions concerning news and minorities. Not examined here for economy of space is research on perceptual, attitudinal, and behavioral effects of news on minority audiences (cf. Armstrong, Neuendorf, & Brentar, 1992; Tan & Tan, 1979).

1. News industry goals for minority *employment* have not been realized;
2. *Representation* of Black and Hispanic Americans in news is consistent with population proportions, but the context of portrayals is questionable;

3. Black and Hispanic Americans *use* television and radio for news more and newspapers less than Whites, and they favor soft news content;
4. *Minority leaders* argue majority media inadequately cover their community and should incorporate more minorities in mainstream news operations; and
5. *Minority publics' attitudes* are positive toward mainstream news, particularly among younger audiences, but they prefer same-race television reporters and anchors.

MINORITY EMPLOYMENT IN THE NEWS INDUSTRY

Minority employment in the news industry does not compare with minority population proportions. Thompson (1989) reported that minorities total 21% of the U.S. population and are expected to comprise 28% by the year 2,000. About 12% of the U.S. population is Black, 9% of Hispanic origin, 3% Asian, and 1% Native American (Bureau of the Census, 1990).

Despite the Kerner Commission's 1968 recommendations to improve news coverage of minorities by bringing more minority reporters, editors, and managers into news organizations, only modest changes have been made in the past quarter-century. Consider separate data for the newspaper and broadcast news industries.

Newspapers

With an American Society of Newspaper Editors' (ASNE) 1978 goal of a threefold increase in the number of minority employees working in newsrooms by the year 2000, there evolved only a modest 1.8% increase from 2,811 minority newsroom professionals in 1978 to 2,862 by 1984. Overall, minorities in 1994 comprised 10.5% of daily newspaper staffs compared with an estimated 9% in 1989 and 1% in 1968 (Sunoo, 1994; Martindale, 1991; Thompson, 1989). Minority composition varies by circulation; however; all U.S. dailies with circulations of more than 100,000 have minorities on their news staffs, whereas only 43% of those dailies with circulations between 10,000 and 25,000 do (Thompson, 1989). According to the most recent ASNE data, 55% of American newspapers employ Black, Hispanic, Asian, and Native American journalists, but 45% have no minorities on staff (Sunoo, 1994).

Thompson (1989) reveals further inequities across job levels. In 1989, 93% of all *copydesk* jobs in U.S. dailies were held by Whites compared with 4% held by Blacks, 2% by Hispanics, and 1% by Asians. The Kerner Commission found that 5% of editorial jobs were held by

Blacks in 1968. Today, Black Americans fill 6% of editorial jobs, Hispanics 2%, Asian Americans 1%, and Native Americans, less than .5%. In 1968, less than 1% of daily newspaper supervisors were Black; in 1989, 95% of newsroom supervisors were White, 3% percent were Black, 1% Hispanic, 1% Asian, and less than 1% were Native American. No Blacks were publishers of major daily newspapers in 1968. In this area there has been progress. By the late 1980s, there were seven Black publishers, three Hispanics, and one Asian American publisher in the United States (Thompson, 1989).

Today, most minority news workers are reporters (53%), 17% copy editors, 17% supervisors, and 13% photographers or artists (Sunoo, 1994).

Television and Radio News

Eleven percent of broadcast newsworkers are minorities (Thompson, 1989). A mail survey of 375 television and 355 radio stations in 1987 showed that 64% of all commercial television stations and 15% of commercial radio stations employed minorities compared with 63% and 16% in 1972 (Stone, 1988); the broadcast industry experienced no additional penetration across individual TV and radio stations in those 15 years.

Numbers of minorities in TV news have been in decline since the mid-1970s when 16% of that workforce was minority (Guimary, 1984). In 1979, 15% of TV news personnel were minorities and in 1982, 14%. Stone (1988) found from his mail survey of TV and radio stations that 13% of TV news professionals and 10% of the radio news workers were minorities in 1987. Women (both minority and majority) increased their share of the TV and radio news workforce, while minority males, especially Blacks, lost ground.

Weaver and others (1985) found that 8% of all television news *reporters and editors* were Black and 1% Hispanic. In radio, 3% of reporters and editors were Black and 1% Hispanic. Stone (1988) found that 10% of TV reporters were Black, just over 3% were Hispanic, 1% were Asian American, and less than .5% were Native American. One job where minority males were overrepresented was news photography, a job that paid the least of editorial positions and was viewed as a career "dead-end."

Of all commercial TV news anchors, 7% were Black, 2% were Hispanic, 1% Asian American, and less than .5% were Native American. In radio news, 5% of anchors were Black, 2% Hispanic, and less than 1% each Asian and Native American.

The proportion of *news directors* in television and radio remained unchanged from 1981 to 1987; 4% were minorities in television and 6% in radio news organizations. Most minority news directors at commercial TV stations were Hispanic (75%), while at radio stations, Blacks filled most (57%) of the minority directorships. No Native American or Asian American news directors were found at TV stations. One percent of radio stations had Native American news directors, while less than .5% had Asian American directors (Stone, 1988).

Of TV *news producers*, 8% were Black, 4% were Hispanic, 2.4% were Asian American, and less than .5% were Native American. Finally, 8% of supervisory positions in commercial TV news operations were held by minorities (Stone, 1988).

The available research suggests that minorities are underemployed in the news industry. While gains are being made in the newspaper industry, progress in broadcasting may be diminishing.

PORTRAYALS OF MINORITIES IN THE NEWS

Content analysis research on minorities in U.S. news is dated and limited in scope. What follows are summaries of research on Black and Hispanic Americans; social science research focusing on Asian and Native Americans has yet to be developed. Although these reviews are necessarily abridged, they suggest increasing numbers of Black and Hispanic Americans with the accuracy of those representations still in question.

To begin, Dodd, Foerch, and Anderson (1988) examined how often women and racial minorities from the United States made the covers of *Time* and *Newsweek* in the decades from 1950 through the 1980s. Women appeared on 15% and minorities on 7% of the 897 covers. Minorities were on 3% of the covers in the 1950s, 12% in the 1960s, and 6% in both the 1970s and 1980s. Women and minorities were portrayed more often in lower status and anonymous roles than majority males; the minorities were most frequently represented in sports (27%) and miscellaneous (13%) categories; they were twice as likely as Whites to be anonymous.

Black Americans

By the early 1970s, Blacks were becoming more visible in the news, and studies suggested they were increasingly seen in at least relative proportion to their representation in the population. Blacks were found in 13% of news magazine pictures by Stempel (1971), in 25% of network television newscasts by Baran (1973), and in 23% of network TV newscasts by Roberts (1975), although primarily in nonspeaking roles on segments dedicated to busing, segregation, and other civil rights issues. In 1979, the U.S. Commission on Civil Rights (1979) reported that less than 2% of the network news stories dealt with minorities, a smaller proportion than two years earlier, and that 8% of the correspondents were minorities.

Martindale (1984) found that coverage of Black Americans in a midwestern newspaper between 1950 and 1980 varied in relationship to the rise and fall of the civil rights movement: total news hole during the 1970s (15%) was less than half of its 1960s figure (33%) and equivalent to the 1950s (13%). She found that among four major metropolitan daily newspapers, coverage of Blacks increased from the 1960s to the 1970s for two of them and remained relatively stable for the other two (Martindale, 1985). In the 1970s, coverage of Blacks in everyday life was the predominant topic. Stereotyped stories comprised 14% of the newshole on Black Americans then. Coverage of Black problems ranged from 3% to 13% across the papers and less space was given to the coverage of Black protest causes and activities.

Martindale later (1987) extracted the category of stereotyped news coverage for more intensive analysis in which she compared coverage of Blacks involved in criminal activities, and of Blacks as entertainment figures, as protesters, and as politicians. Taking as a baseline the total coverage of Blacks in the newspaper, criminal activities coverage ranged from 3% to 12% in the four dailies; Blacks as entertainers ranged from 5% to 9%; Blacks as protesters was exactly 1% in all four papers; and the coverage of Black politicians ranged from 8% to 20%. Overall, there was little change from the 1960s to 1970s in coverage of Blacks in criminal activities, a sharp increase in coverage as entertainers, a sharper increase in coverage as politicians, and a striking decrease in presenting them as protesters (from 15% in the 1960s to 1% in the 1970s).

Elaborating Martindale's finding that newspapers increased their coverage of Blacks in politics, Chaudhary (1980) examined newspaper coverage of Black and White elected officials during 1974 and 1976 elections in 19 metropolitan cities in which the Black population exceeded 200,000. White elected officials received significantly more coverage on election day and two days before the election, and they received more favorable placement on the front page and inside front page above the fold, where most of the election stories were located. Black elected officials received longer stories, averaging 300 words compared to 225 for White officials, but significantly more negative stories appeared for Black elected officials than for Whites.

Womack (1986, 1988) examined the extent of Black participation in network presidential convention broadcasts comparing 1972 and 1976 with 1984 coverage. He found no differences among the networks in their presentation of race and gender, but significantly more Blacks were interviewed in 1984 than earlier. Furthermore, Blacks were interviewed in greater proportion than their relative delegate strength, although interviewees were most likely to be rank-and-file delegates.

In sharp contrast to the coverage of Blacks in politics, Pritchard (1985) examined newspaper coverage of 90 homicide prosecutions in Milwaukee from 1981 to 1983. Pritchard determined that: (a) stories with minority suspects were shorter; (b) although the Milwaukee newspapers overall provided what was assessed as fair coverage of 80% of the homicides, nevertheless minority suspects were less likely to receive fair coverage; and (c) minority suspects were less likely to receive thorough coverage.

Entman recently demonstrated that subtle visual and audio distinctions in television news portrayals of Blacks and Whites accused of crimes appear to be presenting "modern racism" to viewers (1992). Entman reinforced the findings that Blacks are presented often: 37% of the newshole prominently featured Blacks. However, video and audio contexts provide evidence that *how* Blacks are being portrayed is less egalitarian. Entman found video portrayals of Blacks accused of crimes compared with Whites were: (1) more dehumanizing because Blacks were less often shown in motion than Whites (movement indicates more humanity, shows emotion and expression), and (2) more threatening because Blacks were less often well-dressed (suggesting more danger from prison uniforms or "shabby" street clothes), and more often physically held by police (suggesting restraint of a threatening person). Audio elements potentially dehumanized Blacks by presenting fewer pro-defense soundbites for Blacks than Whites. In short, Entman revealed qualitative differences in portrayals of Black and White suspects on television news with more negative video and audio contexts of the former.

Finally, before progressing to studies of Hispanic American portrayals, it is appropriate here to note a study of Black and Hispanic interaction in mainstream news magazines. Shah and Thornton (1994) reported there was little reportage of interaction between the two minorities in the 11 national publications they examined. Over the 13-year period from 1980 through 1992, only 21 articles appeared, 8 of these in 1991 when rioting beleaguered an area of Washington, DC. Fifteen articles included references to Whites and eight to Korean Americans. Whites were commonly placed in the context of victims, mediators, or analysts, while Korean Americans were covered in the context of victims of the Los Angeles riots. Across the 21 articles, the most common themes of coverage were conflict and racism.

Hispanic Americans

In six southwestern U.S. cities with Hispanic residents comprising 20–65% of the population, local daily newspapers were analyzed for locally written Hispanic news, sports, editorials, photos, and bulletin listings (Greenberg, Heeter, Burgoon, Burgoon, & Korzenny, 1983). Newspapers varied greatly in their coverage of Mexican Americans across locations and news topics, but the following trends were observed. While these papers filled their local newshole with Hispanic news stories in proportion to the percentage of Hispanics in their community, largely as a function of stories that contained a Spanish surname, stories that focused primarily on Hispanics averaged only 10% of the local news. Hispanic sports stories filled more of the local sports newshole (42%), with virtually all qualifying because the story contained one or more Spanish surnames. Bulletins such as births, deaths, and community events announcements were one half or less of the proportion of the Hispanic population. Hispanic photos filled 19% of the total local photo newshole. Editorial page content carried one Hispanic referent every other issue, filling 13% of the local editorial page.

Examining two Southwest papers for 1982, 1984, and 1986, Turk and others (1989) found that Hispanics were present in those newspapers at least in proportion to their presence in the population. The three single-year samples were not different from one another within each paper; coverage in 1986 was equivalent to the other 2 years. In one city, half the newspaper space was devoted to Hispanic coverage, although the population was one-third Hispanic. Hispanic stories and photos were generally longer, with bigger headlines and more prominent placement. But Hispanic news coverage tended to focus on Hispanics as "problem people," although the slant on White stories was less favorable than that on Hispanic stories.

A cross-media study in communities with at least 20% Hispanic population (Heeter et al., 1983) compared local Hispanic news coverage across newspapers, radio, and television on parallel criteria. On a typical day, news that involved Hispanics averaged a little more than one half-page of text in the daily paper, 1 of 5 minutes devoted to local news on radio, and a little more than 3 of the 14 minutes of news on evening television news. No Hispanic studio newscasters were found for either radio or television. Overall, local radio gave less of its newshole and focused more on crime and name dropping. Newspapers gave newshole and television gave time equivalent to Hispanic population proportions; newspapers covered many more kinds of issues for more varied reasons; television coverage was present and was at least as strong as radio.

These studies of minority portrayals in the news media indicate a reasonable presence of Blacks and Hispanics in news stories and news presentations. While more visible than two decades ago, questions remain about how minorities are being presented, especially Hispanic minorities. Although new stereotypes may be replacing older ones (e.g., Black suspects are less human, more dangerous, and less trustworthy than White suspects; Blacks as athletes and entertainers run amok; Blacks are victims of big-city police oppression).

Emerging work from a critical perspective is well suited to answering questions of content meaning. Goshorn and Gandy (1995), for example, looked at reportage of a single national news event in 1991 announcing that Blacks were less likely than Whites to obtain home mortgages. Headlines in the 57 stories analyzed, tended to frame the issue in terms of Black loss rather than White gain. Leads, however, more often cast the story in terms of White success for getting mortgages, demoting the perspective of Black risk (but this was less likely in newspapers where the Black community was larger). Similar critical research includes Campbell's contemporary analysis of racial news myths (1995), phases of news portrayals by Wilson and Gutiérrez (1995), Swenson's analysis of Rodney King and Reginald Denny news (1995), and Fiske's cultural view of news of the Los Angeles uprisings (1994).

USE OF NEWS BY MINORITIES

Nielsen annually reports that Blacks are much more avid television consumers than Whites; viewing in Black households exceeds White households by 1–2 hours per day. Black adolescents view television at least 2 hours more per day than White adolescents (Greenberg, Brown, & Buerkel-Rothfuss, 1992). But this national evidence is based on studies of exposure to television entertainment programs, not television news; there is no greater affinity for Blacks to attend to television news. In fact, Blacks watch less TV news than Whites. Recently, however, specialized Black cable programming such as the Black Entertainment Network (BET) has provided a minority orientation to entertainment and news. Where available, it has drawn strong viewership, particularly among younger Black Americans and those concerned with the importance of knowing Black history or issues of the Black extended family. BET receives one third of the viewing time among these groups (Jones, 1990).

Hispanics too are heavier entertainment television viewers than Whites and watch national and local news as frequently and for as long as Whites (Greenberg, Burgoon, Burgoon, & Korzenny, 1983). Hispanic youth watch significantly more of all television program types, including local and network news. Both Hispanics and Whites listen to radio news for 20 minutes a day. Hispanic youth also did not differ from White youth in radio listening time, for news, music, or sports.

For more than two decades, research has supported the contention that Blacks do less newspaper reading than Whites. Examining low-income Blacks and Whites, Sharon (1974) found less reading of newspapers was paralleled by less reading of magazines. Whites were more likely to read the main news sections, women's and society pages, editorials, financial news, business news, and regular advertising. Bogart (1972) also identified levels of comparative readership, finding that 80% of his White sample had read a newspaper yesterday compared with 61% in the Black sample; thus, given that more than half were daily readers, it would be erroneous to consider Blacks nonreaders.

Later, Allen and Bielby (1979) focused on the relationships that subgroups of Black adults have with the print media. More educated and wealthy Blacks spent more time with mainstream print media. These Blacks also were exposed more to Black establishment magazines such as *Ebony*, and to Black nonestablishment magazines such as *Black Scholar*, but avoided Black entertainment magazines such as *Jet*, which were more the selection of younger and more alienated Blacks. Older Blacks spent more time reading majority newspapers and less time with all categories of Black magazines. Total newspaper reading was positively correlated with trust in Black establishment and nonestablishment magazines and it was negatively related to perceptions of newspaper bias (heavier readers judged the paper as less biased). To obtain information about the Black community, more educated Blacks avoided mainstream newspapers, whereas those who did more newspaper reading were more likely to seek such information from the mainstream.

Cobb (1986) conducted interviews of 1,355 11th and 12th graders, 71% White and 22% Black. An initial finding was that one in five did not read a newspaper, especially those in minority households or with less educated parents. One in three read the newspaper infrequently and briefly; they did not have a time or place for reading, were generally negative toward the newspaper, and 90% chose some other medium as most valuable. They were the least regular readers of any content area and had the second least exposure to the other three media examined. This apathetic group was predominantly White. Black youth were less likely to have a newspaper available in their home, looked at fewer issues for longer periods of time, and more regularly read and held positive attitudes toward advertising; they also were most positive toward radio advertising (Cobb & Kenny, 1986).

Weber and Fleming (1984) found that White and Black youth

claimed television was their primary source of information with the newspaper in second place by a 2-1 margin among Blacks and a 3-1 or 4-1 margin among others. Thus, newspapers were a stronger second choice among the Black youth.

Hispanics also are less likely than Whites to be newspaper readers (Greenberg et al., 1983). Readership was especially low among predominantly Spanish-speaking Hispanics. Forty-five percent of Hispanics were regular newspaper readers and 30% were nonreaders, compared with 68% and 12% of the Whites. Hispanic newspaper readers, however, spent as much time as Whites with the paper—about 40 minutes. While only 59% of Hispanic households had access to a newspaper, 80% of White households did; 50% of the former subscribed, compared to 77% of the latter. A major contributor to this difference was the greater occasional reading among the younger Hispanics.

Among Hispanic adults, there was a stronger preference than among Whites for news of crimes, accidents, and disasters; news of Mexico and Latin America; job opportunities; advertising; stories about discrimination; problems in the schools and bilingual education; news about youth gangs; advice on personal problems and on health issues. Whites exceeded Hispanics in their interest in politics at all levels, editorial elements of the newspaper, business news, and humorous stories and features (Greenberg et al., 1983).

These studies illustrate that minority groups prefer television over other mass media at least as an entertainment medium, and inferentially as a news medium. Radio also is used more intensively by Blacks and Hispanics. Combining both electronic media, these minorities dedicate several more hours each day to them than Whites.

MINORITY LEADERS' PERCEPTIONS OF THE NEWS

Four studies offer insight into Black, Hispanic, and Native American leaders' attitudes toward the news media; no research assesses Asian minority leaders' attitudes. Concerns of these leaders include lack of employment opportunities for their communities, stereotypic coverage of their populations and a media focus on negative news, and mainstream press ignorance of issues faced by their publics.

Employment

Sneed, Riffe, and Van Ommeren (1988) surveyed 396 Black state legislators' evaluations of White-owned newspaper performance in their communities in coverage of news about Blacks and the Black community. Among the legislators, 89% thought more Black reporters should be hired and 74% said that understanding of minority concerns and perspectives would increase if the White-owned press in their community hired a Black editor.

Based on interviews with Hispanic leaders in six southwestern communities, Korzenny and others (1983) reported that "lack of accessibility with respect to employment and coverage were at the top of the list of complaints" leaders had of media relations with the Hispanic community (p. 67). Minority leaders further argued that Hispanics were rarely involved in administrative or decision-making media jobs and that they often were hired into media jobs from outside the community, leading to no identity with issues relevant to Hispanics in their new location.

Eighty-six percent of Puerto Rican elected and appointed public officials, business people, educators, and religious and grassroots leaders reported that newspaper and TV coverage of Puerto Ricans would be better if more Hispanics reporters were hired in newsroom jobs (Nicolini, 1987). In his exploratory study of Native Americans' relationships with public television and radio, Eiselein (1982) reported that Native Americans were more likely to be members of advisory boards than employees of stations.

Stereotypic Coverage, Focus on Negative News

Sneed and others (1988) found that Black legislators universally agreed press coverage of Blacks in athletics is fair and balanced but that news about crime involving Blacks was not. There was "strength of the agreement among Black legislators that press coverage in their communities is inadequate" (p. 6).

Local Hispanic community leaders blamed employment patterns and traditional stereotypes for an overemphasis on crime and negative news, a shortage of positive news, and less frequency and prominence given Hispanic than majority news. They also believed that radio offered the most local coverage, while television coverage was minimal. Leaders faulted negative media portrayals of Hispanics for "poor self-concept" and lack of pride in Hispanic communities (Korzenny et al., 1983).

All Puerto Rican leaders were dissatisfied with newspaper coverage of the Hispanic community, most (85%) were dissatisfied with TV coverage and 75% were dissatisfied with radio coverage (Nicolini, 1987). These leaders believed "that either the general public must form a negative impression of the Hispanic community, or, perhaps, no impression at all" (p. 599).

According to Eiselein (1982), "Native American organizations and tribes felt that broadcasting did not provide adequate coverage of Native American events and concerns" (p. 4). Only 6% of organization representatives and 17% of tribal representatives said that TV coverage of their communities was "adequate." The proportion indicating adequate radio coverage was 9% and 17% for organization and tribal respondents, respectively.

Ignorance of Minority Issues

Sneed and others (1988) reported Black legislators had strong agreement that the "White-owned press does not understand some issues that involve Blacks in their communities" (p. 6). Seventy-seven percent thought the mainstream press in their communities did a poor job of covering the Black community and 82% thought the press failed to report stories of interest and importance to Blacks. Moreover, 79% of the leaders agreed that papers in their towns did not understand Black issues; half the respondents concluded newspaper publishers are not concerned about Black issues.

Nicolini (1987) found 88% of the Puerto Rican leaders she surveyed felt that non-Hispanic reporters were ill-informed about the Hispanic community; that non-Hispanic reporters were "arrogant," "demanding," and "only interested in getting superficial facts"; and Hispanic reporters they knew were knowledgeable and positive about the Hispanic community and that they asked "the 'right questions'" (p. 600).

Eiselein reported that 61% of Native American organization leaders and 59% of tribal leaders said that news about their communities was "very important," while only 8% of public TV stations and 12% of public radio stations held this view.

Overall, relatively limited documentation of minority leaders' attitudes toward the mainstream press (and none related to Asian Americans) illustrates neglect of an area of scholarship with significant policy potential. In all, minority leaders regret negative coverage of minorities, lack of employment in mainstream news organizations, and pervasive insensitivity toward news that matters to their publics.

MINORITY PUBLICS' PERCEPTIONS OF NEWS

If social science suggests news content of minorities is inadequate and minority leaders are critical of the news industry, minority publics themselves are *not* dissatisfied. In general, secondary analysis of two national data sets by Becker, Kosicki, and Jones (1992) found that Blacks and Whites hold similar opinions of the news media. Although Blacks gave their newspaper and local television a lower favorability rating than Whites, both groups were not different in their favorability ratings for magazines, network television, or radio. Moreover, both groups held similar views of believability of the daily paper, news magazines, and radio and both held similar views of political and social issues coverage in the press. And, while both Blacks and Whites judged Blacks as having the least influence over how news organizations report news, Blacks feel they are particularly not influential on news content compared to other groups.

Race is not a predictor of evaluation for the local daily newspaper (Burgoon, Burgoon, & Shatzer, 1987). Race, however, does predict important distinctions in judgments of individual newspaper attributes. In large urban centers, Blacks and Whites gave higher ratings than non-Black on how accurate, lively, timely, and bland the news was. In small to medium cities, Blacks were most positive on how lively and courageous the newspaper was; both Blacks and Hispanics were more positive than Whites on judging the newspapers' competency; on every single significant difference, one or more of the minority groups had the most positive image evaluation. In southwestern cities, Hispanics gave higher ratings—the newspaper was more competent, influential, courageous, lively, powerful, and had the latest news; on three items, Blacks gave higher ratings than Whites. Generally, then, Hispanics said these local papers were more credible than did the Blacks, who in turn were more positive than the Whites.

Hispanic viewers exceed Whites in overall satisfaction with local TV news, in satisfaction with local TV coverage of social news in their communities, and the likelihood of believing television reports if they conflict with other local media (Greenberg et al., 1983). Hispanics also exceed Whites in the level of their satisfaction with local radio coverage of social news in the community, whereas Whites are more satisfied with local radio coverage of crime.

A study of Chicago Blacks, Hispanics, and Whites (Faber, O'Guinn, & Meyer, 1987) revealed Blacks were most likely to say there were too few Blacks on TV, both Blacks and Hispanics perceived too few Hispanics, and all three groups perceived that Hispanics were the most underrepresented. Interestingly, amount of viewing contradicted perceptions of the *fairness* of these portrayals; heavy-viewing Whites were more likely to perceive that the representations of Hispanics were fair; heavy-viewing Hispanics expressed the opposite perception, and for Blacks there was no correlation between viewing and perceived fairness of Hispanics; heavy-viewing Blacks, however, were more likely to say there were too few Blacks on television.

Comparatively, Greenberg and others (1983) found that fifth- and tenth-grade Hispanics assessed the portrayal of Mexican Americans, Mexican American families, and Black Americans on television as substantially more realistic than did their White classmates. Hispanic more than White youth reported their belief that local newspapers and television news shows portrayed good things; the two groups did not differ in the extent to which they judged the media as showing bad things, although it must be noted that their overall assessment was that there were more bad than good portrayals. The White youth also were more likely to believe the newspaper in case of conflicting reports from different media; Hispanics more often believed TV reports.

PERCEPTIONS OF THE JOURNALISTS

Two thirds of Black households chose Black newscasters as more believable than White newscasters (Johnson, 1984, 1987); half chose a Black male as most believable, one fourth chose a White male, one fifth a Black female, and 6% a White female—a clear preference for male newscasters over females as well. Nine in ten said that Blacks were more attractive newscasters. While Blacks rated Black and White newscasters equivalently in competency, Whites rated White newscasters as more competent in a study of both competency and social distance (Kaner, 1982). There was a preference for opposite-sex and same-race newscasters as potential neighbors; higher ratings were given to same race as potential kin and this same-race preference was especially pronounced among Whites. Neither TV news viewing frequency nor socioeconomic status were correlated with evaluations. In contrast to Johnson's findings, Black males rated female newscasters higher than male newscasters, but White males did the opposite.

Across these studies, evaluations of daily newspapers produce attitudes that are at least as positive as those of Whites among Black and Hispanic readers. Among minority adults, same race newscasters were judged to be more believable and as competent as majority newscasters.

CONCLUSIONS

A sparse number of studies covering a wide time period, with a myriad of samples, a variety of study goals, a complete absence of research on Asian Americans, and minimal evidence from Native Americans greatly limit the opportunity for firm statements. This literature provides a basis for the following conclusions:

On Employment in the Media

Goals set within the industry for employment of minorities have not been met. Growth in minority employment has slowed and development and placement of minorities in key editorial positions is not evident. Poignant is a management consultant's comment cited by Sunoo (1994, p. 106): "Minorities no longer need a boarding pass. What they need is an upgrade." Perhaps the goals and the processes by which minorities are attracted into journalism should be reexamined.

On Portrayals in the Media

Black and Hispanic Americans are present in the news in proportions equal to or greater than their presence in the population. Now that they are visible, the issue is no longer how many there are, but how they are portrayed. Blacks are not being presented disproportionately as criminals, but relatively new stereotypes may be replacing older ones—for example, Blacks as troubled athletes and entertainers, as victims of the police, and as questionable politicians. Here, evidence is emerging more in the critical literature than the social science literature. Hispanics appear regularly in sports news and soft news of America's papers, but less regularly in hard news. How fully minorities are being mainstreamed into the news remains to be determined.

On Media Use

Blacks and Hispanics prefer and depend on television for entertainment and for news more than the majority. Radio is also used more intensively by Blacks and by Hispanics. As a result, they give an additional one to three hours *more* each day to these electronic media. Blacks and Hispanics read newspapers less than Whites. Black adolescents read the newspaper sporadically, at best. These minorities were less oriented to the general news sections and youth especially favored the softer news content.

On Minority Leaders' Attitudes

Leaders of minority populations condemn majority media coverage of their communities. They feel there is not enough coverage, what coverage exists is overly negative, the media are not sensitive to the minority community and do not understand minority populations' problems. These leaders argue such shortcomings could be alleviated by greater minority employment in mainstream news organizations.

On Minority Publics' Media Attitudes

Minority publics do not demonstrate particularly negative attitudes toward mainstream news. Evaluations of daily newspapers produce attitudes among minority readers that are at least as positive, if not more so, than those of Whites. Blacks who read newspapers are satisfied with the job the newspaper does in covering the Black community. Television has greater credibility in the minority communities than any other medium. Hispanics, especially, are quiescent about the coverage they obtain from TV and radio. Minority youth perceive the media to be realistic in their race portrayals. Among minority adults, same race newscasters were preferred and judged to be more believable than, and as competent as, majority newscasters. Thus the complaints levied consistently by minority community leaders are not echoed in studies of their constituents.

FINAL REMARKS

Martindale (1991) made four recommendations for improving news coverage of minorities and minority issues:

1. Increased accuracy and more representative coverage
2. Less stereotypical coverage
3. More coverage of minority achievements and contributions
4. More coverage of problems faced by minorities

Martindale proposed that these improvements would develop primarily through increased employment of minority reporters, editors and supervisors in news organizations. As she states,

> the presence of minority journalists in a newsroom tends to sensitize White reporters and perhaps may enlarge their awareness and lead them to new sources. But not until minorities obtain editorships are they in a position to influence coverage decisions, to determine what gets covered and how it is played. (p. 10)

To her list of suggestions, the following is proffered. The only systematic research in this area on a regular basis is that which is federally mandated and examines minority employment in the licensed broadcast industries; to this, the newspaper industry regularly provides an update of its voluntary efforts. In the other areas examined in this paper—media use, media portrayals, and leader and public attitudes toward the media—research is scarce and spasmodic. Unless there is some programmatic effort at an organized body of research undertakings, readers can expect little better in the next review a decade hence. In fact, interest in these kinds of issues may be decreasing among social scientists, who must move on to issues for which funding is available.

The news industry itself could underwrite such a research program. For a relatively small investment, the newspaper, magazine, radio, and television industries could embark on the kinds of research abstracted here, extend beyond those with a cadre of thoughtful scholars, and make a significant contribution to both themselves and the minority communities they wish to serve. Those communities consistently speak of the need for more and better information on which to base their efforts and those communities will soon comprise nearly half the U.S. population (Sunoo, 1994). An industry-organized and funded program of research on *minorities and the news* would produce, at best, a responsive service to minority citizens and at the least represent a significant marker in the industry's effort to alter the history of their relations with minority groups in the United States.

REFERENCES

Allen, R. L., & Bielby, W. T. (1979). Blacks' relationship with the print media. *Journalism Quarterly, 56*(3), 488–496.

Armstrong, G. B., Neuendorf, K. A., & Brentar, J. E. (1992). TV entertainment, news, and racial perceptions of college students. *Journal of Communication, 42*(3), 153–176.

Baran, S. (1973). Dying black/dying white: Coverage of six newspapers. *Journalism Quarterly, 50*(4), 761–763.

Becker, L. B., Kosicki, G. M., & Jones, F. (1992). Racial differences in evaluations of the mass media. *Journalism Quarterly, 69*(1), 124–134.

Bogart, L. (1972). Negro and white media exposure: New evidence. *Journalism Quarterly, 49*(1), 15–21.

Burgoon, M., Burgoon, J. K., & Shatzer, M. J. (1987). Ethnic differences in the evaluation of newspaper image. *International Journal of Intercultural Relations, 11*(1), 49–64.

Campbell, C. P. (1995). *Race, myth and the news.* Thousand Oaks, CA: Sage.

Chaudhary, A. (1980). Press portrayal of black officials. *Journalism Quarterly, 57*(4), 636–641.

Cobb, C. (1986). Patterns of newspaper readership among teenagers. *Communication Research, 13*(2), 299–326.

Cobb, C. J., & Kenny, D. (1986). Adolescents and the newspaper—Images in black and white. *Newspaper Research Journal, 7*(3), 1–8.

Dodd, D., Foerch, B., & Anderson, H. (1988). Content analysis of women and racial minorities as news magazine cover persons. *Journal of Social Behavior and Personality, 3*(3), 231–236.

Eiselein, E. (1982). *Native Americans and broadcasting.* Lincoln, NE: Native American Public Broadcasting Consortium. (ERIC Document Reproduction Service No. 235929)

Entman, R. M. (1992). Blacks in the news: Television, modern racism and cultural change. *Journalism Quarterly, 69*(2), 341–361.

Faber, R. J., O'Guinn, T. C., & Meyer, T. C. (1987). Television portrayals of Hispanics. *International Journal of Intercultural Relations, 11,* 155–169.

Fiske, J. (1994). Radical shopping in Los Angeles: Race, media and the sphere of consumption. *Media Culture & Society, 16,* 469–486.

Gandy, O., & Coleman, L. G. (1986). The Jackson campaign: Mass media and black student perceptions. *Journalism Quarterly, 63*(1), 138–43, 154.

Goshorn, K., & Gandy, O. H. (1995). Race, risk and responsibility: Editorial constraint in the framing of inequality. *Journal of Communication, 45*(2), 133–151.

Greenberg, B., Burgoon, M., Burgoon, J., & Korzenny, F. (Eds.). *Mexican Americans and the mass media.* Norwood, NJ: Ablex.

Greenberg, B. S., & Brand, J. E. (1994). Minorities and the mass media: An update. In J. Bryant & D. Zillman (Eds.), *Perspectives on media effects.* Hillsdale, NJ: Erlbaum.

Greenberg, B. S., Brown, J. D., & Buerkel-Rothfuss, N. L. (1992). *Media, sex and the adolescent.* Cresskill, NJ: Hampton Press.

Greenberg, B. S., Heeter, C., Burgoon, J., Burgoon, M., & Korzenny, F. (1983). Local newspaper coverage of Mexican Americans. *Journalism Quarterly, 60*(4), 671–676.

Guimary, D. (1984). Ethnic minorities in newsrooms of major market media in California. *Journalism Quarterly, 61*(4), 827–830, 834.

Heeter, C., Greenberg, B., Mendelson, B., Burgoon, J., Burgoon, M., & Korzenny, F. (1983). Cross media coverage of local Hispanic American news. *Journal of Broadcasting, 27*(4), 395–402.

Johnson, E. (1984). Credibility of black and white newscasters to a black audience. *Journal of Broadcasting, 28*(3), 365–368.

Johnson, E. (1987). Believability of newscasters to black television viewers. *Western Journal of Black Studies, 11*(2), 64–68.

Jones, F. G. (1990). The black audience and the BET channel. *Journal of Broadcasting & Electronic Media, 34*(4), 477–486.

Kaner, H. (1982). Adolescent reactions to race and sex of professional television newscasters (Doctoral dissertation, New York University). *Dissertation Abstracts International, 43*(02–A), 298.

Korzenny, F., Griffis, B.A., Greenberg, B., Burgoon, J., & Burgoon, M. (1983). How community leaders, newspaper executives and reporters perceive Mexican Americans and the mass media. In B. Greenberg, M. Burgoon, J. Burgoon, & F. Korzenny (Eds.), *Mexican Americans and the mass media.* Norwood, NJ: Ablex.

Martindale, C. (1984, August 5–8). *Being Black in America: The press portrayal.* Paper presented at the annual meeting of the Association for Education in Journalism and Mass Communication, Gainesville, FL.

Martindale, C. (1985). Coverage of Black Americans in five newspapers since 1950. *Journalism Quarterly, 62*(2), 321–328, 436.

Martindale, C. (1987, August 1–4). *Changes in Newspaper Images of Black Americans.* Paper presented at the annual meeting of the Association for Education in Journalism and Mass Communication, San Antonio, TX.

Martindale, C. (1991, April 25–28). *Improving images of African-Americans in the Media.* Paper presented at the annual meeting of the Eastern Communication Association, Pittsburgh, PA.

Nicolini, P. (1987). Puerto Rican leaders' views of English-language media. *Journalism Quarterly, 64*(2–3), 597–601.

Pritchard, D. (1985). Race, homicide and newspapers. *Journalism Quarterly,* 62(3), 500–507.

Roberts, C. (1975). The presentation of blacks in television network newscasts. *Journalism Quarterly,* 52(1), 50–55.

Sharon, A. T. (1974). Racial differences in newspaper readership. *Public Opinion Quarterly,* 37(4), 611–617.

Shah, H., & Thornton, M. C. (1994). Racial ideology in U.S. mainstream news magazine coverage of Black-Latino interaction, 1980–1992. *Critical Studies in Mass Communication, 11,* 141–161.

Sneed, D., Riffe, D., & Van Ommeren, R. (1988, July 2–5). *Press coverage of Blacks and the Black community: The minority legislators' perspective.* Paper presented at the annual meeting of the Association for Education in Journalism and Mass Communication, Portland, OR.

Stempel, G. (1971). Visibility of blacks in news and news-picture magazines. *Journalism Quarterly,* 48(2), 337–339.

Stone, V. A. (1987, August 1–4). *Minority employment in broadcast news, 1976–1986.* Paper presented at the annual meeting of the Association for Education in Journalism and Mass Communication, San Antonio, TX.

Stone, V. A. (1988, July 3). *Pipelines and dead ends: jobs held by minorities and women in broadcast news.* Presented to the annual convention of the Minorities and Communication Division of the Association for Education in Journalism and Mass Communication, Portland, OR.

Sunoo, B. P. (1994, November). Tapping diversity in America's newsrooms. *Personnel Journal,* 104–111.

Swenson, J. D. (1995). Rodney King, Reginald Denny, and TV news: Cultural (re-)construction of racism. *Journal of Communication Inquiry, 19*(1), 75–88.

Tan, A. S., & Tan, G. (1979). Television use and self-esteem of blacks. *Journal of Communication, 29*(1), 129–135.

Thompson, G. (1989). Prying open closed-minded newsrooms. *Social Education, 53*(3), 163–164.

Turk, J. V., Richard, J., Bryson, R. L., & Johnson, S. M. (1989). Hispanic American in the news in two southwestern cities. *Journalism Quarterly, 66,* 107–113.

U.S. Commission on Civil Rights. (1979). *Window dressing on the set: An update.* Washington, DC: U.S. Government Printing Office.

Weaver, D., Drew, D., & Wilhoit, G. C. (1985, August 3–6). *A profile of U.S. radio and television journalist.* Paper presented at the Radio Television Division at the annual meeting of the Association for Education in Journalism and Mass Communication, Memphis, TN.

Weber, O. J., & Fleming, D.B. (1984). Black adolescents and the news. *The Journal of Negro Education, 53*(1), 85–90.

Wilson, C., & Gutiérrez, F. (1995). *Race, multiculturalism and the media* (2nd. ed.). Thousand Oaks, CA: Sage.

Womack, D. L. (1986). ABC, CBS, and NBC live interview coverage during the Democratic National Conventions of 1972, 1976, and 1984: A content analysis (Doctoral dissertation, University of Southern Mississippi). *Dissertation Abstracts International, 47*(06-A), 2786.

Womack, D. L. (1988, July 2–5). *Black participation in live network television interviews at the 1984 Democratic Convention.* Paper presented at the annual meeting of the Association for Education in Journalism and Mass Communication, Portland,OR.

CHAPTER 2

Minority Representation and Portrayal in Modern Newsprint Cartoons

Scott McLean

All Comic characters, from Dagwood to Ming of Mongo, are
socially significant in the sense that they propagate images that
play up our prejudices.

—Jules Feiffer

MINORITIES IN NEWSPRINT CARTOONS

From the introduction of cartoons in newsprint, blatantly racist and
derogatory minority stereotypes have been portrayed as the objects of
hostility, ridicule, and humiliation. From the "savage natives," representing indigenous cultures from North America to the Polynesian
Islands, to black "Sambo" or "Mammie" depictions, minority characters have played the roles on the receiving end of physical and verbal
abuse. Over time, minority characters have changed in both role and
presence in newsprint cartoons, due to the author's intentions, the editor's directions, the syndicate's control, and the consumer's preference.
This study will examine newsprint cartoons in eight newspapers, representing daily strips and focusing on the role and presence of minority
characters in comparison to those of earlier depictions.

"Any drawing that encapsulates a complete thought can be called a
'cartoon'," according to Maurice Horn (1980; Harrison, 1981, p.17),
who compiled and authored *The World Encyclopedia of Cartoons*
(1980) and *The World Encyclopedia of Comics* (1976). Richard Harrison (1981) notes cartoons both simplify and exaggerate, representing a
three-dimensional world in two dimensions. For this discussion, cartoons are works of art and/or words that depict characters and narrative

themes or jokes in newsprint. Cartoon strips come out every day, and portray social commentary, or observations so true they are tragically hilarious. They state a simple punchline, play on words or pictures, or sometimes the point is simply impossible to get, but the ideas they communicate can cross cultures and language. They tell us about our world, and sell papers. Arthur Asa Berger (1973) wrote a serious essay, *The Comic-Stripped American*, on comics as social commentary, and concluded that "any medium that has the continued attention of hundreds of millions of people deserves serious attention and study" (p. 15).

Across this century, minority characters have progressed from blatant and common, to rare or nonexistent, only to reemerge in the 1960s and 1970s with new and less derogatory depictions. To a large extent, this trend has been ignored. There are a number of texts, such as Randall Harrison's *The Cartoon: Communication to the Quick (1981)*, that focus on cartoon strips in newsprint as part of popular culture and an aspect of mass communication. Each text contributes understanding and insight to this important medium, but as in many works, what is absent speaks volumes. Through each work, the consistent lack of attention to the issue of derogatory depiction appears to be an avoidance of an uncomfortable past. While the early minority depictions were, in many cases, derogatory, recent cartoons have made great strides toward a more representative depiction of perspectives and characters. This ongoing development, however, requires a frame of reference, which includes past depictions, in order to chart the substantial progress.

EARLY REPRESENTATION

Richard Felton Outcault is generally credited with the distinction of being the creator of America's first comic strip character in 1897 (Kanfer, 1994). *The Yellow Kid* incorporated humor, pidgin English messages on his yellow "nightshirt," and physical humor to delight readers and sell papers. "From his earliest work, Outcault displayed racist tendencies: In 'The Yellow Kid's Great Fight,' the hero hit his little black opponent so hard that he suffered a dislocated jaw. In the penultimate panel, the boy lies supine, while a billy goat munches on the 'wool' on his head" (Kanfer, 1994, p. 37).

Arthur Asa Berger, in his 1973 landmark analysis of comic strips, describes African American character portrayal in *The Katzenjammer Kids*:

> The blacks in the strip fitted into the stereotype of the time—the African savage with a fancy little loin dress and names like "Captain Oozy-Woopis" or "King Doo-Dab." In an adventure dealing with pranks at school, one little boy is called "Sammy Snowball." The Kids

get their friends all dirty, when they start playing around ink, but Sammy, because he is already black, is not punished by the irate teacher. As he leaves, he says "Ise glad ise black." (Berger, 1973, p. 39)

Berger (1973) continues to note the context of the strip in the time it was produced, stating:

> Actually, blacks were not really objects of ridicule in the strips. They were drawn according to the cartoon convention of the time (which still exists to this day, in many cases), but in the stories they didn't play the "Sambo" role, and possessed a certain amount of dignity and authority, given the strip. (p. 39)

It is important to note the qualification, "given the strip." Like many strips of the era, it was an accepted practice to portray characters of color as ignorant, dependent, and absurdly comical. *The Katzenjammer Kids*, like its peers, was written and drawn from a majority perspective, including power hierarchies. Within that framework, any degree of dignity or authority portrayed above subservient could be deemed progressive. Regardless of the degree of dignity or authority that a character of color occasionally exhibited, the "puppeteers" and their caricatures nonetheless reflected this majority perspective with all its inherent exaggeration and racism.

One notable exception is the acclaimed *Krazy Kat* strip by George Herriman, a mulatto and "the first person of color to achieve prominence in cartooning" (Harvey, 1994, p. 179). The strip started under the title *The Dingbat Family* in 1910, but when the activities of the upstairs neighbor's became a peculiar point of interest, the strip was retitled (Harvey, 1994). Kat, mouse, dog, and a brick were the primary characters in a strip that expertly combined physical humor with word play and puns. Though rough and line drawn, the strip portrayed the desert Mountain Valley in southeastern Utah and human characters, many that spoke pidgin Spanish. In *The Art of the Funnies: An Aesthetic History*, Harvey (1994) points out that African American scholars have indicated there are aspects of life in Black America in *Krazy Kat*, particularly the comedy of reversal. Harvey (1994, p. 179) details an observation made by William W. Cook of Darmouth College in which Krazy Kat's color and size in relation to Ignatz, the diminutive mouse, are reminiscent of vaudeville characters. The vaudeville stage was populated by comic racial stereotypes held over from minstrelsy, an earlier form of comical stage acting. The narrative theme was often a large African American woman berating her diminutive husband, and his skill at evading both obligations and punishment was central to the comedy. *Krazy Kat*, according to Harvey (1994), follows this pattern, repeating the central themes, between Kat and mouse.

Before 1943, strips such as *Gasoline Alley* featured main protago-nist's like Walt Wallet being cared for by a Black "Mammie" (Reit-berger & Fuchs, 1971). The main characters represented the majority culture, and interpersonal communication between majority (main) characters and minority (secondary or tertiary) characters was often "top down," giving instructions and the like. This model of communi-cation between the characters implied an organizational hierarchy, just as the Yellow Kid related to his opponent.

Al Capp, the creator of *Li'l Abner*, a successful adventure drama strip that started in 1934, noted "newspaper publishers had discovered that people bought more papers, more regularly, if they were *worried* by a comic strip than if they were merely amused by one" (Byrnes, 1950; Harvey, 1994, p. 70). Drama strips, like many cartoon strips, included minority characters for a purpose. Milton Canliff, the creator of *Terry and the Pirates*, details this purpose succinctly:

> Heroism cannot thrive without rascality. Slinky, oily Malayans and sundry other Eastern types had been standard for years. Why not twist it a bit and make the Number One Menace a woman? One who com-bines all the best features of past mustache twirlers with the lure of a handsome wench. There was a woman pirate along the China coast at one time, so it wasn't beyond reality. She's fabulously wealthy. [Her name,] Lai Choi San, means Mountain of Wealth. That's too much for readers to remember. Call her that once to establish the atmosphere, but the Occidentals have nicknamed her the Dragon lady. (Canliff, 1937; 1945, p. 85; Harvey, 1994, p. 138)

In the strip's narrative line, characters of color and varying cultures were both caricatured as bandits, thieves, "the traditional Chinese ogre" (Harvey, 1994, p. 140), and protagonists. Caniff's strip featured Con-nie, the "number one boy" of the lead characters Pat and Terry, whom Harvey (1994, p. 140) describes as a "Chinese goofer" with large ears and teeth, a bald head, and pidgin English, "Plenty wise headclocker belong like Confucius." Connie serves as comic relief in his "wild attempt to ape American ways" (Harvey, 1994, p. 140). Big Stoop, a giant Mongolian mute, joins the cadre as a silent, loyal follower.

In the 1920s to the 1960s, comics changed and developed dramati-cally. Society itself underwent a transformation, a migration from rural to urban areas (Berger, 1973). Calvin Coolidge and an era when "the business of America is business was the prevailing philosophy" (Berger, 1973) contributed to themes, characters, and conflicts in cartoons. George E. Mowry, in *The Urban Nation*, states "The rapid evolution during the twenties of the 'ad mass,' or the mass-production-consump-tion society, tied together big business and the masses in a symbiotic relationship so close that the health of one was the health of the other"

(Mowry in Berger, 1973, p. 76). It is no wonder then that "Daddy War-bucks," a capitalist trillionaire father figure who argued the dangers of governmental bureaucracy and sought to save democracy, became a popular character in *Little Orphan Annie*. It is curious to note, however, that "he is aided in his work by two mysterious Orientals, both of whom are killers" (Berger, 1973, p. 84). These killers both did the "dirty work" and served their majority master, not unlike Connie in *Terry and the Pirates*, save the humor. This strip is also representative of its era in its reference to Japanese "Japs" and Germans "Krauts" by Annie and other main characters in the strip (Berger, 1973).

The year 1929 saw the debut of Buck Rogers, a 25th-century soli-tary hero, saving humanity from aliens, many of which were Asian. The onset of World War II brought anti-Japanese sentiments to the strip (Berger, 1973), like cinema and other mass media of the era. Berger (1973, p. 98) states, "Foreigners, strangers, those who look different (the Orientals) or who have not accepted American values (the half breeds and other kinds of 'degenerates') present a danger" in *Buck Rogers*. This system of Other as strange and threatening continues through many strips of the era. Dick Tracy, aggressive enforcer of the "good," strikes out after ugliness (bad) in the form of Ugly Christine, The Mole, Spots, Flattop, and many others. *Dick Tracy* as a strip employs violence against evil, both on and off stage, and the climate of Us and Them is actively cultivated. Berger (1973, p. 120) notes the role of grotesque characters is a "characteristic of American literature, as well as popular culture," but nonetheless, this perpetuation of Otherness as evil contributes to degradation of Other characters, confining them to the submissive or evil roles.

Harrison (1981) notes, however, that not all representations were derogatory. During World War II, *Mr. Bigott* cartoons poked fun at prej-udiced people, he notes, though many readers missed their point and interpreted them "as applying to someone else" (Harrison, 1981, p. 123).

In the late 1940s and 1950s, characters of color seemed to disap-pear. "Like all the other media, comics offered a world of social myths to the recipient and contributed among other things to the fact that the 'Black man' became to many Americans an 'invisible man'" (Ellison in Reitberger & Fuchs, 1971). Francis E. Barcus (1961, 1963) conducted a survey of Sunday strips from 1943 to 1958, finding only one African American character among 458 in 1958 (Reitberger & Fuchs, 1971; Harrison, 1981). One significant strip, though minor in terms of distri-bution, that was not included in the survey was Tom Little's *Sunflower Street*, which ran from 1934 into the 1950s. African Americans were the main protagonists, though portrayed as the "naive, always jolly, Sambo type" (Reitberger, & Fuchs, 1971, p. 147).

In 1950, both *Peanuts* and *Beetle Bailey* debuted. *Peanuts*, by Charles Schulz, incorporated a simple graphic style with humor about childhood, and eventually became a very successful and popular strip. *Beetle Bailey*, by Mort Walker (see Figure 2.1), was also a content strip that focused on characters, relationships, and gag humor but quickly evolved. Spider, the early version of Beetle, started out in a academic setting, with odd professors and peers serving as vehicles for punchlines with which many could empathize. The Korean War came along early in the strip, and the renamed Beetle Bailey left his collegiate dress for a military one. This initially lead to a significant increase in the number of papers that picked up the strip (Harvey, 1994), and also set the stage for later events. The military represented a place where many people, and many races, came together. The strip's setting and characters, to a large degree, represent a hierarchy and authority figures present in modern life. Much of its humor was derived from poking fun at authority figures such as inept General Halftrack, who ran the camp (poorly) by day and was run by his wife at night. Every character takes his or her turn revealing quirks in personality that level them all to the same playing field, bouncing off each other as "buttons" are pushed and reactions ignite.

FIGURE 2.1

In 1970, after syndicate deliberation and strong assertion on Walker's part, Lieutenant Flap, the strip's first African American character, walked on stage. Flap, with his goatee, Afro hairstyle, and in-your-face manner, was a lieutenant with rank and privilege. On October 5, 1970, his debut, he walked into Sergeant Snorkel's office and shouted "How Come There's No Blacks In This Honkie Outfit?!," poking fun at Walker's own admission of a homogeneous cast (Harvey, 1994, p. 206). Soon after, Flap assimilates and becomes part of the cast, as if he'd always been there. His integration, however, was not as easy off the page. There was significant discussion as to whether his introduction would lose readership, but Walker explained: "The Army had been integrated for years. Blacks exist. Beetle Bailey's army was phony.

I was a coward if I didn't try it. The trick was to do an honest job of it, come up with a character that was not offensive yet was as funny as the rest of my characters" (Harvey, 1994, p. 206).

As examples of successful strips in the 1970s, Harrison (1981) mentions Gus Arriola's *Gordo* as a successful strip with ethnic appeal, and lists Morrie Turner's *Wee Pals*, *Friday Foster* by Jim Lawerence and drawn by Jorge Longaron, a Spanish artist, Ted Shearer's *Quincy*, and Ray Billingsley's *Lookin' Fine* as other cartoons with minority characters.

A STUDY OF MODERN NEWSPRINT CARTOONS

Bill Watterson, creator of *Calvin and Hobbes*, discusses his strip, from characters to content, in *The Calvin and Hobbes Tenth Anniversary Book*. Watterson provides great detail and numerous examples to illustrate the technical side of creativity and the production of cartoon strips. One useful frame he outlines, in describing *Calvin and Hobbes*, is the role of primary, secondary, and tertiary characters. In this popular strip, Calvin and Hobbes are the lead, or primary, characters. Secondary characters include Calvin's rival, Susie, and his parents. This level of characterization features development, both in relation to the main characters and as independent characters. Susie has a definite personality, as does his mother and father. They are, however, second string. Calvin's mother and father lack names. Tertiary characters, roles that lack development in the strip, include Calvin's teacher, babysitter, principal, and uncle. They possess attitude, but do not develop beyond one dimension. The exception to this frame occurs when a tertiary or secondary character is allowed to develop. The babysitter, for instance, starts out early in the strips as Calvin's nemesis. Across the battles, power struggles, and repetitive scenarios, Watterson allows them to become friends. She develops, and although she does not "walk onstage" often, when she does, the readership is familiar with her developing character. She's moved to second string.

This frame of reference, rather than an either/or orientation, allows this study to examine where the characters are in relation to the overall strip and each other, noting their development, presence beyond one dimension, and extent to which they resemble early stereotyped caricatures.

SURVEY

In Table 2.1, newsprint cartoons are listed in order of primary, secondary/tertiary minority characters. The cartoon strips are then com-

TABLE 2.1
Newspaper Cartoons and Minority Characters

Cartoon Strip	1	2	3	4	5	6	7	8	9
PRIMARY									
The Fusco Brothers								x	
Jump Start				x	x		x		
Herb & Jamaal	x								
Curtis	x		x	x	x	x			
Safe Havens	x								
Thatch						x			
SECONDARY/TERTIARY									
Doonesbury*	x	x	x						
Foxtrot	x	x				x			
Luann	x		x		x				
Sylvia	x	x				x	x		
Beetle Bailey	x	x	x	x	x	x	x		
Funky Winkerbean						x			
Tank MacNamara**				x					
Peanuts	x	x	x			x	x	x	
Terry and the Pirates		x			x				
Phantom				x					
Bound & Gagged	x	x			x				
Mister Boffo		x					x		
Subtotal	10	8	5	5	7	6	5	2	18
Total	34	28	17	26	38	35	38	28	98
S/T (rounded)	29%	29%	29%	19%	18%	17%	13%	7%	18%

1 *The Oregonian* — 9/05/95
2 *Chicago Tribune* — 9/01/95
3 *San Francisco Chronicle* — 10/10/95
4 *Seattle Post* — 10/09/95
5 *The Denver Post* — 10/04/95
6 *St. Louis Post-Dispatch* — 10/06/95
7 *LA Times* — 8/02/95
8 *The Washington Post* — 9/25/95
9 Total cartoons with minority characters over all strips present.

* *Doonesbury* is sometimes published in the opinion/editorial section.
** *Tank McNamara* is sometimes published in the sports section.

pared to a series of regional newspapers in which they appear. The cartoons that feature minority characters are subtotaled, and compared to the total number of cartoons in the newspapers.

Tertiary Characters

In the 1950s, Charles Schulz, creator of *Peanuts*, broke away from the action adventure and drama strips, and built a cast of characters linked with little more than their common insecurities and relationships with each other. This took comic strips in a new direction in the fifties, and *Peanuts* quickly became prominent, today reaching 69 countries through 2,600 newspapers (Wilson, 1995). *Peanuts* became the benchmark comic for up-and-coming comic artists. Both Lynn Johnston (*For Better or Worse*) and Cathy Guisewite (*Cathy*) indicated *Peanuts* had a significant influence on them as children and comic artists (Wilson, 1995). The strip featured a cast of characters with distinct personalities, most notably a troubled Charlie Brown, and willful, selfish Lucy. Humor in the strip is sometimes physical, with Lucy playing upon Charlie Brown's trust strip after strip. She holds the football, he runs and tries to punt, only to have her pull it away, and he helplessly lands on his back. The long-suffering nature of Brown has been long attributed to the strip's success, with Schultz noting happiness isn't so funny. Characters often reflect on the troubles of being children, fearing the speech in front of class, or make subtle commentary on social issues. *Peanuts*, as a "classic," includes Franklin, an African American character the same youthful age as the others. He is the only character of color, and generally enters the stage on or around Martin Luther King Jr. Day. While Lucy is central, and her will well known, Franklin is a tertiary character, sometimes secondary, and his character is not developed to the same extent. His presence is important in that it illustrates not all the kids in Charlie Brown's neighborhood look the same. His lack of development reflects the era of the strip, and while childhood is timeless, this portrayal is representative of the 1950s. To a large extent, this cartoon strip is representative of modern strips with tertiary minority characters. Absence of minority characters, like strips of the 1950s, is the dominant pattern. When the minority character is present, however, the derogatory depiction has largely been omitted.

Secondary Characters

Cartoon strips like *Luann* and *Foxtrot* integrate minority characters more prominently in certain scenes, but the main characters are White. The distinct difference from earlier secondary characters, like Connie in *Terry and the Pirates*, is the lack of power heirarchies. In *Luann*, an

African American teenager and classmate often adds commentary that makes the main character, Luann, stop and think. One cartoon strip featured Luann's efforts to capture a boy's attention on Valentine's Day with a large, homemade card. Luann was frightened, but her classmate helped her to get noticed. Of course, things didn't work out smoothly, but Luann's friend was a positive part of the story line. In *Foxtrot*, one of the main characters, Jason, a young boy, interacts with his African American friend. They play as equals, and their friendship is normal, without the power heirarchies associated with earlier cartoons. While the secondary role continues to define the minority character by his or her relationship to the majority characters, the depiction is less derogatory than earlier caricatures.

Doonesbury represents an integrated cast of characters. Early on, characters challenged stereotypes. Ginny, an African American female, ran for Congress in the strip in the mid-1970s. Around the same time, Duke, an older White male renowned for his love of hallucinogens, accepts a position in Samoa as governor while representing the American bureaucracy, and later moves to China. His belligerence pokes fun at racial issues and changing social trends. MacArthur, a native Samoan, plays his assistant with humor and dry wit. Honey, his Chinese assistant, takes liberties with her translations of his boorish and culturally insensitive comments. Nate (Hale) and Sammy, an African American character, discuss the meaning of "All men are created equal" during the American Revolution (Trudeau, 1978).

Primary Characters

The more prominent the character, as a general rule, the less stereotypical the portrayal. Bacus (1961, 1963), in his study of cartoons from 1943 to 1958, found that domestic relations were the number one focus. It's not surprising, then, that recent successful strips would involve family issues like sibling rivalry or school-related challenges. It is noteworthy, however, to highlight the increased role of African American characters, as they outnumber other minority characters significantly.

Jump Start, by Robb Armstrong, follows the classical model of a family, with Marcy (Mom) and Joe (Dad) as lead characters, and family relations as a primary vehicle for dialogue and humor. The Cobb family struggles with issues that most families encounter, like intergenerational differences, issues with kids, finances, and employment. *Herb & Jammal*, by Stephen Bentley, features two main African American male characters. Humor revolves around relationships with women, Jammal's NBA efforts, or the confrontations in everyday life. *Curtis* (see Figure 2.2), like *Jump Start*, is a family-oriented strip, but deals with more serious issues in a straightforward manner. The Wilkin's family, created by Billingsley, deals with inner-city violence, gang violence at school, a miscarriage and subsequent grief, and religious issues. Some issues are handled seriously, while others add humor to the narrative. Curtis is patted on the head by the Pope, and he and his hat become the focus of significant media attention, with crowds at the door. People go to great lengths just to touch Curtis, and he must eventually appease the crowd by tossing his hat to them.

FIGURE 2.2

Bill Holbrook also incorporates family issues, and has created a world in which Samantha, the main character, excels at lawyer camp for kids as well as hockey. *Safe Havens* debuted on October 3, 1988. It was set in a daycare center, and Samantha was a minor character. "In the next four years she completely took the strip over to the point that in 1993 King Features and I seriously considered changing the title to *Samantha*" (Holbrook, 1996), remarked creator Bill Holbrook (see Figure 2.3). Now we see Samantha deal with the world on a daily basis, whether she's contemplating removal of the very real heart on her wrist, for all to see, which clearly reads she loves Dave, or she gets first place in the science fair by entering feverish Roger, the lottery ball mascot, as an example of global warming. She's smart, witty, and funny. She relates to world as it presents itself, the ups and downs of

FIGURE 2.3

childhood, and readers can clearly identify with her experiences. In contrast to earlier depictions of minority characters, Samantha is an accessible, positive character. In an e-mail exchange, Holbrook stated:

> Despite much work that still needs to be done, we have made great strides during my lifetime toward developing a more tolerant society. Popular culture reflects these changes, of course, and I try to make *Safe Havens* a positive force. While my main priority is to be funny, I also realize the impact even a comic strip can have on peoples' attitudes. (Holbrook, 1996)

This improvement in depiction, however, is not universal. In the Sunday comics of *The Oregonian*, December 3, 1995, Dana Summers features a Native American as the lead character. *Bound & Gagged* is a gag cartoon, in which the characters and the punchline are different in each strip. The round character, wearing a headband with a pointed feather, is shown finger to mouth in an expression of being perplexed in front of a sign that reads "Telegraph Ahead." The character stares at the telegraph pole with a thought balloon featuring a question mark in the second frame. The third frame shows him, in leather leggings and a skirt cloth, chopping down the pole with a stone hatchet. In the fourth frame he's making smoke signals with a blanket over a fire of pole logs. The indication that he couldn't read the sign and had to resort to "primitive" means in order to communicate is the punchline, and the character and his actions are the "joke." This depiction perpetuates the myth of ignorance and comical buffoonery of comics past.

CENSORSHIP

One central issue to the question of content in newsprint cartoons is who decides the content. In a "free-market society," one might surmise the consumer would be the decision-maker. When it comes to newsprint cartoons, the syndicates to a large extent control the content, theme, direction, and characters before the consumer ever views the product.

At the National Cartoonist Society gathering in April 1962, "Hal Foster told delegates of the many furious letters of protest he had received, because he had included Nubian Negro slaves, a Jewish Merchant and a Irishman in his [strip] *Prince Valiant*" (Reitberger & Fuchs, 1971, p. 144) and went on public record at the meeting as saying "the only people you can draw are white, rich Protestants." Dale Messick had his drama strip, *Brenda Starr*, pulled from southern states after including an African American girl in a group of youths (*Time*, 1965; Reitberger & Fuchs, 1971). Alfred Andriola, of *Kerry Drake*, had to change a proposed character's name from Jet Black to Sable Black because his syndicate's censor objected to possible controversy (*Giff Wiff*, 1966; Reitberger, & Fuchs, 1971), and Charles Schultz was restricted from allowing Linus's blanket from coming to life, with the fear it would be deemed violent and lose readership (*Time*, 1965; Reitberger, & Fuchs, 1971).

Reitberger and Fuchs (1971) detailed Foster's controversy, noting that it "only confirmed the syndicates in their policy to distribute only comics which did not give offense to any section of the public" and "all strips . . . were therefore cleaned of any controversial matter" (Reitberger, & Fuchs, 1971, p. 144).

In addition to the syndicates, there is an additional gatekeeper before the consumer may view the strip: the newspaper editors (Harrison, 1981). *Beetle Bailey*, for instance, was banned from *Stars and Stripes* from 1954 to 1955, for moral issues, and again in October of 1970, when Mort Walker introduced Lieutenant Flap, an African American soldier (*Time*, 1970; Reitberger & Fuchs, 1971). There is a finite amount of space allocated to the strips, and for one to be included, another must be removed. Removal of a strip could provoke a response from readers, and editors are hesitant to take actions that might affect revenue. Introduction of a new strip, that contains characters, depictions, or narrative themes that may be controversial, runs the risk of offending advertisers and readers. Newspaper editors, often biased on the side of the status quo, have financial concerns and multiple audiences to please.

BEYOND NEWSPRINT: ELECTRONIC CARTOONS

One area of cartoon strips that exploded in recent years is on the World Wide Web. Rather than print-based strips, this format for access and presentation has immediate, colorful appeal, and the potential to increase all forms of representation. From *Alley Oop*, where "The Stone Age meets the Information Age,"[1] to the *Dysfunctional Family Circus*, where Bil Keane's wholesome strip meets twisted new dialogue, the medium is changing the nature of cartoon strips. A 90s version of *Terry and the Pirates* gives life and less violent content to an early strip. *Doonesbury Electronic Town Hall* allows the reader to participate in polls, chat with others of similar interest, and browse through archived strips. The interactivity of the medium brings action and excitement to an otherwise two-dimensional frame. For example, *Yeah! Cool Sites* fea-

---

1. http://www.unitedmedia.com/comics/alleyoop/

tures the *World Wide Web Fights,* a parody of the World Wrestling Federation, in which Chewbacca, of *Star Wars,* is pitted against *Star Trek: The Next Generation*'s Worf. Bill Holbrook, of *Safe Havens* and *On the Fastrack,* pairs a herbivore, Kevin the rabbit, and a carnivore, Kell the wolf, as a married couple with two children, ages 17 and 12. The characters met online, and the strip itself is distributed exclusively online (Rothman, 1996).

The great majority of strips, as mentioned, are versions of print-based works, and therefore represent the majority. One noticeable exception is a Hatbag Productions feature, *Hippy and the Black Guy,* a strip that debuted in 1994 on the campus of the University of Mississippi. It is self-described as "no holds barred satire of the way in which modern Americans are guided by stereotypes."[2] This simply drawn cartoon strip features college humor, and strikes out at traditional representations with potency.

Market segmentation and reaching readership has never been faster. Chris Kelly's *Fried Society,* a weekly Generation X comic strip out of Los Angeles, combines wit and perspective to successfully attract a niche audience. Overall, this medium is one to explore and observe a trend that will undoubtedly feature an increase in minority characters over time.

CONCLUSION

This chapter outlines the depiction and portrayal of minority characters in subservient and derogatory roles. From *Terry and the Pirates* to *Prince Valiant* and *Little Orphan Annie,* minority characters have been the object of ridicule. While not every cartoon cast them in the same roles, the trend serves to inform us of earlier perspectives and depictions. Across this century, minority characters have moved from secondary and tertiary roles to central figures in the landscape of newsprint cartoons. Some cartoon strips, like *Peanuts,* incorporate a single character in order to diversify their cast while holding onto a framework that better represents the 1950s than today. Others, like *Beetle Bailey,* also represent this earlier era as well and include numerous stereotypes, from the Latin lover to a Chinese American, all equally limiting but nonetheless representations less inflammatory than those of the 1920s to the 1940s. Finally, *Herb & Jammal, Safe Havens,* and others portray a modern society, where individuals interact without the hierarchies of yesteryear, and audiences can appreciate the characters and their narratives themes

---

2. http://www2.netdoor.com/~lainh/hatbag.html

with recognition, respect, and a laugh. There is a need for more study of this trend and cartoons, from the World Wide Web to the dusty archives, in order to lend insight and understanding to how cartoons represent our world and how we represent ourselves in them.

REFERENCES

Bacus, F. E. (1961, Spring). A content analysis of trends in Sunday comics, 1900–1959. *Journalism Quarterly, 38,* 171–180.

Bacus, F. E. (1963). The world of Sunday comics. In D. M. White and R. H. Abel (Eds.), *The funnies: An American idiom* (pp. 190–218). New York: Macmillan.

Berger, A. A. (1973). *The comic-stripped American: What Dick Tracy, Blondie, Daddy Warbucks, and Charlie Brown tell us about ourselves.* Baltimore, MD: Penguin Books.

Blackbeard, B., & Williams, M. (Eds.). (1977). *The Smithsonian collection of newspaper comics.* New York: Harry Abrams.

Byrnes, G. (1950). *A complete guide to professional cartooning* (pp. 71–72). Drexel Hill, PA: Bell Publishing.

Canliff, M. (1945). On Sunday you can see the blood in color. *The Magazine of Sigma Chi,* February–March (rpt. from *The Quill,* 1937).

Feiffer, J. (1965). *The great comic book heroes.* New York: Dial Press

Giff Wiff. (1966, May 20). "Pas question de faire ça." No. 20, p. 30.

Harrison, R. P. (1981). *The cartoon: Communication to the quick.* Beverly Hills, CA: Sage

Harvey, R. C. (1994). *The art of the funnies: An aesthetic history.* Jackson, MS: University Press of Mississippi

Holbrook, B. (1996). An e-mail exchange on February 15, 1996 between Bill Holbrook and McLean concerning the development of this chapter. The quotes are used with permission.

Horn, M. (Ed.). (1980). *The world encyclopedia of cartoons.* New York: Chelsea House

Kanfer, S. (1994, May/June). From The Yellow Kid to yellow journalism. *Civilization: The Magazine of the Library of Congress, 2*(3), 32–37.

Rothman, H. (1996, March). A daily comic—minus the paper. *CompuServe,* p. 11.

Time. (1965, April 9). Cover story on *Peanuts,* p. 84.

Time. (1970, November 2), p. 37.

Trudeau, G. B. (1978). *Doonesbury's greatest hits.* New York: Holt, Rinehart, and Winston.

Watterson, B. (1995). *The Calvin and Hobbes tenth anniversary book.* Kansas City, MO: Andrews and McMeel.

Wilson, A. (1995, October 30). Charles Schulz has earned more than peanuts. *The Spokesman Review,* pp. C1, C5 (rpt. from the *Detroit Free Press*).

CHAPTER 3

Disney Does Diversity: The Social Context of Racial-Ethnic Imagery

Alan J. Spector

The films of Walt Disney studios are widely acclaimed as exhibiting positive, constructive social values. Common themes include the importance of honesty, of hard work, and of loyalty. Yet a critical viewing of Disney's animated films shows that far from being a leader in constructive social values, they generally reflect racist stereotypes typical of the period in which they were produced. No cultural work, even an animated children's film, can be evaluated in a one-dimensional way, of course. The Disney animated films generally have a variety of characters, some of which display no particularly negative ethnic stereotypes, others that are mildly negative, and some that reflect and reinforce the most vulgar racist stereotypes. Any discussion of this topic necessitates some general background discussion about the use of ethnic characters and especially ethnic humor in literary works.

ETHNIC CHARACTERIZATIONS OR RACIST CHARACTERIZATIONS?

Because the Disney animated films are directed at children, humor is a basic part of their characterizations. We find three criteria central to defining "ethnic" humor as "racist" humor. First, the stereotype must be negative. Second, if the target of the humor is an oppressed, subjugated, or otherwise subordinated group, the impact of that stereotype is significantly more potent. Finally, if the stereotype feeds into or reinforces a common fallacious stereotype of the group, the impact is all the more damaging because it can add to the subjugation of the targeted group.

Consider the first criterion. One might read a folk tale about a tall Norwegian or a clever Irishman. While those are stereotypes, they are not necessarily negative. There are tall people and clever people in all ethnic groups, and in any case, these characteristics are not necessarily objects of scorn.

The second criterion adds more complexity to the discussion. Equating all erroneous ideas about race and ethnicity is superficial. Recent scholarship has emphasized the power dimension—taking into account how much power there is to *implement* particular ideas about race-ethnic relations (Cox, 1959; Blauner, 1972). For example, a Disney movie might portray an Englishman as stuffy, repressed, or pompous. The stereotype is negative, according to the discussion in the previous section. On the other hand, the intensity of the criticism is somewhat muted because Anglo-Americans are not a particularly oppressed group in the United States today (except perhaps for some Appalachians, who are often characterized in such extreme ways as to approach being regarded as a quasi-biological subgroup of American society; but this is not germane to the issue of so-called "pompous Englishmen"). For Anglo-Americans to defend their right to engage in racist stereotyping against Blacks or Hispanics, for example, by responding that they do not object to stereotypes against their British origins misses the point. The effect on the targeted groups is quite different if one group is substantially subjugated and the other is not. Another metaphor might be instructive here. Consider the example of a woman, alone on a dark street, suddenly surrounded by five men who demand that she obey them or she will be hurt. The woman manages to escape unharmed, and the men are apprehended. At that point, the men say:

> We never actually harmed her or even touched her. All we did was to say words. So, let her stand there and say the same words back to us. She can tell us that we have to obey her or we will be harmed. Then, after she says those words, we will be even.

Very few people in our society would accept that line of reasoning. It is clear that the same words, in one setting, are nothing but irrelevant bursts of sound into the air, while in another setting, they constitute a very direct threat, attempting to force someone into behavior against her will. Words have different impacts on people, depending in large part on the ability to back those words up with force. That is the key point that antiracists make in the context of opposing racist verbal abuse. Those who defend this abuse on the grounds that words are innocuous are either being inconsistent, since they would disagree with the excuse of the five men discussed above, or, they simply want to deny that members of certain racial-ethnic groups are still being victimized, and that racist culture intensifies it. Therefore, rather than making abstract appeals to a vaguely defined "diversity," it is more effective to either point out their inconsistency, or directly challenge their assumption that there is no discrimination against members of certain groups. Furthermore, the use of the word "offensive" to object to racist stereotypes is often ineffectual because it misses the point. Some things are offensive to some people, but they are appropriate and their use should be defended; those who object may well be expressing hypersensitive sensibilities that are not valid reasons for censorship. Racist stereotyping is worse than "offensive"; it is *abusive*. Calling it "offensive" opens up the door to the charge that the critics are hypersensitive censors. Moreover, calling it "offensive" is actually too mild of a criticism. This stereotyping adds to the oppression of victimized people.

REINFORCING COMMONLY HELD STEREOTYPES

A third characteristic, beyond negativity and victimization of a subjugated group, relates to the nature of the stereotype. If the stereotype reinforces what is a commonly held negative stereotype about a group, then that stereotype is helping to build a consensus of public opinion toward, at best, tolerance or indifference to oppression, and at worst, active participation in that oppression. For example, consider if someone put forward the following ethnic stereotype: "The problem with Irish Catholics is that they are so tall that their brains can't get enough oxygen." Although Irish Catholics are discriminated against in certain situations, such as Northern Ireland, and although the comment is a negative comment, the impact of the comment is diminished because there is no common stereotype of Irish Catholics being particularly tall. There is, however, a common erroneous stereotype of Native Americans as being prone to violence, and there is a common stereotype of many subjugated ethnic minorities as being comical figures, primarily suitable for use as mascots.

If one can interchange Lassie, the dog, with Gunga Din or the loyal African American, or Mexican, or Asian "sidekick" (who often dies while saving the White hero), or if one can interchange a comical pet ("Alf" from outer space) with a comical child actor from an ethnic minority group (Webster, Arnold, or Urkel), one can see that the stereotypes are not "innocent," "neutral" humor, but rather reinforce perceptions that members of those groups are inferior to the more dominant ethnic group.

Discerning the difference between ethnic humor that explores the positive aspects of various ethnic groups and ethnic humor whose purpose is to demean certain groups is not a simple matter. One can find wisdom in Arab fables, in Yiddish short stories, in Norse and Greek mythology, in African, Irish, or South Asian folk tales, German fantasy stories, East Asian parables, or the legends of different indigenous people. Often these works reflect cultural folk traditions of the people. It does not necessarily reinforce racist oppression to describe folk traditions or even to critique it, if it is done in a constructive way. Yiddish folk tales, for example, are often self-critical in an affectionate, bittersweet way. When the stories, archetypes, and stereotypes serve to denigrate certain groups, especially groups who are subordinated because of their ethnicity, then those works can rightly be criticized as "racist," whether those stereotypes are perpetuated by a nonmember of the ethnic group, such as Rush Limbaugh ridiculing the language of urban African Americans, or by members of the subordinated ethnic group itself, such as Martin Lawrence portraying young Black men as being obsessed with sex.

There is no reference work that can be used to evaluate whether ethnic humor or ethnic folk tales are racist or not. There is no simple barometer or template that can be mechanically utilized to measure the amount of racially or ethnically prejudiced ideology in a particular expression. On the other hand, one need not have a Ph.D. in social psychology to discern the impact of various forms of expression. If the stereotype is negative, if the target is a subordinated group, and especially, if the stereotype reinforces a commonly held fallacious negative stereotype of an oppressed group, then such stereotyping can legitimately be called "abuse," and its promulgation can justifiably be opposed by those who oppose racial prejudice and racial discrimination and who seek a world where people are valued, rather than devalued, for the special contributions they can make to society. Within this context, we can discuss some of Disney's most popular animated children's films.

FRENCH CHEFS AND STUFFY ENGLISHMEN

Disney's work has been critiqued from a variety of perspectives. Ariel Dorfman has done a pointed, controversial analysis of Disney's comic books, arguing that many of the stories are celebrations of U.S. imperialism, with Third World characters appearing as naive savages at best, and corrupt villains at worst. More recently, the Disney organization has come under strong criticism for the actions of one ABC radio station that Disney controls. The station's programming includes a talk show host notorious for his overt, explicit racist comments about African Americans and other ethnic groups, and is involved in sponsoring a conference that includes staunch advocates of the biological inferiority of Black people. But the negative racial-ethnic content in Disney's animated films is far more complex than the overt political commentary of a talk show host.

One way to examine the Disney animated films would be to describe the major films in chronological order. For purposes of this discussion, however, we will discuss various types of ethnic characters as they have manifested themselves across a number of different films. Our purpose is not to systematically inventory every Disney animated production, recording evidence for the purpose of indicting the Disney studio, but rather to simply demonstrate the persistence and pervasiveness of the different types of stereotyping. The Disney films mentioned here are a selected sampling from the many Disney animated films, and the discussion is intended to use these selected images as ways to illustrate certain types of ethnic stereotyping for purposes of a sociological discussion, rather than an aesthetic appreciation or journalistic exposé of Disney.

Ethnic stereotyping is common in most animated Disney films. Often, the stereotyping is of the less blatant kind. Geppetto, the puppet maker in *Pinocchio* (1940), is portrayed as a positive figure, although he manifests some of the common stereotypical characteristics often attributed to Italians. He is a good man, but a bit simple. The archetypical "stuffy Englishman" is also a common character in Disney movies. Generally, they are portrayed with primarily good characteristics as well as some minor negative ones (although in *Pocahontas* (1996), some of the English are depicted as being rigid to the point of being brutish). Another similar type of ethnic stereotype can be found in *The Little Mermaid*. A principal character, Sebastian, is portrayed the way that stereotypical Frenchmen are often portrayed—temperamental and comical. And in *Lady and the Tramp* (1955), Southern Europeans are again portrayed as temperamental, comical chefs. This "less obvious" ethnic stereotyping is so common in Disney's animated films that it becomes a trivial exercise to list the examples. The ethnic stereotyping sometimes had a more obvious presence, however.

Among the most controversial was the presentation of the black crows in the film *Dumbo* (1940). The crows are meant to represent African American men, streetwise, sarcastic, standing around on a street corner making comments and giving advice. One defender of Disney describes the controversy this way:

> There has been considerable controversy over the Black Crow sequence in recent years, most of it unjustified. The crows are unde-

niably black, but they are black characters, not black stereotypes. There is no denigrating dialogue, or Uncle Tomism in the scene, and if offense is to be taken in hearing blacks call each other "brother," then the viewer is merely being sensitive to accuracy. There is another interesting aspect to the crow sequence, as Ward Kimball tells it. "I was in charge of the crows, [and] I wanted to make each crow a separate character. One example was the little crow with the big horn-rimmed glasses. When he rolled his eyes, the eyes went out beyond the head mass, they rolled around inside the big glasses." (Maltin, 1973)

Even Maltin feels compelled to qualify his defense of this characterization with the words: "There has been considerable controversy over the Black Crow sequence in recent years, *most* of it unjustified" (emphasis added). However, he does not choose to tell us what aspects of the controversy might be justified. As discussed earlier, there is a gray area between ethnic characterizations and denigrating ethnic stereotypes. It is true that the crows are not shown murdering anyone, or tap dancing, or eating watermelon, but the stereotype of wisecracking Black men standing around on street corners does play into the popular negative stereotype that Black men (presumably unemployed?), in contrast to White men, spend an inordinate amount of time standing around on street corners doing nothing constructive. It is true that some Black men stand around on street corners, and in that sense, the film might claim that it is accurately depicting "some" Black men. But that is a common, and unconvincing, defense used by those who are accused of ethnic stereotyping. To take typical, but real, characters from any ethnic group and *imply* that these characters are typical is a common practice that allows the writer/artist to claim "historical accuracy" for his or her distorted stereotype. Perhaps if there had been a few other "African American" characters depicted in other ways, the film might be able to effectively use that defense. But when all the characters fall into the commonly accepted stereotype, the criticism of ethnic stereotyping carries more weight.

The Disney studio was certainly aware of how it was utilizing ethnic characteristics. While many lay people take for granted characterizations in films, those who study film production know that very little happens by accident. This is even more true in animated films. Evidence of Disney's attention to this detail can be found in the following quote from two Disney artists:

The little girl in *The Jungle Book* (1967) has large pupils surrounded by a dark, dusky iris. We wanted to get the rich look of the East Indian eye, and, hopefully, a seductive quality as well. (Thomas & Johnston, 1981, p. 449)

The ethnic stereotyping is not always simplistically done. Other animated Disney films manifest negative, but mixed images of ethnic groups. In *Peter Pan* (1953), the villain, Captain Hook, is obviously British. But unlike the good characters of the film, who are endowed with physical features more generally identified with Northern European characters, the Captain Hook character would appear to be more Southern or Eastern European. Again, one might object to this comment, because there are many British people with those types of physical characteristics. And, more importantly, if we are working to overcome racial and ethnic stereotyping, then why should we play into that stereotyping by objecting to the fact that Captain Hook is portrayed as dark haired with a large nose? On the other hand, he is the villain, and the writers and artists chose to give him physical characteristics that somehow reflect his villainy; this is a common practice in many films. So it is doubtful that Captain Hook was given those particular characteristics as a purely random assignment that came out of the artists' attempts to reflect the physical diversity of the British population.

Beyond Hook, there is also the issue of the "Indians." It is true that the Indians are on the side of good, rather than evil. It is also true that one of the more memorable moments in the film depicts the Indians as dancing around and generally behaving in the typical Hollywood stereotype of how Indians supposedly behaved. And the famous song: "What Makes the Red Man Red?" undermines any attempt to portray Native Americans with dignity, as the equals of all other people.

The Jungle Book has come under criticism for its portrayal of various characters, as mentioned earlier. Sometimes the racism is more subtle. For example, the villain, a tiger, is not portrayed as having any particular stereotypical ethnic characteristics. However, his name is Khan. The East Asian as villain, common to Hollywood in general, is not uncommon in Disney's productions.

There is one other animated Disney film that sends mixed messages about ethnic relations. In a sense, it is different from the films described above, because the characters do not display physical features or mannerisms that are commonly associated with distinctive ethnic groups. But in *The Fox and the Hound*, the ultimate message is: "Stick to your own kind." It is a tragic message, a reluctant message. Clearly, everyone would be happier if we lived in a world where there was more tolerance. But in the face of this, the characters have no choice but to give in. It is tragic and hopeless to have serious relationships with those who are not "of your own kind." Admittedly, many of the examples discussed above have mixed messages. But in some of Disney's movies, the racist stereotyping is of the most blatant, vulgar variety.

OF CATS AND MEN

Disney's film *Lady and the Tramp* ranks among his classics. It is truly an "All-American" story, complete with a message of morality and democracy, as the aristocratic dog, Lady, overcomes all odds, including the antidemocratic elitism of others in the film, in order to realize her true love. Her true love is Tramp, a regular "Joe," a working-class, plain folks kind of dog with the kind of open, friendly, honest personality that was commonly associated with actors such as Jimmy Stewart. But amidst this sea of triumphant American democracy are the villains. The worst villains are the Siamese cats. This is not just a cat and dog story, however. The cats prance around arrogantly in a Hollywood-invented style that is supposed to represent what the audience should assume are the mannerisms of aristocratic Siamese or Chinese. (Disney's films, like many Hollywood films, often tended to lump ethnic groups together into a kind of undifferentiated mass—Asians, Chinese, Japanese, Siamese, for example, or Arabs and East Indians as another example.) The cats even proudly sing of their supposed ethnic heritage while they threaten an innocent baby:

> We are Siamese if you please.
> We are Siamese if you don't please.
> We are former residents of Siam.
> There is no finer cats than I am.

There is, of course, the denigrating humor in listening to the Asiatic cats butcher the English language. Beyond that, the stereotype of the Asiatic as evil, but cunning, utterly deceitful without morals or princi-ples was a staple of Hollywood. *Lady and the Tramp* helped "educate" millions of young Americans to embrace that stereotype. In this case, it was clearly a stereotype that encompassed all three criteria outlined above: negative, directed at a subjugated or discriminated group, and building upon commonly accepted "folk" stereotypes of that group.

Some might object that *Lady and the Tramp* is an old film, reflec-tive of the attitudes of its times. That is, of course, no excuse. Even then, there were some Hollywood films that depicted Asians with dignity; there were objections to the racist stereotyping even when the film was first released. In any case, this kind of gross stereotyping is not, unfor-tunately, just an artifact of Disney's past.

Disney's recent film, *Duck Tales: Secrets of the Lost Lamp*, is truly a throwback to the worst kind of Hollywood racist imagery. The heroes, all relatives of Donald Duck, are white as snow. There are two villains. The most immediate villain is depicted as an Arab. He is evil, but he is also a bumbling fool. In one scene, for example, he is seen wearing billowing pants, stuffed with stolen silver, so heavy that he stumbles around dropping it all over the place. His evil is superseded by his stupidity. There is one particularly archetypical scene where the white ducks and the brown Arab are all running around excitedly chasing each other and they all suddenly stop, and the audience sees the one brown face of the comic villain sticking out in the group of all-white "good guys."

But behind the scenes lies the worst villain—a magical being with Asiatic characteristics, perhaps part Persian, but most likely East Asian. This villain is again, the evil, but clever, cunning character type so commonly associated with East Asians in Hollywood films. The portrayal of Europeans as the "civilizers" or good guys, the Asiatics as evil, and the Arabs as a sort of combination of mainly African mixed with European and perhaps a touch of West or South Asian appeared in a number of Hollywood movies. The common stereotype of Africans was not of evil, cunning genius, but rather of an "uncivilized" nature that supposedly gives rise to a comic stupidity. There were a number of films in past decades depicting Arabs fighting off the invading "hordes" of Asiatics. But by the 1990s, one might have hoped that Disney studios would have abandoned this kind of gross ethnic stereotyping. Here too, the depictions fit all three criteria discussed above.

POCAHONTAS: DISNEY TRIES "PC"

The release of the Disney film *Pocahontas* was hailed by many liberals as a triumph of antiracism. Some conservatives felt that the film was following a trendy, liberal, so-called "political correctness." The hero is a heroine—a woman and an Indian. She is portrayed as intelligent and courageous. Many of the White men in the movie, British, are portrayed as bullying and coarse. Pocahontas is at one with nature, with humanity, with goodness in a struggle against imperialist invaders from Europe. In historical terms, the film has come under stinging critique, however. The real Pocahontas was forced to go Europe and died there within a few months. The intense brutality of imperialism is actually minimized in this sugar-coated fable. But what if the film were not based on distortions of history? What if it were a work of fiction to be considered as art, rather than as history? Would it then finally signal a recognition by Disney studios of the dignity and equality of all ethnic groups? Some might still remain skeptical. It is true that the character in the film is a woman and an Indian. And it is true that she is portrayed with intelligence, grace, and dignity. But she is also gorgeous, by popular Hollywood standards. To hedge their bets, the studio gave *Pocahontas* many of the physical features and mannerisms of a typical Hollywood leading lady. In the same sense that Sidney Poitier was able to break the color line in Hollywood films as a black man by initially portraying characters that were assimilated, so too did Disney have to make sure that Pocahontas would remind children of a Native American Barbie doll.

CONCLUSION

This essay has been an attempt to sensitize the reader to different types of negative ethnic stereotyping. We have used some of Disney's animated films as illustrations of these different degrees of stereotyping. Some might object to some of the examples, arguing that we overreached and that films should be taken as face value entertainment, rather than subject to sociological or political scrutiny. But if films are making social or political statements, overtly or via stereotypes, then they are fair game to that kind of critique. Others might object that Disney also had some positive characterizations of minorities. To use Disney's films to illustrate the negative ethnic stereotypes perpetuated in children's films is the focal point of this essay. There are many other examples that could be explored in more depth: *The Lion King* (1995), *Aladdin* (1993), Disney's short cartoon features, and many others. That would be a worthwhile endeavor, possibly a longer article, a book, or even a documentary film.

REFERENCES

Allport, G. W. (1954). *The nature of prejudice*. Cambridge, MA: Addison-Wesley.

Bennett, L. (1988). *Before the Mayflower*, (6th rev. ed.). New York: Penguin.

Blauner, R. (1972). *Racial oppression in America*. New York: Harper & Row.

Bonacich, E. (1972). A theory of ethnic antagonism: The split labor market. *American Sociological Review, 37,* 547–559.

Cox, O. C. (1959). *Caste, class, and race: A study in social dynamics*. New York: Monthly Review Press.

Doob, C. B. (1993). *Racism—an American cauldron*. New York: Harper Collins.

Feagin, J. R., & Feagin, C. B. (1996). *Racial and ethnic relations* (5th ed.). Upper Saddle River, NJ: Prentice Hall.

Gordon, D., Edwards, R., & Reich, M. (1982). *Segmented work, divided workers*. Cambridge: Cambridge University Press.

Maltin, L. (1973). *The Disney films*. New York: Crown.

Omi, M., & Winant, H. (1986). *Racial formation in the United States: From the 1960s to the 1980s.* New York: Routledge & Kegan Paul.

Thomas, F., & Johnston, O. (1981). *Disney animation: The illusion of life.* New York: Abbeville Press.

Willie, C. V. (1978, July/August). The inclining significance of race. *Society, 15,* 10–15.

Wilson, W. J. (1980). *The declining significance of race* (2nd ed.). Chicago: University of Chicago Press.

CHAPTER 4

Beyond Employment Diversity: Rethinking Contemporary Racist News Representations

Christopher P. Campbell

Covering most of the front page of the Sunday (New Orleans) *Times-Picayune* on the morning of February 9, 1995, was a story that outlined the criminal pathology of a 20-year-old African American man suspected of murdering a White attorney in a highly publicized carjacking case. In all capital letters, the headline read "A LIFE OF CRIME." A three-by-four-inch "mug shot" of the man was centered between the text of the story and a huge graphic that outlined the man's juvenile and adult criminal records.

In oversized type, the story began (again, in all capital letters): "A PLEA BARGAIN HERE. A DROPPED CHARGE THERE. Once, in a sad commentary on the times, he got off lightly because the cop who arrested him was himself arrested for murder. Through 10 years, at least 23 arrests and five convictions, Percy Hawthorne slipped through the system. Finally, police say, he killed."

Above the newspaper's nameplate, a "teaser" for a story in that day's Living section featured a picture of Sybil Morial, mother of New Orleans mayor Marc Morial and widow of former mayor Dutch Morial. Beginning on the front page of that day's Living section were three stories related to Mrs. Morial, replete with a number of family photos and a five-by-seven-inch color photo of her seated in her home's solarium. The cutline under that photo told us that the solarium was "Morial's favorite room for hanging out and watching the herons and ducks and squirrels that visit her backyard, as well as the bayou that meanders behind it."

Like Percy Hawthorne, Sybil Morial is an African American. Unlike Percy Hawthorne, Sybil Morial enjoys a life of privilege, of affluence, of superb education, of social prominence, and of political status. As the stories tell us, she has five grown children: a mayor, a doctor, an investment banker, a fund-raiser, and a law student. Though one of the stories tells us that Sybil and Dutch Morial grew up in segregated New Orleans and were active participants in the battle for civil rights, the theme of the coverage was the impressive educational, political, and social success of the Morial family.

Without doubt, Sybil Morial and her family are deserving of the flattering coverage they received in that day's *Times-Picayune*. And the crime that Percy Hawthorne is accused of committing is a heinous one that also may have merited the attention it received. But the coverage of these two people on the same day also serves as an example of the two primary representations of African Americans that news organizations cling to and that may be obliterating more accurate, comprehensive, and multidimensional representations.

Sociologist Herman Gray identified similar "twin representations" (1991, p. 304) in his study of prime-time television's images of African Americans. That study compared the middle-class imagery of television sitcoms with the underclass imagery of nonfictional television. I will argue here that the two images also exist side-by-side in American news coverage, and that they may be dominating American discussion and thought on matters of race. I will also argue that these two representations persist despite the news media's efforts to racially diversify their newsrooms. I will suggest that the news industry needs to carefully re-examine the "common sense" with which it goes about the business of covering African Americans and African American communities.

CONTEMPORARY RACISM AND THE NEWS

The aforementioned article by Gray (1991) contrasts the upper-middle-class Black life portrayed on *The Cosby Show* with the underclass black life portrayed in a 1985 PBS documentary entitled *The Vanishing Family: Crisis in Black America*. Race as it is portrayed on fictional television, according to Gray, is consistent with the American Dream, and "appeals to the utopian desire in blacks and whites for racial oneness and equality while displacing the persistent reality of racism and racial inequality or the kinds of social struggles and cooperation required to eliminate them" (p. 302).

The underclass Black life of nonfictional TV, on the other hand, fails to "identify complex social forces like racism, social organization, economic dislocation, unemployment, the changing economy, or the welfare state as the causes of the crisis in [the urban underclass] community" (p. 300). Gray concludes that these representations "displace" more accurate representations that would show us that most members of the underclass have the same values we saw on *Cosby,* but many "lack the options and opportunities to realize them" (p. 303).

So while the images and themes reflected in prime-time shows with majority African American casts often mean positive portrayals of minority life, the "commonsense" understandings they contribute to are not void of problematic meanings. Similarly, when news coverage includes such portrayals as a sort of counterbalance to the far more frequent coverage of criminal pathology in the African American community, it legitimates the mythical "reality" of American racial harmony and cooperation. In doing so, it offers no explanation for the members of the underclass who have somehow not opted for the American Dream but for a life of crime, poverty, hopelessness.

Entman (1990) has suggested that the frequency of African American local television news anchors reinforces the contemporary racist belief that Americans who are members of minority groups have the same opportunities to succeed as White Americans, and that those who don't succeed are solely responsible for their failure. He is very likely correct; the two most common images of African Americans on local TV news are (1) well-paid journalists, and (2) violent criminals. And as this essay will demonstrate, both White and African American journalists cling to common sense notions about underclass African Americans that categorize them as menacing, immature, and unintelligent.

A number of studies have identified problems with news coverage of African Americans (see Bagdikian, 1983; Boskin, 1980; Dates & Barlow, 1990; Entman, 1990, 1992; Gist, 1990; Kerner Commission, 1968; Martindale, 1986, 1990a, 1990b; Nelson, 1993; Pease, 1989; Wilson & Guttiérez, 1985). Most of those studies point to the "invisibility" of minority communities in the news and of the prevalence of stereotypes in the news that does get covered.

Recent studies have also cited the existence of contemporary racist coverage by news organizations with racially diverse newsrooms. Cose (1994) argues:

> Even if newspapers can manage to achieve demographic parity [in their hiring of minority journalists] with the general population, that alone will not guarantee a more honest and representative brand of reporting. The problem lies as much in our attitudes as in our statistics. (p. 10)

I have argued (Campbell, 1995) that minority journalists may indeed be inadvertently playing a role in advancing the subtle attitudes of contemporary racism. Stories by journalists of all colors reflect the dominant newsroom values, which dictate similar coverage of events by minority and nonminority newspeople.

News coverage by organizations that are racially diverse can still reflect the attitudes of contemporary racism. Those attitudes are more subtle than the overtly racist attitudes of traditional racism. For Americans of all colors, some of those attitudes may go unrecognized.

Two types of contemporary racism have been identified as "symbolic" (by McConahay, 1986) and "enlightened" (by Jhally & Lewis, 1992) racism. Symbolic racism (also called "modern" racism by Sears, 1988) has three basic characteristics: first, a general animosity among Whites toward African Americans; second, a resistance to Black political demands—for instance, affirmative action or hiring quotas; and third, a belief that racial discrimination is a thing of the past. Numerous studies have found the portrayal of crime on local television news to contribute to the first characteristic; that is, the frequent menacing images of African American criminals contribute to a modern racist hostility toward African Americans. Entman (1990) also found that local television coverage "exaggerated the degree to which Black politicians (as compared with White ones) practice special interest politics" (p. 342), contributing to the second characteristic of modern racism: resistance to Black political demands. Entman also argues that the presence of Black anchors and authority figures on the news contributes to the third characteristic of modern racism, the belief that racial discrimination no longer exists.

This characteristic is also at the root of enlightened racism (Jhally & Lewis, 1992), a contemporary form of racism that allows Whites to simultaneously hold the view that they are liberal-minded and pro–equal rights yet still hold the belief that underclass minorities are themselves solely responsible for not seizing American equal opportunity. Jhally and Lewis, who analyzed the reactions of viewers of *The Cosby Show*, found

> In the apparently enlightened welcome that white viewers extend to the Huxtables, [we end up with] a new, sophisticated form of racism . . . who have not achieved similar professional or material success. Television, which tells us nothing about the structures behind success or failure, leaves white viewers to assume that black people who do not measure up to their television counterparts have only themselves to blame. (pp. 137–138)

News coverage that also "neglects the structures behind success or failure" similarly contributes to the attitudes of the enlightened racist. For such viewers who regularly see successful African American anchors and reporters, they can only surmise that their success is a reflection of the triumph of American social progress and racial tolerance. When coverage highlights the achievements of some fortunate African American, racists are given additional rationalization for their attitude. Certainly, I am not recommending that coverage of successful African Americans should be eliminated. I am arguing, however, that when that coverage is included to somehow counter the far more common coverage of underclass African American criminals—especially at the exclusion of coverage of the huge majority of underclass African Americans who themselves are not criminal—then the two representations will fuel continued racist attitudes.

The problem is possibly as much about *class* as it is about *race*. That is, news organizations rarely cover underclass members of *any* race (outside of coverage of violent crime). Newsroom common sense prescribes coverage of prominent societal figures rather than members of low-income communities who may very well have the same values—like determination, compassion, and desire for excellence—that are almost solely attributed to Americans of privilege. When journalists of color arrive in newsrooms where coverage reflects a hegemonic understanding of class, the racial diversity they bring may not be equally diverse in terms of class.

Journalists of color covering news about non-White Americans similar to White Americans indicates the powerful, implicit common sense that dictates the routines and conventions of the newsroom. News organizations (especially local television news organizations) are obsessed with the instantaneous coverage of violent crime—crime that happens to be more common in the African American community. The coverage rarely considers the political, social, historical, educational, or economic roots of such crime, and therefore constructs individual episodes of violence as stories with no history, entirely void of perspective.

When racially sensitive news organizations attempt to balance that kind of coverage with "positive" coverage of successfully assimilated African Americans, they show us the "reality" of the American melting pot. Audiences are left with two conflicting images. One is of Percy Hawthorne, sociopath. The other is of Sybil Morial, superwoman. If America is a place where equal access is available to all (as explained in the routine coverage of people like the Morial family), only one explanation remains for the behavior of the country's Percy Hawthornes, and that is that they somehow lack the values, initiative, or intelligence to seize the many wonderful possibilities available to them in this land of opportunity. What is missing is coverage of the many factors—educational neglect, political ineptitude, racism, economic disparity (to name a few)—which would show audiences that many young African American men do not live in a land of opportunity.

What follows are textual analyses of a series of local TV news stories that—like the Hawthorne/Morial coverage—reflect the news industry's commonsense portrayals of race. As cultural anthropologist Clifford Geertz once observed, "Common sense is not what the mind
cleared of cant spontaneously apprehends; it is what the mind filled with
presuppositions . . . concludes" (1983, p. 84).

KING DAY IN SYRACUSE

In 1993, I began a study of local television news which included analysis
of coverage in 29 American cities on the Martin Luther King Jr. holiday
(Campbell, 1995). The theme of the coverage in 28 of those cities was that
King Day was a day to celebrate America's triumph over its racist past.
American racism was consistently relegated to images of old black-and-
white footage from the civil rights era. Hints at the persistence of racism
were regularly absorbed into the "positive" aspects of the coverage. King
Day on local TV news was a day to celebrate America as a haven of inte-
gration and tolerance, fueling the notions of enlightened racism.

One story I analyzed typifies that approach. Syracuse's WTVH
acknowledged the holiday by concluding its 5:30 p.m. broadcast with a
3½-minute feature on an African American family and its members'
views on King. The Pollard family is a financially and socially successful one, the father the dean of a college at a major university. American
racism is largely depicted in images of the past, black-and-white film-
clips of another time—the White men who taunt the civil rights
marchers and wave a Confederate flag represent the bigotry of an era
gone by. William Pollard recalls the injustice of the segregated South of
his youth, but his present status as an esteemed academic speaks to
America's triumph over that injustice.

The Pollard family—like the fictional Huxtable family—attests to
the attainability of the American Dream. Their strong sense of values is
stressed, and becomes the commonsense explanation of why they are
different from those who are less fortunate. The family's successful
assimilation into the financial and moral high ground of middle-Ameri-
can society is lauded by the doting White journalists who cover the
story: "Quite a family," says the anchor. "Very, very impressive,"
responds the reporter. "They're wonderful," adds the anchor.

The Pollards mythologically represent an open American society in
which dreams can be fulfilled for those with the right values. The Pollards are real-life Huxtables. Their success carries similar connotations
to that of Bill Cosby's fictional family, which as Jhally and Lewis (1992)
argued, implied "the failure of a majority of black people . . . who have

not achieved similar professional or material success" (p. 137). They stand in stark contrast to the impoverished and criminal images of African Americans, which are far more common in the news.

In fact, the Pollard family story was followed by a story that led off the station's 6 p.m. newscast about a woman whose son was killed when her home was destroyed by a fire that was apparently caused by a cigarette she had lit before falling asleep. The story begins with videotaped pictures of a burned-out house and emphasis on the propounded similarity of this fire with another one that had led to a trial that had been covered by the station the previous week.

The story's narrative draws clear lines between races. The Whites we see include three WTVH journalists, a police captain, and the Syracuse district attorney. It is their common sense that dictates the story's conclusions about mothers who leave their children "home alone," a phrase anchor Ron Curtis uses three times in his introduction to the story. The story's African American sources include Victoria Dunbar, who is accused of having been out drinking when her son died in a fire at their home, and a man who comments that his neighbor should be held accountable for leaving her children unattended. His comment supports the story's dominant culture understanding of the event: How could a mother leave her children home alone to die in a fire?

That understanding is hammered home in the reporter's interview with the Syracuse district attorney, whose volatile reaction to the incident exceeds that of the African American source. The reporter tells us that the death of a child makes Bill Fitzpatrick "particularly mad," and his feelings stand in stark contrast to the brief comments of Victoria Dunbar, whose words are described by a reporter as a "chillingly true" harbinger of the latest fire: "I'm quite sure I'm not the only parent that stays out or goes out sometimes and leaves their kids at home by themselves." Her comments become the African American interpretation of the events. Dunbar's image contrasts with the White sources and journalists whose outrage at the events becomes the manifest interpretation, and the story reinforces what Wilson and Gutiérrez (1985) call "the old stereotype of ethnics as . . . too lazy to work and who indulge in drugs and sexual promiscuity" (p. 139).

That stereotype is also evoked earlier in the story when a reporter says that "Shirley Avery left her kids alone in the early hours Sunday while she drank at a friend's house," and a police source tells us she left "to go out to find her boyfriend." In describing racist sexual stereotypes, West (1993) describes the dominant culture perception of Black sexuality in terms of "the exotic 'other'—closer to nature (removed from intelligence and control) and more prone to be guided by base pleasures and impulses" (p. 88).

The story's commonsense theme of outrage—reflected in the comments by the White journalists and sources—seems dictated by stereo-typical thought processes that have mythologized Black behavior: Look at how horrible these mothers are, out carousing instead of tending to their children. Again, the stories are based on police accounts, not com-pleted court cases. We are not told of the results of Dunbar's trial, and Avery's trial is not likely to occur soon. But the stories implicate the guilty mothers. Their existence is seen as a disparate one from the out-raged White observers. White life—displayed in the familial banter among the journalists (co-anchor Ron Curtis twice referring to reporter Scott Atkinson as "Scotty") and in Fitzpatrick's colorful verbalization of his infuriation—is hardly the same as Black life.

When reconsidering the journalists doting reactions at the end of the Pollard family story, we understand their awe at an African American family that has achieved such remarkable success. And we are left with two distinct images of African American life: the Pollards, wholesome, assimilated, financially and socially successful; and Shirley Avery/Victo-ria Dunbar, mothers whose criminal, amoral behavior led to the death of their children. For the enlightened racist, it is simply a matter of choice for the two mothers to live a life of slovenliness, when in fact they could have opted for the wholesome life of the Pollards. Since the news robs stories of any historical or social context, the images hardly pro-vide any perspective that could demonstrate otherwise.

KING DAY IN COLUMBUS, OHIO

The Syracuse stories were told by White journalists, but coverage by African Americans can embrace similar racial representations. Coverage of the King holiday by Columbus's WSYX was typical of the kind of stories local news audiences nationwide saw January 18, 1993. It shows how the "twin representations" of race can exist within one story and how African American reporters can reflect majority-culture common sense in their own coverage.

WSYX sent two Black reporters to cover the King holiday in that city. On a connotative level, the Columbus coverage—like that in Syra-cuse and 27 other cities whose coverage I viewed in 1993—assigns American racism to the past. Reporter Charlene Brown describes the day's march as "very symbolic" in that it commemorated "the marches that Dr. Martin Luther King, Jr. himself led." The marchers "braved the cold weather to come out and join in [honoring] . . . a peace-maker and a man that worked for equality for all." The children who are inter-viewed contribute to the story's commonsense understanding of the struggle for racial equality as a part of American history. In introducing the kids' remarks, reporter Tanya Hutchins says "their generation" listened to church service speakers "more intently than most would think," and that they "understand what Martin Luther King was all about."

One of the children says King is "very special to me because he fought for our rights so we could sit at a lunch counter and eat." Another says, "He helped Blacks and Whites make friends." The children's innocent failure to fully grasp the true nature of race relations in America is understandable. But their simplistic explanations of King's apparent triumph over racism is little different from the mythological theme espoused by the station's journalists. As co-anchor Deborah Countiss remarks at the story's conclusion, "One of the very sad chapters in our nation's history . . . has been turned into a celebration."

Like coverage in many cities, the Columbus coverage contains allusions to the persistence of racism, but they are overshadowed by the story's more prevalent assimilationist ideology. For instance, city councilman Michael Coleman, in his speech at a Catholic church, echoes King in saying, "We are not free until all of us are free." And in the reporters' "live" discussion of the day's events, Brown tells Hutchins that the participation of young people is "the kind of thing that you don't expect . . . given so much of what we cover everyday and so many of the problems that we have with our young people." Hutchins agrees. But these hints at the persistence of a society plagued with racial problems fail to contradict the story's assimilationist narrative.

Although Coleman suggests "we are not free," his status as a successful African American politician speaks to an America of equal access for all of its citizens. Similarly, the images of the African American reporters who admit to "the problems we have with our young people" confute the notion that those problems may be linked to racism. The Black civic leader and journalists contribute to the mythology of enlightened racism. As Jhally and Lewis (1992) observe,

> Among white people, the admission of black characters to television's upwardly mobile world gives credence to the idea that racial divisions, whether perpetuated by class barriers or racism, do not exist. Most white people are extremely receptive to such a message. (p. 135)

The story's focus on the celebratory nature of the day's events is compounded by the journalists' frequent references to the diversity of the participants. We see two shots of the day's march. The first one, a long shot from above the marchers, does seem to show a number of White participants in the crowd. The second is a full shot of five marchers, one of whom is White. Brown describes the participants as "young, old, Black, White, people from many different religions." In introducing coverage of the church service, Hutchins says, "People of all races and denominations came to worship at St. John the Evangelist Church in East Columbus." The shots of the ceremony indicate the crowd does appear to be well integrated. The assimilationist ideology continues in the children's responses to the reporter's questions. A ten-year-old African American boy says King symbolized for "justice, well, for Black people, standing up for Black and White."

The approach of the WSYX journalists to the story suggests that the children's interpretation of race relations is an accurate one. Brown concludes the story by agreeing with Countiss's assessment of the celebratory nature of the events as "a positive thing." Says Brown,

> I think that's one of the most important things to keep in mind about this celebration. It is a celebration of [King's] life, and not just a memorial to his slaying, and that gives it a much more upbeat and—for a lot of people—much more meaningful message.

Among that "lot of people" are clearly the station's journalists. While a celebration of the life of Dr. Martin Luther King Jr. is appropriate, the tone of the coverage smugly denies America's failure to attain his dream. In its words and images, it presents a contrived understanding of racial harmony. Both the White and Black journalists contribute to the mythical existence of the American melting pot. Perhaps most significant are the remarks made by the African American reporters who contribute to the stereotypes that local TV news routinely reinforces. Hutchins says the participation of young people—and almost all of those we have seen are Black—in the days events "was a great example . . . of kids not on the streets but actually performing and participating in activities all throughout the city." And Brown adds that that participation is "the kind of thing that you don't expect young people to do given so much of what we cover everyday and so many of the problems that we have with our young people." Although the coverage of the events could serve to counter the stereotypes, the emphasis on their uniqueness simply compounds the standard notions of negative behavior. Because of the station's interpretation of King Day as a celebration of America's triumph over racism, Brown's comments (and her status, as well as Hutchins's, as successful television journalists)—however she may have intended them to be understood—directly reinforce the beliefs of enlightened racism: Prejudice and discrimination no longer exist; Americans of color who fail to achieve financial and social success have only themselves to blame.

MIDNIGHT BASKETBALL IN MILWAUKEE

I witnessed a similar narrative in coverage by Milwaukee's WITI of a midnight basketball league that was forming in 1993. I have since

witnessed remarkably similar coverage of midnight basketball programs in New Orleans, my hometown, by both White and African
American journalists. If there is a midnight basketball league in your
town, I bet you have seen it too; the conventions of local television
news make it easy to predict how stories are covered. The coverage
demonstrates the proclivity of local television news to feed mythical
thinking about race. The stories make assumptions that are rooted in
stereotypical thinking and are shrouded in the journalistic common
sense that dictates what news organizations choose to cover and how
that coverage is handled.

In Milwaukee's coverage, WITI anchor Vince Gibbens tells viewers
that that city's midnight league is "aimed at getting young men from the
inner-city on their feet." Live from courtside, reporter Phil Harris tells
us that the league's goal is "to give 18– to 25–year-olds something positive to do in the late night hours. One benefit to the community is keeping these young men off the street and out of potential trouble." The
men we see behind Harris all appear to be Black.

Certainly, the intention of WITI was not to reinforce negative
stereotypes about African American men. In fact, a story like this one
could actually debunk the myths that are reinforced by standard crime-
related news by focusing on a constructive program designed to improve
inner-city life. But in the context of typical local television news coverage—coverage that is preoccupied with crime news while generally
ignoring less lurid stories in minority communities—the story contributes to contemporary racist mythology.

We do not find out from this story how many of the league's participants actually need to "get on their feet." We do not know how
many of them are unemployed. No explanations are offered that might
help us understand the "potential trouble" that these men might get
into. If, indeed, these men are prone to do "negative" things, what is the
reason? While these issues are possibly too complex to explain in a short
television news story, by neglecting them journalists contribute to a perpetuation of stereotypical thinking about African American life in the
inner-city. Sure the crime rate is high. So is the unemployment rate.
(Remarkably, the news rarely makes the obvious link between the two.)
But crime is committed by a very small percentage of inner-city residents.

The public's willingness to buy into hoaxes in which Black men are
blamed for violent crimes (for instance, the Susan Smith case) is rooted
in the stereotypes reinforced by local TV news. Writing about such
hoaxes, *Philadelphia Inquirer* associate editor Acel Moore (1994)
acknowledged that African American communities suffer from a higher
rate of violent crime, but

ignored is the reality that 98 percent of all black Americans are law-abiding citizens. If you compute all the African Americans who are arrested for violent crimes, they represent less than 1 percent of the black population. (p. B-7)

Milwaukee's midnight basketball league is certainly a "good idea," as Gibbens announces in concluding the story. It will very likely contribute to a better life for its participants, especially because the program encourages continuing education and includes job-training. But this does not mean that its participants are "off their feet" or "on the street." Those who are participating in the program are just as likely to be employed, productive members of society. But the story's mythical implications—that the participants are destined to otherwise behave negatively—contribute to racist notions that continue to foster the poverty and despair of urban life in America.

The Milwaukee story was handled by an African American reporter, Phil Harris. New Orleans coverage was handled almost identically by White reporters. Clearly, America's newsrooms need to increase the number of journalists of color if they are to successfully cover *all* of America's communities. But those newsrooms also need to rethink their approaches to coverage, especially when that coverage reinforces racist attitudes.

Local TV news does have the capacity to resist the stereotypes. Another of the stories I critiqued in my study—a murder covered by WTKR in Norfolk, Virginia—focused on the mother of the African American victim. Rather than getting the standard police account of the murder (which is often followed with shots of suspects being walked through a police station—solely for the sake of the local TV news cameras), WTKR reporter Patti DiVincenzo conducted an extensive interview with the mother, who was profound in her indictment of a society in which such things happen. But that coverage was highly unconventional; by resisting the conventions, it also resisted the commonsense interpretations of crime and race that dominate the evening news.

CONCLUSIONS

Newsroom conventions are powerful and unquestioned, and journalists—generally overworked and harried by deadline pressures—spend little time considering the more subtle implications of their work. There are also economic ramifications. The kind of perspective missing from stories would require in-depth, time-consuming investigation and reporting. This is least likely to happen in local television news, where big money dictates a kind of rapid-fire, mindless coverage intended to draw the largest number of viewers. And the current "twin representations" of race are satisfying for those viewers; newsroom common sense feeds America's common sense.

These representations can affect the American political system dangerously. The resurgence of racism and right-wing political thought clearly has roots in media portrayals—fictional and nonfictional—that reinforce the notions of contemporary racism. The news media, then, is hardly doing its job, which is to provide Americans with the kind of information on which sound political decisions can be based.

One could argue that I have read too much into too little in this analysis. I have analyzed only a handful of stories as evidence of the racist representations of race that flourish in the news media. While plenty of other research exists to support my findings, I would agree that it is an area that cries out for more analysis, both qualitative and quantitative. Academics need to continue the work that has been done in this area and to encourage their students to "read" the news in a critical fashion. Racial representation is an area of academic critique that needs further scholarly investigation, especially by academics of color. I would also argue that journalists themselves need to begin seriously reconsidering the way they do their job, especially considering how they portray America's minority communities.

The push for racially diverse newsrooms has certainly led to improved coverage of ethnic minority Americans. Anyone familiar with the award-winning race projects completed by *The Times-Picayune* or the *Akron Beacon-Journal* knows just how insightful coverage can be. But those projects were clearly beyond what we can expect in routine news coverage, even in the most racially diverse newsrooms.

What is far more likely is the continued racist coverage with which we are bombarded each night on the local evening news and more newspaper stories like the ones about Percy Hawthorne and Sybil Morial. Newsroom conventions need to be reconsidered and reinvented if American journalism is going to live up to its job, which is to provide a democratic populace with accurate and insightful coverage that will lead to wise, fair public policy.

REFERENCES

Bagdikian, B. (1983). *The media monopoly*. Boston: Beacon Press.

Boskin, J. (1980). Denials: The media view of dark skins and the city. In B. Rubin (Ed.), *Small voices and great trumpets: Minorities and the media* (pp. 141–147). New York: Praeger.

Campbell, C. P. (1995). *Race, myth and the news*. Thousand Oaks, CA: Sage.

Cose, E. (1994). Seething in silence—the news in black and white. *Media Studies Journal, 8*(3), 1–10.

Dates, J. L., & Barlow, W. (1990). *Split image: African-Americans in the mass media*. Washington, DC: Howard University Press.

Entman, R. M. (1990). Modern racism and the images of blacks in local television news. *Critical Studies in Mass Communication, 7*(4), 332–345.

Entman, R. M. (1992). Blacks in the news: Television, modern racism and cultural change. *Journalism Quarterly, 69*(2), 341–361.

Geertz, C. (1983). Common sense as a cultural system. In *Local knowledge: Further essays in interpretive anthropology*. New York: Basic Books.

Gist, M. E. (1990). Minorities in media imagery. *Newspaper Research Journal, 11*(3), 52–63.

Gray, H. (1991). Television, black Americans, and the American dream. In R. K. Avery & D. Eason (Eds.), *Critical perspectives on media and society* (pp. 294–305). New York: Guilford Press.

Jhally, S., & Lewis, J. (1992). *Enlightened racism: "The Cosby Show" audiences, and the myth of the American dream*. Boulder, CO: Westview Press.

Kerner Commission. (1968). *Report of the National Advisory Commission on Civil Disorders*. New York: E. P. Dutton.

Martindale, C. (1986). *The white press in black America*. New York: Greenwood Press.

Martindale, C. (1990a). Changes in newspaper images of black Americans. *Newspaper Research Journal, 11*(1), 40–50.

Martindale, C. (1990b). Coverage of black Americans in four major newspapers, 1950–1989. *Newspaper Research Journal, 11*(3), 96–112.

McConahay, J. B. (1986). Modern racism, ambivalence, and the modern racism scale. In S. L. Gaertner & J. F. Dovidio (Eds.), *Prejudice, discrimination, and racism* (pp. 91–125). Orlando, FL: Academic Press.

Moore, A. (1994, March 25). Hoaxes, black males and false accusations of crime. *The Times-Picayune*, p. B-7.

Nelson, J. (1993). *Volunteer slavery: My authentic Negro experience*. Chicago: Noble Press.

Pease, E. C. (1989). Kerner plus 20: Minority news coverage in the Columbus Dispatch. *Newspaper Research Journal, 10*(3), 17–38.

Sears, D. O. (1988). Symbolic racism. In P. A. Katz & D. A. Taylor (Eds.), *Eliminating racism* (pp. 53–84). New York: Plenum Press.

West, C. (1993). *Race matters*. Boston: Beacon Press.

Wilson, C. C. II, & Gutiérrez, F. (1985). *Minorities and media: Diversity and the end of mass communication*. Beverly Hills, CA: Sage.

PART II

Mass Media and Ethnicity

CHAPTER 5

Hegemony in Black and White: Interracial Buddy Films and the New Racism

B. Lee Artz

W. E. B. DuBois's observation in the early 1900s that the problem of color is the problem of the 20th century retains the same unsettling validity at the end of the century. Shifting political currents have allowed government policymakers to open an assault on affirmative action, make severe cuts in education, health care, and other social programs, and radically increase punitive measures against "urban" crime. The ability to initiate and institute such changes requires that the American people believe that racism has been overcome and that inequities in economic and social progress are the consequence of culture, biology, or individual life choices.

Such public perceptions have been reinforced, if not developed, by mass media images of real and fictional successful African Americans. The 4,500 Black elected officials recruited to established government institutions on the local, state, and federal level underwrite claims that Blacks now share in decision-making at all levels. News reports featuring General Colin Powell commanding American troops, Mayor Thomas Bradley defending Los Angeles police actions, and African American legislative, city council, and school board members participating in policy decisions bolster perceptions of race equality. These prominent news images of Black political leaders have been supplemented with a host of successful fictional Black characters on television—from George Jefferson and Bill Cosby to important black officials on *NYPD Blue*, *Law & Order*, and *Homicide*, among others. Complementing these small screen images, Hollywood has released dozens of well-publicized and popular movies depicting Black-White friendships—*Silver Streak, 48 Hours, Beverly Hills Cop, The Last Boy Scout, Die Hard, Lethal Weapon,* and *The Money Train,* among others. In the last two decades, these big-budget interracial male-bonding movies have been Hollywood's contribution to the discussion on race in America. In "buddy movies" there may be individual instances of prejudice, but overall, American society does not represent film heroes as racist.

Mass popular culture in late-20th-century America is characterized by this "new" racism. The emergent Black middle class and the recognizable additions of Black representatives to government bodies are accented in a corporate-run mass culture, while the conditions of life for poor and working-class Blacks are discounted or avoided. Celluloid images of successful Blacks working in established institutions help construct perceptions of harmonious race relations. Buddy movies, in particular, help Blacks (and Whites) accept existing social conditions. Behind the facade of entertainment lies a persuasive political argument that Blacks are benefiting materially, politically, and culturally from existing social arrangements and practices. Through the production, distribution, and consumption of fictions that include entertaining, innocuous interracial narratives, Blacks appear to be "movin' on up." Pleasing to Blacks and comforting to Whites, the fictions of interracial buddy movies simplify race relations, reassuring America of its continuing goodness. Viewed by millions of Americans, cultural vehicles such as interracial buddy movies help negotiate popular consent for the "new" racism—touting equality while ignoring the actual condition of race relations.

CULTURAL HEGEMONY'S RACIAL SEGREGATION

Mass popular culture has always reflected and contributed to the preferred characterization of race in America. Interracial buddy films are only the most recent cultural manifestation of ongoing political and social negotiations over Black-White race relations. For hundreds of years, American popular culture has been filled with themes, tensions, and humor based on race. Apologists for slavery relied heavily on racial stereotypes in their literature and ever since, Black faces and bodies—in service to White society—have adorned a wide range of cultural objects from cookie jars to tobacco cans (Turner, 1994).

Early movies relied on similar crude racial stereotypes. In the 1920s and 1930s, for instance, child actors called Sunshine Sammy, Farina, Stymie, and Buckwheat popularized the pickaninny stereotype in Hal

Roach's *Our Gang* series. A lively interracial bunch of lower-class kids spent their days playing, conniving, and figuring out life. All of these "little rascals" were charming and comical and the Black kids were accorded a certain respect. Farina was "noted for his common sense and heroic demeanor," Stymie for his "nonchalance and detached shrewdness," while Buckwheat was the "perfect little dum-dum tag-along." Still, these "positive" portraits were outlined by existing stereotypes. "On more than one occasion, Farina was seen banqueting on a colored man's favorite dishes—fried chicken and watermelon" (Bogle, 1994, p. 23). Roach's treatment of Black comics was considered "liberal" at the time. In movies over the next three decades, however, African Americans weren't treated so politely. Blacks were either absent or relegated to offensive roles as "toms, coons, mulattos, mammies, and bucks" (Bogle, 1994, p. 4). Radio (and later television) simply reshuffled these images into programs such as *Amos and Andy* and *The Jack Benny Show*.

It took a massive social movement to rearrange depictions of Blacks in popular culture, a social movement that was powerful enough to socially and politically upset race segregation, discrimination, and inequality. Following the civil rights movement of the 1960s, the news media sharply increased coverage of Black America and, for the first time, devoted stories to the "normal life of the black community . . . showing blacks in the context of the total American society" (Martindale, 1986, p. 106). Liberal television producers entertained audiences with the fluff of *Julia* and the fiction of *Good Times*. Hollywood responded to the new social and political climate by releasing a series of format-driven Black superhero films now known as "blaxploitation" movies.

The movie industry's sudden interest in Black themes came at a time when public and private institutions were under political attack by an increasingly radical Black movement. From universities to local governments, hegemonic institutions were rearranging the terms of domination-subordination. Adjusting to Black demands was pragmatically cost-effective, socially and politically. Changes in movie narratives were no exception. Hollywood's Black superheroes came out just at a time when the mass Black audience needed them.

Heroes who defiantly challenge authorities have long been admired in Black folklore, so movies that starred tough, Black heroes were well received. Hollywood simply packaged their modern-day characters in imagery that glamorized the ghetto and elevated the pimp/outlaw/rebel to folk hero, while ignoring the actual social conditions of Black life (Bogle, 1994, p. 236). The old stereotypes of Black bucks "simply resurfaced in new garb to look modern, hip, provocative, and politically relevant" (Bogle, 1994, p. 232)—all for hegemonic effect. Dominant studios "played on the needs of black audiences for heroic figures without answering those needs in realistic terms" (Bogle, 1994, p. 242). "Black" power was de-politicized and embodied in *individual* heroes like Richard Roundtree as detective John Shaft, Fred Williamson in *Black Caesar* (1973), and the Black female superwoman Pam Grier. Significantly, while Black heroes and heroines "self-righteously gave lip service to the idea of political commitment" (Bogle, 1994, p. 241), they invariably dealt with social and community ills as personal obstacles.

Despite the distortions, patronizations, and service to dominant interests, Black-oriented films from this period retain a certain edge. "Their collective subtext attracts or sometimes repels us. Often political and social messages crept through, providing insights and comments on the quality of life in America. They touched on the mass hope for an overturn of a corrupt racist system" (Bogle, 1994, p. 242). The films of the 1970s illustrate how hegemony was constructed through the incorporation of Black concerns (racism, discrimination, power) and Black-oriented images (urban scenes, strong males, ghetto life) in representations that carried concepts (individualism, family values, hard work, authority) preferred by dominant groups. This construction takes a different form in the 1980s, when social movements faltered and political alliances shifted.

CULTURAL HEGEMONY'S RACIAL INTEGRATION

Not surprisingly, by the 1980s, Hollywood was out to rid films of the rebellious Black character. Having largely been marginalized in daily life, such figures could no longer exist in movies, or if they did, they had to be "tamed, disposed of, or absorbed into the system" (Bogle, 1994, p. 269). Obvious stereotypes resurfaced in *Caddyshack* (1980) and *Weird Science* (1985) while blackface and "neo-minstrelsy" appeared in *The Blue Brothers* (1980) and *Soul Man* (1986) (Guerrero, 1993, p. 237), but the more prevalent practice was to use Black stars like Richard Pryor, Louis Gossett Jr., and later Eddie Murphy and Danny Glover, in supporting roles. Indeed, the 1980s became the era of "buddy pictures" as friendly pairs of White and Black men frolicked from adventure to adventure.

Just as the "blaxploitation" movies of the 1970s reflect race relations of the time, so too, the new buddy movies reflect the tension of contemporary race relations and their popular conceptions. Of course, interracial buddies are not new to Hollywood—Will Rogers had Stepin Fetchit and Jack Benny had Eddie "Rochester" Anderson, but these were clearly unequal relationships based on the overt prejudices of

1930s and 1940s. Sidney Poitier modified the format somewhat in the 1950s and later it was refined with the comedy team of Richard Pryor and Gene Wilder. The buddy storyline finally settled on interracial teams of equal partners—partners who shared the film's intellectual, physical, and comic responsibilities—partners who "bond."

Black-White male bonding characterizes action-adventure movies of the 1980s and 90s: Carl Weathers warms to Sylvester Stallone in the *Rocky* series. Billy Dee Williams appears as Stallone's equal in *Nighthawks* (1982) and as a peer to the Star Wars heroes in *The Empire Strikes Back* (1980) and *Return of the Jedi* (1983). Gregory Hines fulfills the buddy role for Mikhail Baryshnikov in *White Nights* (1985) and Billy Crystal in *Running Scared* (1986). Eddie Murphy befriends Dan Akroyd in *Trading Places* (1983). Denzel Washington helps Donald Woods fight apartheid in *Cry Freedom* (1987). Joining his *Die Hard* Black buddies, Damon Wayans works with Bruce Willis against the bad guys in *The Last Boy Scout* (1991). The most popular movies of this genre feature Eddie Murphy as the sarcastic leading buddy in *48 Hours* (1982), *Beverly Hills Cop* (1984), and the sequels to each. Finally, in 1987, audiences were introduced to what must be the model interracial male team of the new age—Danny Glover and Mel Gibson as partner cops in *Lethal Weapon*. There are other examples of Hollywood's buddy genre—and there will be many more—because a public fascinated by and fearful of actual race relations needs the escapist fare pushed by major movie studios.

Beyond their attraction as action-adventure pictures, interracial buddy films are "wish-fulfillment fantasies for a nation that has repeatedly hoped to simplify its racial tensions" (Bogle, 1994, pp. 271–272). Indeed, buddy films are immensely popular and profitable because they permit and provide multiple meanings and interpretations for culturally and racially diverse audiences. Yet buddy movies effectively reinforce existing racial hegemony because couched within the myriad representations and readings of interracial images lies a clear message that presents the American status quo as preferred and natural. With occasional variation, these interracial "buddy films" follow an identifiable format that can only be characterized as a narrative and visual "strategy of containment" that subordinates Black characters and images and "subtly reaffirms dominant society's traditional racial order" (Guerrero, 1993, p. 237).

ATTRACTING THE RESISTIVE BLACK AUDIENCE

Perhaps most importantly we must understand why interracial "buddy" films that promote existing race relations can be so popular with Black audiences. The answer lies in the incorporation of four general characteristics attractive to Black audiences: (1) Black culture is recognizable and important to the story, (2) White characters often appear inferior to Black stars, (3) Black stars exhibit strength, dignity, and intelligence, and (4) Black-White cooperation appears possible. These ingredients vary from film to film, are buffered by certain dominant readings, and are even overturned in several instances. Nonetheless, these ingredients predominate in buddy films and help explain Black consent for the narratives and themes appearing in these films. These characteristics are best explained through example.

Recognizable Black culture. Because race provides the dramatic and comedic tension for all interracial buddy movies, leading Black characters always exhibit Black cultural identifiers in language, style, and attitudes. In *Silver Streak* and *Stir Crazy*, for example, Richard Pryor is funny and irreverent as Gene Wilder's fast-talking buddy. He's hip and irrepressibly Black, comically instructing Wilder on how to be "bad" and urban tough. Eddie Murphy is loose and jive-talking in *48 Hours*, his exchange of insults with Nick Nolte suggesting the verbal sparring of "playing the dozens" to Black audiences. In *Beverly Hills Cop*, Murphy sports a Detroit urban high school jacket, sneakers, and a hip urban style—loud talk sprinkled-with-vulgarity and a cool posture smacking of insubordination. Like the characters portrayed by Pryor, Murphy, and Weathers in *Rocky*, most Black buddies since the 1980s converse in the lyrical style of Black English, frequently using contemporary African American slang terms. Modern-day Black buddies are stereotypically boisterous and singularly unimpressed with White authority.

Weak White characters. Narratives for buddy pictures always contain a number of White characters who are weak, naive, or dishonest and easily upstaged by the Black star. A bumbling Gene Wilder needs the guidance of a clever Richard Pryor in *Silver Streak*. Eddie Murphy's film career has been built on fooling, deceiving, and intimidating a variety of White characters. In *Beverly Hills Cop*, for example, he befriends two dippy unsophisticated White cops, easily tricking and maneuvering them throughout the movie. In *48 Hours*, single-handedly Murphy scares a barroom full of White "crackers." Socialite Dan Akroyd is utterly incapable of fending for himself without Murphy in *Trading Places*. In *Grand Canyon*, Kevin Kline is powerless when confronted by a few Black teenagers. It takes a tough Danny Glover to rescue the defenseless Kline. With a (feminist?) twist, Rosie Perez has to protect a naive Woody Harrelson from Wesley Snipe's "hustle" in *White Men Can't Jump*. In short, a multitude of White characters provide convenient foils for the street-smart wiles of the Black buddy.

Strong, smart Black characters. Black characters possess a certain crude dignity in all buddy pictures. Richard Pryor is resourceful and clever in *Silver Streak* and *Stir Crazy*. Eddie Murphy is "quick-witted, sharp-tongued, undaunted, and unconquerable" in *48 Hours* (Bogle, 1994, p. 281). "Irreverent, insubordinate, and disrespectful" of White culture in *Beverly Hills Cop* (Guerrero, 1993, p. 243), Murphy successfully catches all of the bad guys when the White cops can't. Throughout the 1980s, audiences cheered on a parade of tough Black buddies. Disciplined and strong, Louis Gossett Jr. taunts and then trains Richard Gere to be *An Officer and a Gentleman*; an unarmed, but resourceful, Damon Wayans rescues Bruce Willis in *The Last Boy Scout*; and a dignified and wise Danny Glover calms and defends a wacky Mel Gibson in *Lethal Weapon*. In Hollywood's new interracial buddy films, dozens of characters give positive representations of single Black males to an appreciative African American audience.

Pleasing interracial fantasy. From the perspective of Black audiences, respectable Black characters work with their White counterparts on an equal footing. "There are no significant cultural gaps or distinctions for [buddies] to bridge" (Bogle, 1994, p. 276). Black characters are respectable and influential over White characters, who become wiser, more relaxed, and more expressive. Wilder learns to be "cool" from Pryor. Tutored by Murphy, Beverly Hills cop Judge Reinhold loosens up his behavior and demeanor. Gossett grooms Gere. With Weathers' help, Stallone becomes a better fighter. And Gibson calms down with Glover's guidance. In this buddy world, individual Black men bring intelligence and skill to their relationships with supportive White men. Audiences are attracted to this narrative of interracial inequality, sincerity, and trust. Unfortunately, these images do not "portray the complexity of social, political and cultural forces that structure relationships between Blacks and Whites" (Giroux, 1994, p. 81).

PROTECTING HEGEMONY AND RACIST SENSIBILITIES

The four characteristics of buddy films that invite Black appreciation are woven into story lines that invite White audience approval of existing race relations: (1) featured Black culture appears as stereotypically "jive"; (2) White authorities are ultimately in charge; (3) the lone Black hero is separated from his community; and (4) the fantasy of Black-White cooperation appears possible within the context of the status quo. These characteristics contain and overcome any resistive impulses within the films' narratives. The more popular buddy films provide some of the best illustrations of these palliatives that make the movies' "Blackness" acceptable to hegemony.

Stereotyped Black culture. With some exceptions, such as Danny Glover in *Lethal Weapon*, Black characters are hustlers (e.g., Snipes in *White Men Can't Jump*) criminals (e.g., Murphy in *48 Hours*), or athletes (e.g., Weathers in *Rocky* and Wayans in *The Last Boy Scout*). Black stars are jive, frequently rude, sexually promiscuous, and generally disrespectful to authority and polite society. Indeed, much of the humor of buddy movies stems from the juxtaposition of expected acceptable behavior and the refusal (or inability) of Black characters to comply. In other words, the appearance of Black culture in mainstream movies is not unequivocally progressive, nor does Black culture in general appear as singularly oppositional. Rather, Hollywood's buddy movies have emasculated, diffused, and mocked Black resistance. Quite frequently, Black roles have almost cartoonish dimensions. In the Rocky series, for example, Carl Weather's early Apollo Creed and Mr. T's later role are little more than caricatures of Black boxers posturing, prancing, and boasting for fight promoters.

Of course, different Black actors and their buddy performances carry more or less social critique than others. For instance, despite similarities between Richard Pryor and Eddie Murphy, the two comedians represent quite different takes on the African American experience.

Because of his humorously biting social insights on race, Pryor had a large Black following long before he appeared as a "buddy." As White audiences "discovered" him, Pryor tempered his ethnic humor because he realized it was reinforcing racist attitudes. Notably, he only became a star to White audiences after Hollywood trimmed his social critique and cast him as a bumbler.

Eddie Murphy, in contrast, had a large White following from the very beginning—perhaps because his comedy lacks the social outrage of Pryor's. Murphy may be a "loose, jivey, close to vulgar Black man" but he doesn't "threaten the White audience's feelings of superiority. Nor does he challenge (through insightful anger) racial attitudes" (Bogle, 1994, p. 281). One look at Murphy as "Farina" on NBC's *Saturday Night Live* should demonstrate that while he speaks out against racism his comedy takes no stands at all. Notably, Eddie Murphy's buddy roles offer up a condescending vision of Black culture as immature and unserious.

Beverly Hills Cop (1984) even treats racism as a joke. In one scene, Eddie Murphy as Alex Foley, the slick Detroit cop, bops in to an upscale Beverly Hills hotel and overhears the receptionist tell someone on the phone that no rooms are available. Murphy asks for a room anyway and then breaks into a loud, fast-talking, outrage-faking Black guy routine. Using the charge of racism as a ploy to intimidate Whites at the hotel makes for an easy laugh and the Black audience may even feel that race is part of the issue, but this scene also graphically recreates the complaint that Blacks find racism in places where it doesn't exist.

When Murphy charges into a country-western bar pretending to be a pushy Black cop—a White racist's "worst nightmare"—he not only delights Blacks who yearn for some social authority, he actually acts out what every White supremacist believes—Blacks with authority would be dangerous and irrational. Likewise, Wesley Snipes's double-cross of Woody Harrelson in *White Men Can't Jump* pokes fun at Woody's naiveté, but it also suggests that Black men are inclined to cheat Whites who befriend them. Such is the contradictory nature of buddy films that seek to please Black and White audiences without upsetting dominant stereotypes or disrupting the preferred reading of race relations in America.

White authority. "Good guys wear white hats" is a given in American culture. In the case of buddy movies, "good guys have white faces" and good guys are in charge. Whatever individual Black authority appears in the film, White authorities are ultimately in charge. Eddie Murphy is literally in the "protective custody" of Nick Nolte for 48 hours and his escapades in Beverly Hills restore the "natural" order of White authority. Pryor has been most successful as a "meek clown in the protective cultural custody of a White buddy" (Guerrero, 1993, p. 241). Weathers wins in the first *Rocky*, but is soon reduced to manager and fan.

Even in science fiction buddy narratives, White authority is sacrosanct. Billy Williams remains an outcast as Luke Skywalker (blond, blue-eyed, and dressed in white) defeats the evil empire and Darth Vader (sinister, faceless, and clad in Black armor). The allegory of Star Wars has nothing on the "realism" of more down-to-earth buddy movies, however. In *Cry Freedom*, White journalist Donald Woods is more important than Black freedom fighter Denzel Washington. In *Running Scared*, Gregory Hines and Billy Crystal resist the bureaucracy, but remain its servants. Perhaps *Die Hard with a Vengeance* best expresses this dominant theme of buddy movies—Samuel L. Jackson portrays a Black nationalist shopkeeper who learns that White authorities are essential to the safety and security of Black children.

Isolated Black characters. With few exceptions, most notably Snipes in *White Men Can't Jump,* Black stars are separated from their community. Pryor, Murphy, Hines, Wayans, and other Black heroes have few, if any, Black friends. Black stars are either desexed or oversexed, but seldom do they have a romantic love interest. In contrast, White buddies usually have girlfriends, wives, or families. In *Lethal Weapon,* which creatively reverses the usual White-Black character roles, Glover's family is made acceptable for the mass White audience "by carefully scrubbing it 'clean' of too strong an ethnic identity" (Bogle, 1994, p. 276).

Hegemonically comforting interracial fantasy. Mocking Black culture, maintaining White authority, and isolating leading Black characters, buddy movies narratively incorporate oppositional imagery and posturing into acceptable hegemonic limits. Although race undoubtedly provides the tension for each movie's success, the complex and contradictory dynamics of real interracial friendships are never explored. Either Black characters penetrate "clearly demarcated White cultural, social, or physical space" (Guerrero., 1993, p. 243) like Pryor in *The Toy* and Murphy in *Beverly Hills*, or White characters find themselves lost in a stereotypically defined Black cultural space; Wilder in prison, Kline in South Africa, or Harrelson in an urban Black neighborhood. In general, Whites are "simultaneously portrayed as both victims of cultural change and the only gatekeepers of a society which appears on the verge of self-destruction" (Giroux, 1994, p. 81). Hollywood's fictional Black-White male friendships typically ignore institutional racism and its manifestations in employment, housing, education, and the justice system. Instead, buddy movies symbolically argue that racism is overstated and, more importantly, can be overcome through male-bonding (not incidentally leaving out over half of the population).

BALANCING SUBORDINATE-DOMINANT NARRATIVES

Buddy films creatively blend these two contradictory, yet complementary, sets of ingredients into narratives that attract wide audiences. The richness and complexity of Black culture does not appear in Hollywood's big-budget projects. Instead, simple and stereotypical Black cultural identifiers are represented as part of mainstream mass society. Through their actions, language, and style, Black characters criticize and challenge established authority, thus pleasing Black audiences. But they do so within hegemonically supportive plots—which comforts more conservative audiences. Like small pieces of a puzzle, oppositional narratives are pieced together with dominant readings, resulting in a finished picture that frames contemporary capitalist society as the best of all possible worlds.

Blacks and other opponents of racism may discern a critique of the social order. They may even derive some pleasure from the "bark" of the leading Black characters. But no one feels the bite. The four characteristics of buddy films that reinforce dominant race relations smother any social critique that might arise from the appearance of Black culture in the story line. In other words, the meaning of Black cultural images must be read not only in the context of the viewers' social experience, but also in the context of the film's story line and character development.

CONCLUSION

After almost 90 years of American cinema, distinctly African American stories and styles are finally being widely distributed. Today, Black audiences wield considerable economic power as consumers and (if organized and motivated) hold significant political and social power; consequently media producers and advertisers now seek to attract and please Black audiences. Buddy films have become the primary cinematic vehicle for incorporating Black cultural images into a popular entertainment that is ideologically favorable to today's capitalist hegemony. Undoubtedly, Hollywood has always constructed fantasy worlds for moviegoers, a primary function of the entertainment industry. But three decades after the civil rights movement, at a time when the United States remains severely racially divided, and while major policy questions affecting race relations are being debated and decided, the singular big screen fantasy of interracial heroes triumphing over all is a dangerous fantasy.

Buddy films don't suggest a way out of the central "problem of the twentieth century," but treat society's racial animosities as an excuse for entertainment. As Guerrero writes, "The popularity and number of these films is due, in part, to their ability to transcode, even into terms of fantasy, social unease over rising racial tensions" (Guerrero, 1993, p. 240).

Echoing the political shifts of government policy makers over the last 20 years, the world-according-to-buddy-movies has miraculously overcome institutional racism. The relevance of and necessity for political group struggle is conveniently denied. Because they prominently feature "positive" Black images, buddy movies disguise actual social relations and encourage Black and White acceptance of existing dominant-subordinate practices. In short, while dominant cultural hegemony has made significant adjustments in mainstream depictions of African Americans, the established social and racial order still appears natural and inevitable on the big silver screen.

With *Heart Condition* (1990), *Diggstown* (1992), *Gladiator* (1992), and *Lethal Weapon III* (1992), *Die Hard with a Vengeance* (1994), *The Money Train* (1995), and others that follow, Hollywood continues to downshift social and political meanings into escapist buddy stories.

REFERENCES

Baker, H. A. (1993). Spike Lee and the commerce of culture. In M. Diawara (Ed.), *Black American cinema* (pp. 154–176). New York: Routledge.

Baraka, I. M. (1993). Spike Lee at the movies. In M. Diawara (Ed.), *Black American cinema* (pp. 145–154). New York: Routledge.

Bogle, D. (1994). *Toms, coons, mulattos, mammies, & bucks: An interpretive history of blacks in American films*. New York: Continuum.

Guerrero, E. (1993). The black image in protective custody: Hollywood's biracial buddy films of the eighties. In M. Diawara (Ed.), *Black American cinema* (pp. 237–246). New York: Routledge.

Martindale, C. (1986). *The white press and black racism*. New York: Greenwood.

Turner, P. A. (1994). *Ceramic uncles & celluloid mammies: Black images and their influence on culture*. New York: Anchor.

CHAPTER 6

Black Situation Comedies and the Politics of Television Art

Angela M. S. Nelson

African Americans have been involved in experimental and full-scale television network programming as actors and entertainers since 1939. Over the past 50 years of American commercial television, African Americans have appeared in various forms of action-adventure drama (including westerns and detective dramas) and melodrama (including medical, legal, and family dramas), as well as made-for-television movies, anthologies, soap operas, mini-series, and comedy-variety shows. However, Blacks have appeared in the situation comedy genre more than in any other television formula. American broadcast and cable television have aired approximately 800 situation comedies since 1947 and since then there have been 184 situation comedies that have featured African Americans in either starring, co-starring, supporting, or transient roles. Of this number, a small percentage are Black sitcoms.

Black situation comedies (Black sitcoms) are open-ended series of 30-minute self-contained episodes—made for television network broadcasting and revolving around one or more plots (situations) generally involving misunderstandings—consist of stereotypical characterizations, ritualistic humor (repetition, gags, insults), an irrational approach to reality (Hough, 1981), and feature a regular cast of core characters of African descent and/or producers, directors, and writers of African descent. These sitcoms speak to Black or "American" audiences and emerge from self-conscious intentions, whether artistic, economic, or political, to illuminate African American characters or experiences (Cripps, 1978).

There are three types of Black sitcoms: domcoms (domestic comedies), actcoms (action comedies), and dramedies (dramatic comedies).

As with the majority of American situation comedies, the action takes place in the home, at the workplace, or in such combined home/work locations as colleges and military dwellings. In Black sitcoms, core characters have limited-to-no interaction with characters from other ethnic and racial groups. When they do, it is usually with Whites or Latinos. While Black dramedies are very rare (domcoms are the most common form), there have been four since 1947: *Julia* (NBC, 1968–1971), *Good Times* (CBS, 1974–1979), *Frank's Place* (CBS, 1987–1988), and *South Central* (Fox, 1993–1994).

Black sitcoms are not "Black" in that they exhibit an African American worldview or a Black philosophy of life. Rather, they are Black because the performers are Black, and their characters are supposedly dealing with their sitcom situations from a "Black" perspective. This is seen clearly when issues or concerns that are unique to African American life, history, and culture are explored, including such issues as racism and discrimination. However, more often than not, the cultural contexts of Black Americans are not explicitly evident in Black sitcoms, except when there is an emphasis on Black music, art, and literature as references and the use of Black language and Black verbal art forms. A Black sitcom that is based on an African American worldview might, for example, emphasize the importance of religion in African American culture throughout American history within the series.

The creation and development of Black situation comedies did not occur within a vacuum. Indeed, their very existence was influenced by the politics of television art, which involves the coexistence of three significant forces upon the creation, distribution, and reception of television situation comedy. These constituent groups consist of (*a*) the industry/network, including production companies and network executives, (*b*) the advertisers and sponsors, and (*c*) the audience. Throughout 40 years of Blacks in television situation comedy, the politics of television art have changed little, causing Black organizations, social leaders, and politicians to complain continually about the role of television in American culture and to identify the programs they believe to be beneficial or detrimental to African Americans. As early as 1939, Julius Adams in the *New York Amsterdam News* commented that "It would be suicidal to put a show like [*Amos 'n' Andy*] on television" (Cripps, 1975). And, as recently as 1993, Reverend Jesse Jackson was single-handedly credited for lobbying for the inclusion of the Black sitcom *Where I Live* (ABC, 1992–1993) onto the ABC 1993 fall lineup (Brodie, 1993).

While the overall effects of the politics of television art have changed little, the mere machinery has affected Black sitcoms in ways manifesting various portrayals of Blacks throughout American television history. In particular, there have been four periods of Black representation in Black sitcoms since 1947 (see McDonald, 1983; Reid, 1993; Gray, 1995). Each period signifies the dominant features of Black characterizations in sitcoms, particularly African Americans in Black sitcoms. They are (1) hybrid minstrelsy (1948–1961), (2) assimilationism (1961–1971), (3) assimilated hybrid minstrelsy (1972–1983), and (4) simultaneity and diversification (1984–present).

HYBRID MINSTRELSY (1948–1961)

Scholars commenting on this period of Blacks in sitcoms have opined that Blacks were portrayed as domineering mammies, Uncle Toms, lazy coons, all in subservient positions to Whites. The fact is that the politics of television art demanded that the familiar roles in which Blacks were portrayed, as in the minstrel shows, and the occupational positions Blacks held in American society during the 19th and early 20th century, be continued into radio and television. Perceived racial and occupational roles (see Meehan, 1983) were significant issues to Blacks involved with racial uplift ideology during the early part of the 20th century (Gaines, 1993). As radio and television producers were aware, the best illustration of a White middle-class family's social status was through the use and employment of a Black domestic. The domestic was a symbol that a White family was successful. The domestic was the symbol of wealth and social status. Therefore, it was this decoding of the servant role that antagonized the NAACP and Black middle class. While it is true the new Black middle class were antagonistic toward the portrayals of Black men and women as maids and butlers in film, radio, and television, their quest for a piece of the American dream was the critical element to understanding their strategy for censorship in these popular forms. In addition to *The Beulah Show* (ABC, 1950–1953), there were five other sitcoms that featured a Black domestic, butler, or handyman in a supporting or transient role. These sitcoms included *The Jack Benny Show* (CBS, 1950–1964; NBC, 1964–1965); *The Stu Erwin Show: The Trouble with Father* (ABC, 1950–1955); *My Little Margie* (CBS and NBC, 1952; CBS, 1953; NBC, 1953–1955); *Make Room for Daddy* (ABC, 1953–1957; CBS, 1957–1964; ABC, 1970–1971); *The Great Gildersleeve* (NBC, 1955–1956); and *Father of the Bride* (CBS, 1961–1962).

Even though *Beulah* was the first significant dramatic television series to feature an African American character as well as an African American female in a starring role, *Amos 'n' Andy* (CBS, 1951–1953) has received the most critical attention because of its popularity and longevity in American popular culture. *Amos 'n' Andy* began on the NBC radio network in Chicago in 1929 and was canceled in 1960. Long credited as being the first situation comedy, *Amos 'n' Andy* was created and performed by two White men, Charles Correll and Freeman Gosden. As a radio program, *Amos 'n' Andy* was both praised and reviled by Black journalists and the National Association for the Advancement of Colored People (NAACP). However, it was not until it was revealed that Gosden and Correll wanted to develop a television version of *Amos 'n' Andy* that the NAACP, in particular, solidified opinions against the program. In May of 1949, Gosden and Correll, in cooperation with CBS television, began searching the nation for an all-Black cast for the television version of *Amos 'n' Andy*. As Thomas Cripps (1983) notes, the NAACP used its national convention as a platform of protest that developed into a lengthy campaign. Their strategies included letters of complaint to the sponsor, press releases, a resolution at the NAACP convention in Atlanta in 1951, and nominal support from a small cluster of allies such as the United Auto Workers and the American Jewish Committee. At first, these efforts did nothing to halt the debut of *Amos 'n' Andy* on June 28, 1951. However, over the course of two seasons, the campaign without a doubt affected the status of the show. The last telecast on CBS was June 11, 1953.

As mentioned earlier, *Beulah* was the first television drama of any significance to star an African American. (*The Laytons* on the DuMont network starred Black actress Amanda Randolph from September 1948 to October 1948. However, very little is known about this show). While there were massive campaigns against *Amos 'n' Andy* on radio and television, it remained a popular and successful program, capturing the nation's attention from 7 to 7:15 p.m. when it began in the late twenties (MacDonald, 1979). *Beulah*, on the other hand, was also popular but was criticized because it portrayed a Black woman in a position that was in fact common for Black women of the time to have held in the 1950s. The Black middle class did not approve of Blacks in roles as domestics because they favored roles that were descriptive of the kinds of jobs and occupations more and more Blacks were obtaining after World War II. Indeed, African Americans were college professors, physicians, attorneys, insurance agents, and bank officials, but they were also factory workers, domestics, and farmers. According to Drake and Clayton (1945), on the eve of World War II 50% of all Black women employed in Chicago were servants or domestics. *Beulah* was vilified because it portrayed a tradition from American enslavement. The Black middle class did not see these occupational roles (domestics and servants) on television as edifying to the race. During the broadcasting run of the radio version of *Beulah*, Hattie McDaniel was emotionally burdened by the complaints and letters she received from such Black middle class organizations as the NAACP. She spent much of her time and energy responding to attacks on her character. This burden seemed even greater since McDaniel had also experienced the same criticism of her domestic/servant roles in the almost 300 films in which she appeared (Jackson, 1990). McDaniel's domestic in *Beulah* was unlike her domestic in *Gone with the Wind.* Beulah's situations on radio and on television (played by Ethel Waters and, later, Louise Beavers) involved misunderstandings (a convention also found in White sitcoms of the same time period). In fact, there is nothing inherently Black about Beulah except that she was created to be a Black domestic, had a Black boyfriend (Bill Jackson), and had a Black girlfriend (Oriole). No explicit references to Black culture were ever made in the radio or television series.

Actually, *Amos 'n' Andy* was the only program that portrayed Blacks in diverse, yet, stereotypical roles. However, it is important to note that the characters also had origins in American comedic film. Sapphire Stevens (played by Ernestine Wade) was described as a domineering mammy who was constantly criticizing her husband George. Actually, she was the traditional shrew seen in plays and films before 1951. The NAACP noted this description in their resolution of 1951, obviously overlooking the relationship of this character type to previous and current popular narrative forms. George "Kingfish" Stevens (played by Tim Moore) was described as a lazy and unreliable coon who always was looking for ways to get out of work. Actually, Kingfish was an updated scoundrel character type that dated back to Greek drama. Andy (played by Spencer Williams) was also described as "a coon" but in slightly different ways than George Stevens. However, Andy was actually the dim-witted second banana, the character type popularized in the *Abbott and Costello* routines of the 1940s and 50s. All of the aforementioned characters exhibited aural and visual qualities of the 19th-century minstrel show. Perhaps the only character that offered direct connections to the slave environment was the rarely seen Amos played by Alvin Childress. Amos was an "Uncle Tom" character type. He was soft-spoken, sentimental, and acquiescent. Because of this fact, Amos's role was diminished in the radio version of *Amos 'n' Andy* (and was almost nonexistent on the television version). While Amos had a family (a context not provided for Uncle Tom of slave times), he was nevertheless a character type more easily traced to slavery and minstrelsy rather than to popular American theater. In reverse order, Kingfish's character increased by the time *Amos 'n' Andy* came to television, since plots could be more exciting with a scheming conman.

In essence, from the late 1940s to the early 1950s, the central issues concerning Blacks in television regarded (*a*) the way in which Blacks were and should be represented in television as well as (*b*) a consensus about whose version of Black imagery should represent the race (Cripps, 1975). Unintentionally, the politics of television art demanded that African Americans confront these issues. As the next section will show, African Americans responded to the call, though becoming somewhat unfocused in their journey, toward positive images of Blacks in television.

ASSIMILATIONISM

The issue of Black representation made an almost 360–degree turn in the late 1960s when two new Black sitcoms came to television. *Julia* and *The Bill Cosby Show* (NBC, 1969–1971) were criticized for their portrayals of assimilated African Americans. Instead of the perceived mammy and coon stereotypes of Black characters in the 1950s, Julia Baker and Chet Kincaid were Blacks fully integrated into White American culture. These characters, Julia Baker especially, were criticized for not portraying "real" Blacks. The observations made of *Julia* also were made of all Blacks who were in television during this period. Nipsey Russell's and Ivan Dixon's characters in *Car 54, Where Are You?* (ABC, 1961–1963) and *Hogan's Heroes* (1965–1971), respectively, inaugurated this period of assimilated characterizations. Just as Clark (1969) laments, Russell's and Dixon's roles were with organizations devoted to the maintenance of law and order, either domestically or internationally. Even though Dixon in *Hogan's Heroes* was not actually upholding law and order in Germany during World War II, his character, Sgt. James Kinchloe, a brilliant inventor, never used his expertise to escape the shenanigans of his White Colonel Robert Hogan (played by Bob Crane). Nevertheless, the main thrust of this period was that Black portrayals did not suggest any of the conflict that actually existed in the 1960s. Hence, the politics of television art rendered the Black image as equally as cut off from the real world as with all the other sitcoms of the same period. For Black critics especially, television was still not rendering the kind of service it felt the race required. Unbeknownst to the critics, then, the next period would not prove to be any better.

ASSIMILATED HYBRID MINSTRELSY (1972–1983)

The seventies were an interesting and challenging time in American culture. In the entertainment arena, African Americans became more visible and more powerful in film, music, and sports. Moreover, by the early seventies, Blacks were major characters in a number of situation comedies, particularly those comedies produced by Norman Lear and

Bud Yorkin. "Assimilated hybrid minstrelsy" refers to Lear's penchant for developing buffoonish characters. These comedies included *Sanford and Son* (NBC, 1972–1977), *Good Times* (CBS, 1974–1979), *The Jeffersons* (1975–1985, *What's Happening!!* (ABC, 1976–1979), and *Grady* (NBC, 1975–1976). Critics chastised these programs for the revival of coon characters seen in "George Jefferson," "J. J. Evans," and "Grady Wilson" and mammy portrayals seen in "Louise Jefferson" and "Florence" from *The Jeffersons*, and "Aunt Esther" in *Sanford and Son*.

The majority of the Black sitcoms during this period presented an assimilated hybrid minstrel style by carrying over some of the same aural and visual qualities of hybrid minstrelsy while at the same time appropriating Black power rhetoric (Reid, 1993). All in all, the seventies looked very much like the fifties. Summarizing a common thought, E. Collier (1974) felt that television still evaded the "nitty-gritty" truth and gave Black viewers the "usual slick, well-packaged slop." In other words, the politics of television art that grew to rely heavily on formula was a major area of contention for Black critics.

SIMULTANEITY AND DIVERSIFICATION (1984–PRESENT)

The current period of Blacks in situation comedy began with Bill Cosby's *The Cosby Show* (NBC, 1984–1992). This period is marked by the rise of Black producers and writers and by the diversification and mainstreaming of many Black sitcoms. The sheer number of Blacks in sitcoms rose significantly in the 1980s and the nineties is still the biggest decade for Blacks in television sitcoms. In particular, however, the series responsible for the flourishing of sitcoms in general, *The Cosby Show*, featured Blacks who seemed to be just as regulated as the Black characters of the sixties. The Huxtables were an assimilated upper-middle-class family who enjoyed close associations with people from several racial and ethnic groups. While it was essentially just another domestic situation comedy, it was unique because of its portrayal of a Black nuclear family. Furthermore, the "sambo and mammy" characterizations that the NAACP opposed vehemently in the 1950s were almost entirely eliminated. Finally, with *The Cosby Show*, there was a program that portrayed a "kinder and gentler" Black family. Also, during this period the unique work of Tim Reid bore fruit in the dramedy *Frank's Place*, as well as Cosby's domcom *A Different World* (NBC, 1987–1993), created to showcase the talent of Lisa Bonet. Both series were significant because of their rounder and fuller portrayals of Blacks. While it is true that both series had stock characters, these obviously cardboard caricatures were outweighed by the more serious characters.

In conclusion, the essential dilemma regarding Blacks in sitcoms since 1947 has been the issue of controlling Black images and desiring more diverse Black images. Who does control the Black image on television? The answer has been the same since 1947: television network executives. Furthermore, these executives have been (and still are) White males. While it can be said that actors have always to a certain extent controlled the characters they portrayed, depending on the decade in which they were performed, even those characters were created in a White mind (most often, a White male's mind). The politics of television sitcom art simply do not allow for diverse and broad portrayals of African Americans.

As just stated, *Frank's Place*, as well as the current sitcom *Living Single* (Fox, 1993–present), provide the best examples of fuller and rounder portrayals of African Americans. However, racism still permeates the production of television so that in the late 1980s an innovative program like *Frank's Place* was unable to remain on television for more than one season. Likewise, into the mid-1990s, *Living Single*, an innovative twentysomething comedy series, is almost totally ignored in the White popular press. Rather, the series of note that is referred to as the "first twentysomething series" is *Friends* (NBC, 1994–present), a program that actually began one season after *Living Single* and features all-White cast members. While Warner Brothers Television approached Yvette Lee Bowser, the creator and co-executive producer of *Living Single*, about creating a sitcom about four African American women, *Friends*, another Warner Brothers television production that focuses on the lives of six White friends, has received all of the critical acclaim and publicity. The dissimilar outcomes of two very similar shows suggests that the politics of television art are more complex than the simple issue of images and portrayals. The bottom line of these politics—politics that have historically proven to be inherently racist—form the very foundation of American society and necessarily have required that the television images of African Americans follow suit.

REFERENCES

Brodie, J. (1993, May 17). Black leaders lobby for shows. *Variety*, pp. 1, 122.

Brooks, T., & Marsh, E. (1995). *The complete directory to prime time network and cable TV shows, 1946–present* (6th ed.). New York: Ballantine.

Cripps, T. (1975). The noble black savage: A problem in the politics of television art. *Journal of Popular Culture, 8*(4), 687–695.

Cripps, T. (1978). *Black film as genre*. Bloomington: Indiana University Press.

Cripps, T. (1983). *Amos 'n' Andy* and the debate over American racial integration. In J. E. O'Connor (Ed.), *American history, American television: Interpreting the video past* (pp. 33–54). New York: Ungar.

Drake, St. C., & Cayton, H. (1945). *Black metropolis: A study of Negro life in a northern city.* Chicago: University of Chicago Press.

Gaines, K. (1993). Assimilationist minstrelsy as racial uplift ideology: James D. Corrothers's literary quest for black leadership. *American Quarterly, 45*(3), 341–69.

Gray, H. (1995). *Watching race: Television and the struggle for "Blackness."* Minneapolis: University of Minnesota Press.

Hough, A. (1981). Trials and tribulations—Thirty years of sitcom. In R. P. Adler, (Ed.), *Understanding television: Essays on television as a social and cultural force* (pp. 201–223). New York: Praeger.

Jackson, C. (1990). *Hattie: The life of Hattie McDaniel.* Lanham, MD: Madison Books.

MacDonald, J. F. (1979). *Don't touch that dial! Radio programming in American life from 1920 to 1960.* Chicago: Nelson-Hall.

MacDonald, J. F. (1992). *Blacks and white TV: Afro-Americans in television since1948* (2nd ed.). Chicago: Nelson-Hall.

Meehan, D. M. (1983). *Ladies of the evening: Women characters of prime-time television.* Metuchen, NJ: Scarecrow.

Reid, M. A. (1993). *Redefining black film.* Berkeley: University of California Press.

CHAPTER 7

Crawling Toward Civil Rights: News Media Coverage of Disability Activism

Beth Haller

In March 1990, the Americans with Disabilities Act (ADA) was slowly gaining consideration by the U.S. House of Representatives, after being passed by the U.S. Senate in September 1989. Disability activists descended on the U.S. Capitol that month to meet with the Speaker of the House and Congressional representatives to urge speedy passage of the act. After the meeting, activists staged a demonstration, chaining their wheelchairs together in the Capitol Rotunda. They also staged a "crawl-in," in which protesters left their wheelchairs and crawled up the Capitol steps.

Their actions directly addressed their place as people with disabilities in U.S. society. By breaking from a social category of marginalization and silence, they tried to shock. They were loud—chanting and yelling. They were active, not passive, chaining their wheelchairs and being uncooperative with police. And they deviated from their "handicap" by leaving their wheelchairs and crawling. They knew if they deviated from the silence and passivity society expected of them, they would receive national media coverage. And they did. Both NBC and CBS covered the protest, as did *the New York Times, the Los Angeles Times, the Washington Post,* and *Time* magazine.

The news story of the ADA really began at that activist event. The activists were fighting for the place of the ADA in public discourse because the lack of media attention threatened its viability in the U.S. Congress. The act had received little mainstream media coverage up to that point. Of the elite newspapers that covered the "crawl-in," the

Washington Post wrote two articles on the Americans with Disabilities Act before March 1990; the *New York Times* had two articles, and the *Los Angeles Times* printed one commentary that called the act "more loophole than law" (Bolte, 1989).

This chapter is a qualitative assessment that illustrates the shifting of media frames and themes that were characterizing people with disabilities and their rights movement at the beginning of legislative process for the ADA. This analysis describes the narrative tropes related to media coverage of disability rights, as well as contextualizing media coverage of the ADA within the larger U.S. culture. This illustrates how the disability rights movement is trying to displace older cultural paradigms to which the media and other institutions still adhere. It is argued that the ADA represents a paradigm shift in how the U.S. culture will interact with people with disabilities in the future, and the analysis of the disability activism illustrates how the paradigm begins to shift.

The disability activists at the Capitol in March 1990 had a specific agenda, which they pursued through actions and words. But the rhetoric of the mainstream media is significant. Media act as mechanisms in the social construction of people with disabilities. Disability scholar Frank Bowe (1978) explains that United States has spent its entire history designing a country for nondisabled people, thus excluding people with disabilities from buildings, transportation, educational and recreational programs, and communication methods. Because of these barriers, literature and mass media become crucial components in representing people with disabilities in society.

In 1990, media scholar John Clogston developed models of media representations of disability. These models fit well with assessment of media stories before the ADA existed. In his content analysis of 13 newspapers and three newsmagazines, Clogston created five models of media portrayals of disabled persons. Haller added three more models in 1995, which fit with the post-ADA media environment (see Table 7.1).

These models are not mutually exclusive when analyzing disability coverage. Several models may appear in one story and may even compete. Clogston's models were successfully applied to a previous disability rights event, which laid the groundwork for further disability rights activism. The 1988 Deaf President Now movement at Gallaudet University in Washington, D.C. became a media event centered on the student protest at the world's only university for deaf people. Students shut down the campus for seven days after a hearing woman was appointed as university president over two qualified deaf candidates. She knew no sign language, which is considered their native language by some deaf persons, and had no knowledge of the cultural traditions of deaf people.

Haller (1993) showed how the presentation of deaf people in the

TABLE 7.1
Models of Media Representation of Disability

Traditional Categories

Medical Model: Disability is presented as an illness or malfunction. Persons who are disabled are shown as dependent on health professionals for cures or maintenance. Disabled individuals are passive and do not participate in "regular" activities because of disability (Clogston, 1990).

Social Pathology Model: Disabled people are presented as disadvantaged and must look to the state or to society for economic support, which is considered a gift, not a right (Clogston, 1990).

Supercrip Model: The disabled person is portrayed as deviant because of "superhuman" feats or as "special" because they live regular lives "in spite of" disability. This role reinforces the idea that disability is deviant—that the person's accomplishments are amazing for someone who is not complete (Clogston, 1993).

Business Model: Disabled people and their issues are presented as costly to society and businesses especially. Making society accessible for disabled people is not worth the cost and overburdens businesses. Accessibility is not profitable (Haller, 1995).

Progressive Categories

Minority/Civil Rights Model: Disabled people are seen as members of the disability community, which has legitimate political grievances. They have civil rights that they may fight for, just like other groups. Accessibility to society is a civil right (Clogston, 1990).

Legal Model: It is illegal to treat people with disabilities in certain ways. They have legal rights and may need to sue to guarantee those rights. The ADA and other laws are presented as ways to halt discrimination (Haller, 1995).

Cultural Pluralism Model: People with disabilities are seen as a multifaceted and their disabilities do not receive undue attention. They are portrayed as nondisabled people would be (Clogston, 1990).

Consumer Model: People with disabilities are presented as an untapped consumer group. Making society accessible could be profitable to businesses and society. If people with disabilities have access to jobs, they will have more disposable income and will no longer need government assistance (Haller, 1995).

Washington Post and *New York Times* in the years before, during, and after the Deaf President Now protest shifted. The traditional categories—medical and social pathology—accounted for 62% of the stories in the 2 years before the Deaf President Now protest. Stories reflecting that model dropped to 24% during the year of the protest (1988), and stayed lower at 40% in the 2 years following the protest. The progressive categories—minority/civil rights and cultural pluralism—fit squarely with the kinds of stories written about the Gallaudet protest. Deaf people were presented as a distinctive community with a valid political agenda. This progressive presentation continued in the 2 years after the protest, with the progressive model accounting for 60% of the stories.

Events such as the Gallaudet protest and the creation of the Americans with Disabilities Act began to change the environment in which media cover disability activism. The traditional stereotyping images of disability are competing with newer images supplied by disability rights activism and new federal legislation.

So the activism in support of the ADA at the U.S. Capitol in 1990 had several components: to pull together the people there into a cohesive disability movement and to let legislators and U.S. citizens know the importance of the ADA to the estimated 43 million people with disabilities in the United States. Therefore, drawing national media attention would assist in getting the ADA and disability issues into public discourse.

Their dramatic protest of leaving their wheelchairs and crawling up the Capitol steps was partially successful, especially with the play it received on the network news and in large circulation publications. However, ABC news and the local newspaper denied them a place in the journalistic discourse of that day. The *Washington Post* ran a six-paragraph story that did not mention the crawl-in (Buckley, 1990, March 14). The *Post* reported on the protest completely as a police story, explaining the arrest of about 100 people with disabilities. The only story source mentioned in the story was a spokesperson for the U.S. Capitol Police, who said "they were asked to leave the rotunda, but refused" (Buckley, 1990, March 14, p. B4).

But other national media covered the disability activism as a substantive news story. The *Los Angeles Times* wrote a medium-length story that appeared on page A27 (Eaton, 1990 March 13). It followed up the day after the protest with a one-paragraph story explaining the arrest of disabled protesters ("Officers Arrest 104," 1990). The *New York Times* wrote an 11–paragraph story the day after the protest (Holmes, 1990, March 14), but followed up with an analysis article about disability rights in its Sunday section (Holmes, 1990, March 18). *Time* magazine ran a two-paragraph story in its American Notes section, but ran the most dramatic photo of all the media sources, which pictured a close-up of a disability activist pulling himself up a step of the Capitol ("A Crawl-In at Capitol," 1990). NBC and CBS both ran about 30–second stories on the protest.

More important than the amount of coverage of the crawl-in is the news stories' rhetoric. Tom Brokaw's voice-over on NBC on March 13 declared: "Some other less privileged and less fortunate people were desperately trying to rock the boat on Capitol Hill today. About 60 disabled people demonstrated, demanding passage of a bill to outlaw discrimination against them in employment, transportation, and other areas. The bill passed the Senate last year but is now bogged down in the House." His words about the demonstration illustrate the social pathology model of disadvantage associated with disability. Brokaw tells TV viewers that people with disabilities are "less fortunate," "less privileged," and "desperate." These people with disabilities must appeal to the state to get help. Falling within Clogston's traditional category, the problems people with disabilities face lie within themselves, not within society's barriers.

People with disabilities reside in a peripheral place in society, according to Brokaw's characterization, because they must "rock the boat" to get their demands met. Their demands are presented as valid because discrimination against them is acknowledged, but the legislation necessary to fix their problems is "bogged down," which puts a question mark around their needs. In addition, this NBC story does not construct people with disabilities as if they can speak for themselves. There is no sound bite from any disability activist, only Brokaw's three-sentence voice-over. The sound of activists chanting "ADA Now" does filter into the background, and there is a shot of I. King Jordan, the president of Gallaudet University, who is deaf, signing and speaking.

However, at a broader level, the fact that NBC news decided to cover the protest and show the crawl-in in the story reflects that the larger progressive category of disability rights is making it into journalistic discourse. Although at level of language, this news story still constructs people with disabilities within medical or social pathology models, it is allowing the entry of the minority/civil rights model into the social construction.

Dan Rather's language in CBS news illustrates also the civil rights perspective in the stories: "Several hundred people in wheelchairs demonstrated in the nation's Capitol today. They lobbied for a civil rights act for Americans with disabilities. Even though the U.S. Capitol itself has wheelchair ramps, they dramatized their general problems with access by crawling up the Capitol steps." Rather's words help validate the ADA by calling it a civil rights act. The implication is that these disability activists are following a tradition of activism by oppressed groups to gain broader civil rights.

However, his rhetoric also pacifies the TV audience by letting them know that the activists are crawling up the steps for symbol alone and that the Capitol is accessible. Therefore, the audience may receive a false sense about the accessibility of society, which is largely inaccessible to people who use wheelchairs. Rather fails to put the Capitol steps comment in context. The reason the federal buildings are accessible is because of the Rehabilitation Act of 1973, which disability activists advocated for with sit-ins in government buildings across the country in the mid-1970s.

The language in the print stories embodied some similar claims about the demonstration, shifting between traditional categories and the civil rights idea that Americans can lobby for their beliefs. *Time* magazine wrote with a gee-whiz attitude that "there had never been such a sight at the entrance of the U.S. Capitol" as the crawl-in, but that "the climb was not really necessary" ("A Crawl-In at Capitol," p. 25). The disability activists are framed as "supercrips," who are doing amazing things in the name of protest. They designed a protest that is better than one by nondisabled people because they can use their disabled bodies to shock.

The *New York Times* employed similar conventions, saying that the activists "boisterously demonstrated," and they "had intended to be arrested" (Holmes, 1990, March 14, p. B7). Thus, people with disabilities are constructed within the cultural pluralism model and given the ability to be active and vocal. Disability activists are constructed as being able to manipulate the police for the attention that provides, just as any other activist group might.

The *Los Angeles Times* characterized protesters as "grumbling" about the situation with the ADA (Eaton, 1990, March 13). Their lobbying effort was called "unusual," but that the protest "had some of the fervor of a civil rights rally of the 1960s." Thus, the *Times* combines two conflicting tropes: People with disabilities are unusual in the medical model because of the physical deviations of their bodies, yet they are able to come together to form a minority group with real civil rights concerns.

The analysis of the protest by the *New York Times* tries to reflect the protest within the minority/civil rights model, but falls into traditional rhetoric periodically. Although acknowledged as a cultural and political movement, the disability rights movement is characterized as a product of better technology. But the technology in the *Times* story is not presented as civil rights but as a gift that society gives to "disadvantaged" people with disabilities. The idea of the gift instead of the civil right constructs people with disabilities as dependent.

The Americans with Disabilities Act in actuality allows people with disabilities to fight against this "dependent" role. By working to create this legislation, they are trying to have some control in the legislative system that has so much power to define them. But some of the language in the newspapers reflect that society may not yet understand what this empowerment means to the oppressed disability community.

The *New York Times* story on the protest pointed out how disability activists were breaking laws and practicing deviance. It focused on their demonstration in the Capitol as illegal under federal law (Holmes, 1990, March 14). It explained how police had to dress in riot gear and use chain cutters and acetylene torches to cut the chains linking wheelchairs. This aspect of story shows how the business model of media representation begins to enter the discourse. The story's focus constructs the protest as costing time and money, forcing tourists out of the Capitol and requiring 2 hours for police to unchain the protesters. On the other hand, disability demonstrators are being characterized as just another activist group causing an uproar because of perceived injustices. Their claims of civil rights are being reported in most of the media stories, but are also being defused by their characterization as deviant and breaking conventions on their place in society.

The visual dimensions of the crawl-in continue the narrative with images that show the competing models of media representations. The *New York Times* even took note of the images: "The pictures were striking, just as they were intended to be: Children paralyzed from the waist down crawling up the steps of the Capitol, and more than 100 protesters, most in wheelchairs, being arrested by police officers in riot gear after a raucous demonstration in the Rotunda" (Holmes, 1990, March 18, p. E5). Disability activists knew they had strong, dramatic images for photographers.

On NBC news, the story showed one person pushing another person in a wheelchair in front of the Capitol. The person using the wheelchair has a large U.S. flag attached to the chair. They are followed by a person in an electric wheelchair speeding by and someone walking by. The next shot shows I. King Jordan, the president of Gallaudet University—surrounded by people in wheelchairs and standing—signing and chanting. These images show a calm, not fiery, demonstration. They are framed as Americans using their right of free speech with the images of the flag and speakers before the Capitol.

More interesting is the choice of images related to the "crawl-in." Dozens of disability activists challenged the notion of what a disabled body should do by leaving their wheelchairs and crawling up the Capitol steps. They tried to make access issues visual, showing how stairs deny entry to people who use wheelchairs. However, the NBC story showed only one person crawling up the Capitol steps—8-year-old Jennifer Keelan of Denver.

As NBC showed the blond and smiling Keelan inching up the steps, Brokaw said: "8-year-old Jennifer Keelan left her wheelchair and dragged herself up the steps saying 'I'll take all night if I have to.'" The *Los Angeles Times* story also mentioned Keelan, saying "spectators' attention focused on 8–year-old Jennifer Keelan of Denver, who propelled herself to the top of the steep stone steps using only her knees and elbows" (Eaton, 1990, March 13, p. A27). In light of the attention on Jennifer Keelan, *The Disability Rag*, a disability rights publication, questioned the use of the crawl-in as a media image. It said: "One might question why a movement intent on showing that disabled people are adults, not children, would make their central media image a child" ("The Crawl-In," p. 21).

It is interesting that NBC rejected shots of the numerous adults crawling up the steps for a shot of a child. Nearby to Jennifer Keelan, 33–year-old Paulette Patterson pulled herself up the steps on her back saying "I want my civil rights. I want to be treated like a human being" (Eaton, 1990, March 13, p. A27). But children are deemed by society as cute and nonthreatening. Nondisabled children might crawl up steps while at play, so Jennifer Keelan can create the illusion that she has no disability.

Knoll (1987) developed 83 categories to assess photos of people with disabilities in a qualitative way. One of the interpretive categories assesses whether visual images of people with disabilities portray them as childlike or as children. The use of Jennifer Keelan seems to symbolize people with disabilities as children who need to be taken care of by society. Children with disabilities also evoke greater pity and represent more tragedy in the eyes of society.

In contrast, another image of the crawl-in in *Time* magazine pictured a man sliding up the Capitol steps. He is bearded with long hair and a headband. The two male activists near him look similar. Part of the Capitol is visible in the background, which is not the case in the Keelan shot. The image harkens back to images of the anti–Vietnam War protests of the 1960s. They exude a more radical and a more civil rights image than that of Keelan. The *Time* photo fits with Knoll's "This is Me" category, in which the person with a disability is shown as self-assertive.

The CBS images fit strongly with the minority group/civil rights model. The focus was not on one person but on a group of protesters with the signs and symbols of activism. The shot of the crawl-in pictured five or six adults, of different races and genders, pulling themselves up the steps. The group shot emphasized the issue at hand rather than focusing on one "supercrip." However, this TV story also neglected to give people with disabilities a voice. There was no interview with an activist, only Rather's voice-over.

The only other still photo of the demonstration doesn't depict the crawl-in. It is an Associated Press photo and ran with the analysis article in *The New York Times* (Holmes, 1990, March 18). It shows three people in wheelchairs sitting in a circle. Behind them is a flag and behind that is the U.S. Capitol. The people in the picture look to be calmly chatting. The only radical nature to the photo is that the one person using a wheelchair who faces the camera has on a headband, sunglasses, and a beard, and looks like a "Vietnam era" person. But overall, the photo exudes tranquility and Americana, not protest. The cutline even calls the demonstration "a rally." This photo depicts the disability protesters as passive, not active. It combines the aura of minority group status with the traditional trope of people with disabilities as passive recipients of society's aid.

The use of traditional stereotypes to present people with disabilities may result not only from traditional cultural norms but also from disability activists not pushing to educate journalists. At the crawl-in, it seems shock techniques took some precedence over communicating with media. *The Disability Rag* criticized the organizers of the demonstration for not getting good information to the news media ("Opportunity Lost," 1990, p. 31). *The Rag* acknowledged that the mainstream media were willing to cover the disability rights protest, but disability leaders were organizing, not dealing with the media. Therefore, the representations of disability protest are also a function of a disability rights movement still learning to fashion the news media image of disability.

This qualitative analysis of disability activism illustrates how media frames can potentially shift and slide as cultural situations change. As Hall et al. (1978) have explained, news media frames are "contested terrain" in which different sides of an issue battle for control over presentation and language. The 1990 crawl-in at the U.S. Capitol in support of the ADA shows that the activities of disability activists are resulting in the gradual shifts in news media representation of disability.

As Clogston has shown in his media models representing disability, the traditional representations have been ones associated with medical dependency, superhuman feats, or a disadvantaged status in society. Media stories still maintain these constructions in some of the rhetoric and images about disability activism. However, when people with disabilities engage in vigorous protest for their rights, these traditional tropes become more malleable. The activists plug into the media's news values that reward change, action, and consequence in journalistic discourse. When disability activists pull people together as a minority group, the media accept the civil rights representation delineated. A new media representation of disability results, one that combines some of the old stereotypes with new, more progressive representations.

REFERENCES

Bolte, B. (1989, September 20). Disabled act: More loophole than law. *Los Angeles Times*, section II, p. 7.

Bowe, F. (1978). *Handicapping America*. New York: Harper & Row.

Buckley, S. (1990, March 14). 100 disabled arrested on Hill. *Washington Post*, p. B4.

Clogston, J. S. (1990). *Disability coverage in 16 newspapers*. Louisville, KY: Advocado Press.

Clogston, J. S. (1993). Traditional and progressive models. Handout presented to the Association of Education in Journalism and Mass Communication. Kansas City, MO.

A crawl-in at the Capitol. (1990, March 26). *Time*, p. 25.

The crawl-in. (1990, May/June). *The Disability Rag*, p. 21.

Eaton, W. J. (1990, March 13). Disabled persons rally, crawl up Capitol step. *Los Angeles Times*, p. A27.

Hall, S., Critcher, C., Jefferson, T, Clarke, J., & Roberts, B. (1978). *Policing the crisis*. New York: Holmes and Meier.

Haller, B. (1993). Paternalism and protest: The presentation of deaf persons in the *Washington Post* and *New York Times*, 1986–90. *Mass Comm Review*, 20(3/4), 169–179.

Haller, B. (1995). Disability rights on the public agenda: Elite news media coverage of the Americans with disabilities act. Unpublished doctoral dissertation, Temple University.

Holmes, S. (1990, March 18). The disabled find a voice and make sure its heard. *New York Times*, p. E5.

Holmes, S. (1990, March 14). Disabled protest and are arrested. *New York Times*, p. B7.

Knoll, J. A. (1987). Through a glass, darkly: The photographic image of people with a disability. Unpublished doctoral dissertation, Syracuse University.

Officers arrest 104 disabled protesters. (1990, March 14). *Los Angeles Times*, p. A16.

Opportunity lost. (1990, May/June). *The Disability Rag*, 30–31.

CHAPTER 8

Media Stereotypes of Jews: From JAPs to MDs

Marsha Woodbury

What are our mental images of Jews? This paper asks if we think of Jewish people as a stereotype that we have gained from our exposure to mass media, perhaps a negative image that characterizes these people as offensive, sleazy, aggressive, obnoxious, and laughable. Did we develop our own image of Jews from TV, movies, newspapers, or magazines, or did we gain it from our life experiences, or from our upbringing by our families? Whatever the source, negative Jewish stereotypes need examination.

The paper begins by defining the word "stereotype," then it very briefly reviews the history of Jewish people and their methods of coping with centuries of persecution. Finally, it directs our attention to current media images of Jews, examining the possible impact of public television and other developments in American communications.

To begin, we look at the word *stereotype*, which evolved from printing and the practice of setting type in a printing plate that made it simple to reproduce material. Thus, the word springs from a labor-saving device, a way to avoid repetitive work. Even today, the word carries elements of its origin, for a negative stereotype replaces thinking, making us blind to the unique contribution of Jewish individuals by the stereotype that we project onto them.

A stereotype is not a classification, that, for example, categorizes people by skin color, height, weight, or clothing. This sorting is helpful, for by slotting images into classifications our brains make sense of the world around us. Rather, a stereotype is an oversimplified generalization that typifies a person or a situation. For example, in America, a classification might be "actor" and a stereotype of "actor" might be "homosexual."

Although some stereotypes may contain an element of truth, they often unfairly and inaccurately label an entire culture or people. And because stereotypes simplify our complex environment, they allow us to make sense of the world around us while limiting our experience of it. Mass media behave very questionably when they perpetuate negative stereotypes of any people. The worst outcome is that the people themselves become the victim of the media stereotype.

The following song lyrics draw on a common Jewish stereotype to create commercial humor:

Well I wanna be a lawyer so you know I won't be poor,
But if I fail the bar exam I'll open up a store,
I'll never pay retail, I'll wait 'til there's a sale,
My wife would clip the coupons but she's scared to break a nail,
OYE! (Brown, Vineburg, & Vineburg 1990)

THE DEFINITION OF JEWISHNESS

Who are the Jewish people? This is a complex question and any attempt at a definition will always draw criticism. For the purposes of this paper, Jews are an ancient people who today share some distinctive characteristics such as culture, religion, and language. The word "tribe" well describes Jewishness; yet "tribe" sounds anachronistic when referring to a modern people. The reason this definition is so difficult is that Jews become Jewish through birth or religious conversion, and thus they can be, quite literally, anyone. When we talk about media images of some minorities, the basic question of who and what the minority is does not need to be explained. We can identify a child or a woman or an Asian. Jews are harder to identify. They can have blue eyes, freckles, and blond hair, or be African American, as was Sammy Davis Jr.

Traditionally, a Jew was a person of Hebrew descent whose religion was Judaism. Over the centuries the definition changed. Strictly speaking, a Jew is a person born of a Jewish mother, or a person who has converted to Judaism according to rabbinical law. However, Jews can be much more widely defined, as we learned from the Holocaust, when the definition of Jewishness was considered racial in Hitler's Germany. The Nazi Party held that a Jew was (on or after September 15, 1935) anyone with three Jewish grandparents; someone with two Jewish grandparents who belonged to the Jewish community, or joined thereafter; or was married to a Jew or Jewess, or was the offspring of a marriage or extramarital liaison with a Jew (The Simon Wiesenthal Center, 1996).

Those who were not classified as Jews but who had some Jewish blood were categorized as *Mischlinge* (hybrids) and were divided into two groups: *Mischlinge* of the first degree, those with two Jewish grandparents; *Mischlinge* of the second degree, those with one Jewish grandparent. During World War II, first-degree *Mischlinge*, incarcerated in concentration camps, were deported to death camps (The Simon Wiesenthal Center, 1996). Whatever definition is applied, Jews have a lengthy history of persecution and even planned eliminations (pogroms) by people in countries from Russia to South America. Jews have long been "the other."

Medieval Christianity portrayed Jews as grotesque individuals, ever-ready to steal consecrated wafers, murder innocent children, and mock the rituals and the beliefs of the "true" faith (Glassman, 1975, p. 152). The stereotype of the Jew as an avaricious money-lender was born in medieval time, after Jews were forbidden from doing any business other than lending money for a profit. This constraint on occupation led many Jewish people to deal in money-lending, which eventually led to the verb, "to jew." "To jew" is to cheat or overreach, to drive a hard bargain, to beat down in price. It is a pejorative word associated with a people who were denied access to other occupations.

Jews were driven out of their homes, dispersed, and forced to seek refuge all over the world. Yet almost everywhere they migrated, Jews held to their religion. As they refused to convert to Christianity, their persistence earned them the label "stubborn."

When extermination seemed inevitable, as in Spain during the Inquisition, some people of Jewish origin worked so hard to "go underground" that their descendants lost contact with the faith and customs, as in the case of the crypto-Jews in America. Their story is worth noting, because of the vast distances they covered and the measures they took to stay alive. These Jews traveled from Spain to South America and moved north into the American Southwest and other regions, disguising their religious practices and passing for Catholic.

Returning to the idea of stereotype, the fact that Jewish people are not only widely dispersed but heterogeneous makes the media stereotype unethical. To condense the richness and diversity of a people into a narrow image is to do the Jewish people an injustice. For example, these famous baseball players were identified as Jewish: Sandy (Sanford) Koufax, Hank Greenberg, Al Rosen, and José Bautista. They do not fit a narrow type.

The lack of positive feelings and images about Jewishness, not to mention the pogroms and the Holocaust, have caused many modern Jews to bury their identity. In Hollywood, where image is so crucial, actors have changed their names in part to suppress their Jewishness; some still do, like Debra Winger and Winona Ryder, who often play gentiles (non-Jews) on screen. Actors Tony Curtis, Lorne Green, Gregory Peck, Lauren Bacall, Charles Bronson, Humphry Bogart, Jeff Chandler, and Kirk Douglas are all Jewish. Douglas, for example, was born Issur Danielovitch in Amsterdam, New York, one of seven children of an impoverished immigrant Russian-Jewish peddler and his wife. Among the half-Jewish are Harrison Ford, Paul Newman, and Goldie Hawn.

Negative stereotypes of Jews and fear of anti-Semitism make hiding a heritage an attractive option. Obviously, many Jewish people don't wear identifying garments and have chosen to eschew their roots, marrying gentiles and settling into mainstream American culture. However, one type of Jew is very easy to identify, through clothing and hair, as they wear special garments. A stereotype often seen in the media is the Hassid. Hassidism is a "family" in the Jewish tribe, a group that springs from Polish roots and holds to very strict observance and worship. They are identified by their appearance, for they wear black clothes, with streimels (large black hats), long beards, and long curly sidelocks. Mainstream Jews often feel uncomfortable about Hassidism. In one of Woody Allen's films, *Annie Hall* (1977), Allen spoofs this stereotype in that he recognizes how many people carry it as an image. In the film, when he visits Annie's straightlaced midwestern family, Allen thinks that they are looking at him and seeing a Hassidic, complete with earlocks and a black hat. This image draws laughs at most theaters, as people recognize the caricature.

THE JEWISH WOMAN

What is the female stereotype? The Jewish woman's archetype is a JAP, a Jewish American Princess, pampered, demanding, loud, tasteless. In films, she is *The Heartbreak Kid* (1972), left on her honeymoon while her newlywed husband pursues the gentile he spies on the beach. On TV, she is Rhoda Morgenstern from the *Mary Tyler Moore Show*, or Melissa Steadman from *Thirty-Something*—characters who are smart, neurotic, and sexually undesirable.

The Jewish-American Princess began as a fairly gentle stereotype of an overindulged daughter of a newly prosperous suburban Jew. As with any nouveau riche, the immigrant Jewish family would lack the social skills to go with their new wealth. The JAP jokes caused mirth, spreading to T-shirts, greeting cards, books, and cartoons. Today, JAP stands for a whining, materialistic, small-minded woman averse to sex, obsessed with shopping, and generally repugnant. The image brought on a wave of JAP-bashing (Shapiro, 1988). At Cornell and other colleges, students wear T-shirts reading SLAP-A-JAP! and BACK OFF BITCH, I'M A JAP-BUSTER! "Anti-Semitism masked as sexism is more socially acceptable," says Rabbi Laura Geller, director of the Hillel Jewish Center at the University of Southern California, "because, unfortunately, sexism is still an accepted form of bigotry" ("Definite Place," 1990). Graffiti at Syracuse University read, "A Solution to the JAP Problem—When they go to get nose jobs, tie their tubes as well." This exhibit of hatred is reminiscent of the Nazi images of the 1930s.

The popular TV formula in which male Jews are married or romantically involved with gentile women denigrates Jewish women, because it makes them appear undesirable, and because almost never is the reverse seen. In fact, some Jewish people use the word "shiksa" for a female gentile as a slur to imply that non-Jewish women are merely sex objects. In the popular media, few Jewish women are lusted after by gentile men, save for Barbara Streisand by Robert Redford in the film *The Way We Were* (1973).

Jewish interviewees mentioned TV programs as being the common vehicles for the male Jew–gentile female match-up, including *Bridget Loves Bernie, Sisters, Brooklyn Bridge, Love and War, L.A. Law, Northern Exposure, Seinfeld*, and *thirty-something*. Any Woody Allen film has the same theme. Jewish women appear as strong characters in movies such as *Driving Miss Daisy* (1989) and *Funny Girl* (1968).

THE JEWISH MOTHER

The Jewish mother has been fairly well carved out by novelists like Philip Roth. The Jewish mother archetype is overprotective, loud-mouthed, and pushy. Part of the stereotype comes from the historical roots of Judaism, the closeness of the family, and the struggle for survival in a new country. The Jewish woman had to manage the family while her husband pursued religion, and consequently developed the strong personality and sharp business skills that make up her stereotype. In the process, she also sacrificed herself for the well-being of her children (Ziv & Zajdman, 1993).

Other cultures have the same strong familial bond that Jewish families have. For example, sons and mothers are very close in Asian families, and, often after marriage, the children move into the family home. In America, children usually move out at 18. The dominant U.S. culture has difficulty understanding foreign relationships and sees them as tainted. Sherree Curry, a reporter who writes about issues of stereotypes, remembered that a few years ago, the sitcom called *Chicken Soup*, about a Jewish mother and her family, seemed appealing but didn't last. One problem was scheduling since the show was shown on a Friday night, when devout Jews would not be watching TV.

The media could help by highlighting women like Ruth Bader Ginsburg, President Clinton's appointee to the U.S. Supreme Court, whose opinions have consistently leaned toward religious tolerance. Another role model is singer Paula Abdul, whose mother is a Canadian Jew, and whose father was born of Syrian Jewish parents. As one person said, "See the beautiful things Arabs and Jews can make when they work together."

JEWISH MEN

Jewish men appeared in movies as early as *The Jazz Singer* (1927) in which the plot had Jake Rabinowitz, the son of a Jewish cantor, runs away from home to become a jazz singer. Recently and profoundly, Jewish men appeared in *Schindler's List* (1993), in which the Holocaust is recreated in grim detail. In contrast to that black-and-white saga, *The Birdcage* (1996) featured colorful and humorous men who were both Jewish and gay. In one of the funnier lines the "straight" midwesterner becomes more upset by the Jewish identity of the gay couple than by their homosexuality.

Woody Allen's movie persona is a true stereotype, a male with morose introspection, a fixation upon persecution and the Holocaust, with a restless, questing Jewish intellectuality. His relationships with gentiles are always doomed to fail. Philip Roth's male characters are equally insecure and unsure of their identity.

A Jewish man can appear as a pushy lawyer, such as the attorney on the TV program *Picket Fences*. This type of character is often short in stature and aggressive, lusting after gentile women. Jewish men are "my son the doctor." Remember the smart kid in *Broadcast News* (1987)? After his school graduation speech, the other students beat him up. The stereotypical Jewish father is indulgent and nouveau riche, telling people what to buy wholesale. The most extreme stereotype is Rodney Dangerfield in *Caddy Shack* (1980), with his garish clothes and lack of manners.

Programming is changing. The *Northern Exposure* creators were careful not to make Dr. Fleischman just another nebbishy Jewish guy. He's athletic, not the clumsy stereotype, and open to others, not haughty. "Joel's a strong guy. And he knows how to fix things. That runs counter to the stereotype," said the producer (Richmond, 1992, p. 3). However, the Jewish male did leave his obnoxious old girlfriend in New York, and all signs are pointing in the direction of romance with the spunky, stereotyped gentile.

JEWISH PEOPLE AND THE MEDIA

In today's media, we don't encounter the more devastating Jewish caricatures of the past. In the 1930s, the Nazis widely spread grotesque images of Jews, featuring protruding noses, and mouths salivating at the sight of money. These pictures laid the groundwork for the mass extermination that followed. Today such images are banned in Germany, as is hate speech.

Because of the horrific history of Jewish stereotyping and persecution, American Jewish people are extremely sensitive to hateful portrayals. The Jewish Anti-Defamation League has fought anti-Semitism for 80 years. They have challenged narrow depictions of Jewish people, defamatory cartoons, and job discrimination.

One of the most recent controversies about Jewish images erupted when actor Marlon Brando spoke on the *Larry King Live* show on CNN in April of 1996, saying "Hollywood is run by Jews. It is owned by Jews, and they should have a greater sensitivity." Brando continued, "They should have a greater sensitivity about the issue of people who are suffering because they've [been] exploited. We have seen the nigger, we have seen the greaseball, we have seen the chink, the slit-eyed dangerous Jap . . . but we never saw the kike because they know perfectly well that's where you draw the wagons around."

Later Brando wept as he apologized to Jewish leaders (Tugend, 1996). He evidently had some stereotypes in mind in his vision of a "kike" that he felt had been omitted from films. His statement underlined the material spread by the extreme anti-Semitic organizations in America, and the words were thus extremely unfortunate.

In the end we must return to the issue of narrowing our image of a whole people. Some common stereotypes of Jewish people are accurate generalizations. Yes, they have been high achievers in America. Jewish people take education seriously, and their representation in the professions is out of proportion to their numbers. By 1970, 60% of all employed Jews were professionals, technical managers, or administrators. By 1988, Jews were twice as likely as non-Jewish Whites to report annual household incomes of more than $50,000. "Jews were the richest ethnic group in the richest country in history" (Davis, 1993). These people make terrific role models, yet sometimes the role models aren't clear as when movie stars hide their Jewishness or in literature, as when Albert Einstein was labeled as being German, and not Jewish, in a Chicago public school textbook.

The most common media stereotype depicts Jews as wealthy, grasping, and acquisitive, and Jewish culture as mainly materialistic. For example, the movie *Dirty Dancing* (1987) shows nearly all the Jewish characters as lacking social grace, and all the women, except the leading lady, as unpleasant JAP stereotypes.

In political cartoons, Jews and Arabs often have huge noses. The caricature stereotypes are not merely reflections of bigotry, but are often conscious weapons that are used to isolate and persecute targeted populations. They remind Jewish people of the Nazi propaganda used against them in the 30s. "Suburbanites have learned to live without lawn statuettes of servile Black stablehands. Cartoonists can certainly survive without their pictorial counterparts" (Wasserman, 1994). Caricatures should be biting and revealing, but there is a difference between exaggerating the observable features of an identifiable public figure (Barbara Streisand's nose, for example) and putting nasty, hate-inducing features on all members of an ethnic group.

To broaden and deepen our understanding of the Jewish people, the Holocaust Museum recently opened in Washington, D.C., and attempts to show the essence of heroism and valor of those who died in the camps. In plays and movies, Jews have been depicted as alienated from society, persecuted, isolated within the Jewish identity, and more recently, isolated from the Jewish identity. Steven Spielberg said he made the film *Schindler's List* for himself, to retake his roots. His relatives were Polish and Ukrainian victims of the Nazis. As a boy in Ohio, he says "I was embarrassed because of my Jewishness." He was "smacked and kicked around" at high school. "Two bloody noses. It was horrible" ("Critics," 1993). The alienation of the Jew has led to serious suffering and "going undercover."

AFRICAN AMERICAN ANTI-SEMITISM

Black/Jewish conflict has surfaced sometimes with resulting violence in the last few years. Images in the media confirm and emphasize the issues of prejudice. For example, some observers objected to Spike Lee's portrayal of Black militant Malcolm X in *Malcolm X* (1992) as a whitewash of his character. They felt the film should have shown how Malcolm X disavowed his initial anti-Semitism, and that he eventually rejected racism.

The Jewish clubowners in Lee's film *Mo' Better Blues* (1990) also offended many. The two owners of the club where the main character worked seemed exploitative and cheap, getting rich off of the talents of the Black jazz musicians. One writer called them "undeveloped secondary characters who look like they stepped off an anti-Jewish poster from Hitler's Germany" (Horowitz, 1992)

In 1994, the media highlighted the hate speeches by leaders of a splinter group of Black Islam, the Nation of Islam. These speeches are full of anti-Semitism and portray the Jews as the power behind the African slave trade and as the inveterate enemies of the African race. Many people do not realize that the full text of these speeches spread hate toward other groups as well. For example, Louis Farrakhan talked about "Spook Lee," whom he called a sellout. Black anti-Semitism is often on the front page, yet stories with the full repertoire of all the objects of hate speech aren't as common.

The media could service society more ethically by enlarging the coverage, and rather than emphasizing catchy sound-bites, include the "anti-everyone ramblings of a hate-monger" (Watson, 1994, p. 3). Admittedly, the picture of a Black speaker saying things like "Jew York City" and "Columbia Jew-niversity" are hard to pass up. Dr. Leonard Jeffries of the City College of the City University of New York lost his job because of his inflammatory remarks. In a speech, Jeffries said Jews were central to the slave trade and described a fellow professor as "the head Jew at City College." He also described "a conspiracy" between Russian Jewry and the Mafia in Hollywood, in which the parties "put together a system of destruction of Black people" (Yudelson, 1995).

C-SPAN repeatedly broadcast the entire hate speech from Howard University of Khalid Abdul Muhammad, a Farrakhan follower. Providing the public with the full video further spread the poison from the Howard speech, but by showing it in its entirety, allowed reasonable people to judge its merits.

Currently, the media could pay attention to healing the wounds. For example, the Chicago Historical Society put on a show called "Bridges and Boundaries: African Americans and American Jews," in an attempt to build understanding.

PUBLIC ACCESS TELEVISION

The Cable Communications Policy Act of 1984 specifically restricts any editorial control of public access programming. Cable makes a channel open to anyone who wants to show something, and TV programs that preach racial and religious hatred are being broadcast in 24 of the 100 largest TV markets in the U.S.

Stations show films like *The Eternal Jew*, the forceful anti-Semitic Nazi movie. Citizens have responded with counter-programming, hoping that good speech will drive out bad. Another tactic to counter powerful negative stereotyping is to limit any programs shown to those that are locally produced, or to ask that a local person sponsor the showing (hate groups might have a hard time finding a local extremist sponsor).

Disclaimers help disavow endorsement of objectionable material, as well as airing it at times of low viewership. The Anti-Defamation League worries that young, impressionable viewers will stumble upon the hate-TV and be influenced by it (Anti-Defamation League, 1991).

CONCLUSION

Media are powerful in that they are unavoidable, and only when they present a full picture of Jewishness can they act ethically. Whether we are passing a newsstand or watching TV in an airport, we gather from media a great deal of our knowledge and beliefs about life outside of our direct experience (Elliott, 1996). This pervasive influence carries responsibilities, because media practitioners are constantly educating people. They are responsible for creating negative stereotypes about minorities, even if the error is unintentional. Because media are everywhere, people are vulnerable to misconceptions about the people they don't know well. It would be correct to portray Jewish people as unmistakably Jewish, but only if the people are possessing a common humanity, and experiencing the joys and sorrows of all people. Jewish images should expand our vision, not confine it.

REFERENCES

Anti-Defamation League. (1991). *Special report: Electronic hate bigotry comes to TV*, Anti-Defamation League.

Brown, I., Vineburg, J., & Vineburg, M. (1990). *The Jewish rap, Jew kids on the block*. Self-produced audiocassette by Nuclear Fish.

Critics leave Schindler off best directors' list. (1993, December 17). *The Daily Telegraph* (London, U.K.).

Davis, D. B. (1993) The other Zion: American Jews and the meritocratic experiment. *The New Republic, 208*(15), 29.

Definite place at Penn State. (1990, May 7). *Time*, p. 104.

Dreifus, C. (1993, May). Richard Dreyfuss. *The Progressive*, p. 32.

Elliott, D. (1996). Ethical and moral responsibilities of the media. In P. Lester (Ed.), *Images that injure* (p. 6). CT: Greenwood.

Glassman, B. (1975). *Anti-Semitic stereotypes without Jews* (p. 152). Detroit, MI: Wayne State University Press.

Horwitz, J. (1992, July 19). Hollywood's troubling inability to portray Jews as real people. *The Washington Post*, p. G1.

Multicultural Management Program Fellows. (1989). *Dictionary of Cautionary Words and Phrases*. Columbia, MO: University of Missouri Journalism School.

Richmond, R. (1992, November 27). Jewish characters stop checking their ethnic baggage. *Chicago Tribune*, Tempo, p. 3.

Rosenfeld, M. (1996, April 14). Enough already! Brando & Co.: A gallery of show biz antisemitism. *The Washington Post* , p. G1.

Shapiro, L. (1988, May 23). When is a joke not a joke? *Newsweek*, p. 79.

The Simon Wiesenthal Center. (1996). *36 Questions About the Holocaust.* http//www.wiesenthal.com/resource/36qlist1.htm

Tugend, T. (1996, April). Jewish leaders denounce Brando's attack on Hollywood Jews. *The Jewish Journal of Greater Los Angeles*, pp. 12–18.

Wassermann, D. (1994, February 19). Visually challenging or visually challenged? A p.c. debate by cartoonists. *The Boston Globe*, p. 15.

Watson, R. (1994, February 10). The Muhammad speech from another perspective. *The Buffalo News*, Viewpoints, p. 3.

Yudelson, L. (1995, June 30). Jeffries stepping down from N.Y. City College post. *Jewish Bulletin of Northern California* (Jewish Telegraphic Agency).

Ziv, A., & Zajdman, A. (1993). *Semites and stereotypes: Characteristics of Jewish humor.* Westport, CT: Greenwood Press.

CHAPTER 9

Still Crazy After All These Years: Italian Americans in Mainstream U.S. Films

Theresa Carilli

A few years ago during a session at the Italian-American Historical Association's annual convention, I witnessed a discussion about media stereotyping of Italian Americans that had a profound effect on me. As so often happens with discussions about media stereotyping of Italian Americans, the audience, composed mostly of Italian Americans who are scholars in a wide variety of disciplines, expressed their outrage and frustration over media images of Italian Americans as criminals or pasta-eating buffoons. Having authored a paper about Italian Americans as media scapegoats where I contend that Italian Americans are media targets because cultural members "pass" as White and theoretically have Mafia ties that protect them, thus allowing noncultural members to perceive Italian Americans as invincible and worthy of degradation, I share such outrage. At the same time, as a playwright who has attempted to give insight into the Italian American culture through plays, I have had to grapple with the issue of creating nonstereotypical characters.

My goal in rendering authentic Italian American cultural experience clashes with my viewpoints about media depictions of Italian Americans. Following the dramatistic principle to "write what one knows," my characters, rendered from my own familial experience as a second-generation Italian American, might appear stereotypical. The males burn down churches and smash walls, while the females bemoan their tragic plight as children of immigrants. They deceive, betray, and engage in emotionally charged debate. They are what I know.

Italian American film writer and director Martin Scorsese depicts a

111

violent criminal underworld in his movies *Mean Streets* and *Good Fellas*. Scorsese acknowledges the influence growing up in an Italian American community has had on his work. In a 1993 PBS interview, Scorsese talks about how deeply personal *Mean Streets* was to him and how it was based on his experiences living in New York's Little Italy:

> We had everything there in the neighborhood. We had our own sense of morality, codes, which were based on codes of behavior, and I began to realize this in the late 80s, early 90s when we went to Sicily to visit the hometown of my mother's people and the hometown of my father's people, it was really more or less like the structure of a Sicilian village.

Raging Bull, the story of boxer Jake LaMotta, received wide acclaim for Scorsese when film critics Gene Siskel and Roger Ebert declared it the best film of the 80s. In *Raging Bull*, Scorsese gives insight into the Italian American experience. While on the surface Jake LaMotta might appear to be a stereotypical Italian American male who borders on savagery, *Raging Bull* represents the Italian American struggle with assimilation into American society. Sociologist Joseph Healey (1995), for example, notes that boxing "reflects the concentration of a particular ethnic group at the bottom of the class structure" (p. 475).

This struggle with assimilation into White American society, coupled with the complex history of the Italian immigrant, contain ingredients for the creation of compelling dramatic scripts. Some "stereotypical" representations of the Italian American experience attempt to explore how Italian history has molded the Italian American persona in a manner that has demonstrated the cultural struggle with assimilation in America. The fascination with explaining the process of history in relation to assimilation has resulted in numerous media depictions of Italian Americans.

Italian Americans are overwhelmingly visible on television sitcoms and in mainstream movies because of their historically based paradoxical nature, which marks them as an anomaly among other American ethnics. This paradoxical nature combines spontaneity, expressiveness, and mystery. The exterior of the Italian American persona seems open, friendly, and what playwright Albert Innauarto in a 1978 *New York Times* interview with Elizabeth Stone describes as "right out there" (p. 88). At the same time, there is mystery, which creates some degree of unpredictability.

In this paper, I demonstrate how this paradoxical nature has been the foundation for compelling dramatic situations in numerous American mainstream movies. Movies such as *Saturday Night Fever, Moonstruck, Jungle Fever*, and *My Cousin Vinny*, which span an approximate 20-year period, make a sincere effort to represent Italian American experience. I have selected these movies because they contain little or no violence, render authentic communication between Italian Americans, and explore the struggles facing Italian Americans caught in-between history and assimilation. Prior to a discussion of each movie, I will explore media stereotyping in relation to Italian history and the Italian American struggle with assimilation. After moving through an explanation of how the Italian American paradoxical nature appears "crazy," I will demonstrate how "crazy" operates in the aforementioned films, underlining both the positive and negative angles of these media depictions.

HISTORY AND ASSIMILATION

Most references to and depictions of Italian Americans are drawn from images of southern Italians, particularly Sicilians. Primarily because of poverty and lack of economic opportunity, southern Italians were the largest Italian population to emigrate to America (Covello, 1967; Gambino, 1974). The history of southern Italian Americans is fraught with conflict. Regarded by northern Italians as Africans since Sicily was once geographically connected to Africa (Birnbaum, 1993) and being deemed "racially inferior" by northern Italian scientists (Verdicchio, 1993), southern Italians were not welcomed into America. In the early 1900s, journalistic descriptions of southern Italians included the adjectives excitable, superstitious, revengeful, dishonest, hot-blooded, ignorant, and dirty (Iorizzo & Mondello, 1971). Such adjectives still color the perception of Italian Americans. Words like excitable, superstitious, and hot-blooded threaten the Protestant ethic of being rational, calculating, and controlled. As with so many cultural groups, the negative value judgments implied through these adjectives ignore the historical basis for behavior.

From its origin, Sicily was constantly being invaded and bombarded by intruders such as the Greeks, the Normans, and the Africans. These invasions occurred because of the rich and plentiful land that continues to provide much of the food and resources for Italy. Because of these countless invasions, Sicily was always under the rule of another country and therefore rarely had its own stable government. Instead, families bonded together to form organizations. According to sociologist Andre Rolle (1980), these family organizations "protected their estates against intruders and competitors" (p. 78). By certain accounts, these family organizations were the foundation for the Mafia.

Behavioral remnants acquired from the intrusions include mistrust. Mistrust manifests either as a wariness of outsiders or as silence.

Richard Gambino (1974), in his landmark book *Blood of My Blood*, notes that education implies, to second- and third-generation Italian Americans, trust in outsiders and betrayal of the family:

> The parents of the typical second-generation child ridiculed American institutions and sought to nurture in him [sic] *la via vecchia* [life in the family]. The father nurtured in his children a sense of mistrust and cynicism regarding the outside world. (p. 33)

Because of such ridicule of American institutions, Gambino describes Italian Americans as the "worst equipped for success in American society." Since Gambino's observations, little has changed for Italian Americans. Daniel Monti (1994) writes that as of 1993, Italian Americans had the lowest rates of educational and occupational achievements among European ethnics. According to Monti, 40% of women and 54% of men who are of Italian descent have fewer than 12 years of formal education (p. 26). For many Italian Americans, wariness of outsiders has translated into a lack of education and professional achievement. Novelist Gay Talese (1993) explores this issue by examining the absence of the Italian American literary voice. Reverting to a Sicilian proverb, "Never educate your children beyond yourself," Talese connects southern Italian history with this absence of literary voice:

> This proverb reflects the thinking of impoverished families struggling to survive in the feudal system of class-stratified Italy, a system that existed against exposing [sic] young family members to alienating ideas that might be communicated by teachers or by the written word—ideas that could undermine the solidarity of the family, which was the patriarch's main source of comfort and strength in a land controlled by foreign oppressors. (p. 29)

Talese also acknowledges that this historical reaction has prevented Italian Americans from achieving high-profile status in media-related industries such as publishing. He notes that only individuals with knowledge of organized crime are allowed into this elite circle.

"Omerta," or the code of silence, developed as a protection against outsiders, insures familial allegiance and discourages assimilation. Both novelist Helen Barolini (1985) in her anthology of Italian American writers, *The Dream Book*, and archeologist Ann Cornelisan (1977) in her ethnographic account, *Women in the Shadows*, have written extensively about how women have used "omerta" as a response to poverty. For men, "omerta" carries with it punitive Mafia associations. Men must either maintain the code of silence within the family or be silenced through death.

While many other behavioral factors might result from mistrust, two dominant factors worth noting are fatalism and emotionalism (Carilli, 1989). A wariness of outsiders or silence and poverty resulting from the invasions can create a fatalistic outlook and engender reactive or overly emotional behavior.

Mistrust and such accompanying behaviors as fatalism and emotionalism explain why Italian Americans have failed to assimilate into American society. Italian neighborhoods and enclaves in major U.S. cities still exist as representations of these trials of assimilation. Current media images of Italian Americans are more likely to depict these uneducated and unassimilated cultural members (Conforti, 1994). Television sitcoms have spawned such unassimilated Italian American characters as the Fonz from *Happy Days*, Tony the housekeeper on *Who's the Boss?* and Eldon from *Murphy Brown*. In this paper, I contend that an American fascination exists with this Italian American struggle. Thus, there is an eagerness on the media's part to display these uneducated, unassimilated Italian Americans. My goal is to demonstrate how this struggle, which translates into "crazy" behavior, manifests in film depictions of Italian Americans. I have selected movies that I believe explore this cultural struggle in a meaningful way, demonstrating that such a struggle has inadvertently portrayed a positive way of being in the world. However, I offer caution, asserting that the struggle can have deleterious effects on Italian Americans' self-perceptions. Images of oneself as uneducated, comical, and passionate can reinforce the assimilation struggle.

CRAZY

The term "crazy" carries with it associations of mental illness (Chaika, 1985; Isaac & Armat, 1990) or societal deviance such as cult membership (Ayella, 1990). In communication terminology, "crazymaking" talk (Bach & Deutsch, 1979) refers to sending unclear or indirect messages. Paradoxical therapy or prescribing that clients change their behavior by indulging in their unhealthy behavioral patterns carries the label of "crazy" therapy (Chaika, 1985). In short, *crazy* is a comprehensive term covering marginal activities that are psychotic, deviant, unusual, and out-of-the-ordinary.

The saying "still crazy after all these years," popularized in a Paul Simon song, refers to a less pejorative, perhaps more playful definition of *crazy*. Referring to an individual as crazy might mean that the individual is humorous, fun-loving, and unique. To "drive someone crazy" implies the use of some behavior or trait to please and entice or to disturb and annoy. The excessive or unique use of behavior or a contradiction between behaviors may result in the description of an individual as "crazy." When applied to Italian Americans, this response refers to those behaviors associated with the assimilation struggle. For this paper, the definition of "crazy" behavior is when a character gives unsupportive, unsolicited opinions in an inappropriately expressive or reactive manner or responds antagonistically or reactively either through conflict or silence. In combination, these behaviors, when exhibited, are the foundation for very provocative drama or very amusing comedy. I contend that these combinations of behavior make Italian Americans intriguing media subjects.

SATURDAY NIGHT FEVER

The dramatic 1978 film *Saturday Night Fever*, supposedly an examination of the late 70s disco scene, contains a startlingly authentic depiction of a Bensonhurst Italian American working-class male, Tony (John Travolta). In the movie, Tony lives at home with his family, works at a paint store, and spends his salary at the disco, where he sports his only talent—dancing. He meets a woman, Stephanie (Karen Gorney), who attempts to leave her painful, hopeless Bensonhurst environment for the promise of career success and social mobility in New York City. Together, Tony and Stephanie enter a dance contest. The Verazzano Narrows Bridge, where Tony and his friends playfully leap about, flirting with the danger of falling off the bridge, represents Tony's neighborhood, his life, and his identity as a working-class Italian American.

Stephanie, in turn, represents all his feelings of conflict. She imposes a threat to his very essence. Stephanie's move to the city is a move away from the painful familiar. Stephanie challenges Tony's macho misogynistic attitude by trying to engage him in a friendship, an unfamiliar context for this Italian American male. Also, Stephanie encourages Tony's dancing—an avocation that is a sharp contrast to his machismo. In one of the most sensitive scenes in the film, Stephanie confronts Tony about being stuck in his identity:

> STEPHANIE. I'm out of this scene almost completely, this Bay Ridge scene. I'm moving to Manhattan. I'm getting my own apartment. I'm changing. I'm really changing as a person. I'm growing. Nobody has any idea how much I'm growing.
>
> TONY. Why don't you go on a diet? (*laughs*)
>
> STEPHANIE. OK. Listen. I like you. We could dance together. That's it. We could just dance together and nothing more, nothing personal. I don't want you comin' on to me.
>
> TONY. Why not?
>
> STEPHANIE. Because I don't date guys like you anymore for one thing. You're too young. You ain't got any class.

TONY. Come on. Would you like to know what I do?

STEPHANIE. It's not necessary.

TONY. I'll tell you what I do. I work in a paint store and I got a raise this week.

STEPHANIE. Right. You work in a paint store. Right? You probably live with your family. You hang out with your buddies and on Saturday night, you go and blow it all off at 2001 [a dance club].

TONY. That's right.

STEPHANIE. You're a cliché. You're nowhere on your way to no place.

Though it seems that Stephanie has broken through Tony's unassimilated identity, his "crazy" despairing reaction after the dance contest indicates otherwise. As he begins to come to terms with the injustices experienced by the local Puerto Rican gang, who has been tantalized by his gang, and by the Puerto Rican couple who compete in a dance competition, Tony's response, an attempt to rape Stephanie, is inappropriate and reactive:

TONY. Everybody's gotta dump on somebody. Right. Of course. Everybody can't do us straight. Right. My pa goes to work. He gets dumped on so he dumps on my mother. Right. Of course. And the Spics, they dump on us and we gotta dump on the Spics. Of course. Everybody's dumpin' on everybody.

Tony's "crazy" reaction results from his feelings of entrapment in a lifestyle and neighborhood that present no future for him. Although the film concludes on the optimistic note that Tony will move to Manhattan and become Stephanie's friend, *Saturday Night Fever* depicts the tragic struggles of a man who tries to transcend his Italian American working-class background.

MOONSTRUCK

In contrast to the tragic Italian American world presented in *Saturday Night Fever*, the 1988 film *Moonstruck*, billed as a romantic comedy, demonstrates how the overly reactive melodramatic Italian American persona can appear comic. The movie, which flirts with the notion that to be Italian or Italian American is to be passionate and romantic, tells the story of a young widow, Loretta (Cher), who becomes romantically involved with her fiancé's brother Ronnie (Nicholas Cage), while her fiancé, Johnnie (Danny Aiello), tends to his ailing mother in Sicily. Giving unsolicited advice or telling melodramatic narratives and being dramatic for effect drives the comedy. From the moment we meet Loretta, she gives her unsolicited advice to Al, an undertaker:

AL. I'm a genius. I am a genius.

LORETTA. If you're such a genius, how come you can't keep track of your receipts? Al, how am I supposed to do your income tax with the mess you got here?

AL. Numbers. Taxes. Receipts. I make 'em look better then they did in real life. I'm an artistic genius.

LORETTA. Then how come you got butter on your tie?

In *Moonstruck*, the advice-giving shows a humorous neuroticism. Pushed to an extreme, the unsolicited opinions seem insulting and absurd. Melodramatic narratives, performed for effect, however, at times surpass the unsolicited opinions in their comedic value. At the airport while Loretta watches Johnnie's plane take off, an older woman laments:

WOMAN. You have someone on that plane? I put a curse on that plane. My sister's on that plane. I put a curse on that plane that it's gonna explode, catch on fire, fall into the sea. Fifty years ago, she stole a man from me. Today she tells me she never loved him, that she took him to be strong on me. Now, she's going back to Sicily. I cursed her that the great Atlantic water should swallow her up.

After Johnnie has left for Sicily, Loretta meets Ronnie. Ronnie's greeting is to tell an impassioned melodramatic narrative:

RONNIE. You're gonna marry my brother Johnnie. I have no life. My brother Johnnie took my life from me. And now, he's gettin' married. He has his. He's gettin' his and he wants me to come. What is life? . . . Nothing is anybody's fault but things happen. Look (*showing hand*). This wood is fake. Five years ago I was engaged to be married and Johnnie came in here and he ordered bread from me and I said OK some bread and I put my hand in the slicer and it got caught because I wasn't payin' attention. The slicer chewed off my hand. When my fiancée found out about it, when she found out I had been maimed, she left me for another man.

While the nature of the story is tragic, Ronnie's dramatic rendering of his personal tragedy, like that of the woman in the airport, is comical and not meant to be taken too seriously. *Moonstruck*, one of the few mainstream movies that contains Italian American characters who are not part of the underground world, demonstrates an awareness of how Italian Americans have a unique ability to push the tragic to extremes, thus turning it into comedy that borders on absurdity. While such behavior is alluded to in *Saturday Night Fever*, when, for example, Tony demands that his family take his hairstyle seriously, or when his friends mock his table manners, *Moonstruck* takes this behavior to new heights, as if it were a study of Italian American communication behavior.

Notably, Cher received an academy award for her depiction of Loretta because of the difficulty in showing the dimensionality of such behavior. In an earlier portrayal of Italian American behavior in the Italian American family, the 1963 movie *Love with a Proper Stranger* failed to present this multidimensionality of character. Instead, Natalie Wood and Steve McQueen portray their Italian American characters with a perfunctory sadness and seriousness. While the movie delves into a tragic topic, that of an unmarried pregnant woman who considers an illegal abortion, some of the family interaction, which had a seemingly comic intention, was overplayed and made the characters appear like unsympathetic whiners. *Moonstruck*, however, brought to light the intriguing tension between tragedy and comedy, which in turn made room for another Italian American comedy like *My Cousin Vinny*.

JUNGLE FEVER

As Spike Lee's follow-up to his hit movie *Do the Right Thing*, a negative depiction of Italian Americans, *Jungle Fever* (1991) shows a far more sympathetic view of the Italian American working-class neighborhood of Bensonhurst, Brooklyn. While this movie was made 12 years after *Saturday Night Fever*, Lee renders a very similar world— that of entrapment, surrender, despair, and silence as a response to all such feelings. Publicized as a movie about the relationships between "Blacks and Whites," the movie is about an Italian American female, Angie (Annabella Sciorra), who works as a temp in an architectural firm where she gets involved with a married African American architect, Flipper (Wesley Snipes). As a result of Angie's actions, her boyfriend, Paulie (John Turturro), questions his own desperate life, leading him to date an African American woman and to consider getting an education.

Both Angie and Paulie are ostracized by their friends and family for silently considering options that could lead them out of their miserable Bensonhurst surroundings. By the standards of the Italian American community, Angie and Paulie have done something "crazy," though self-protective. Ironically, their efforts to transcend their Italian American neighborhood are through African Americans, who themselves are struggling with their identity in a world governed by the White patriarchy. In actuality, the behavior of the family and community is reactive and crazy. When Angie's father learns of her involvement with a Black man, he responds by beating her:

> FATHER. What kind of woman are you. I didn't raise you to be with a nigger. I'd rather you'd be a mass murderer or a child molester than fuckin' a

nigger. Don't you respect your mother's memory? I raised you to be a good Italian girl. You're a disgrace. You're a disgrace. You're an Italian girl. You're a disgrace.

The macho bigots who frequent the neighborhood store where Paulie works respond with equal irrational intolerance:

> VINNY. Paulie, We know. You're a jerk-off most of the time but I feel for you. A colored. A spook. Jesus Christ. A fuckin' eggplant. (Translated from Italian word "melanzana" which is a derogatory reference to African Americans.)
>
> FRANKIE. You know Paulie, Jew girls, Jew girls do that all the time but I would've thought better of Angela. I mean she went to Catholic school for eight years, eight years.
>
> JOEY. That's 16 years, you moron.
>
> VINNY. You gonna give her a beatin'?
>
> PAULIE. Her father did that already.
>
> VINNY. I'm not talkin' about her father. I'm talkin' about you. See my girl Denise, she got out of line one time and I stomped her right in the midsection.

Italian American critics like Angelo Mazzocco (1995) condemn Spike Lee for his depiction of Italian Americans in *Jungle Fever*:

> In his portrayal of Italian Americans, Lee exploits all the stereotypes associated with this ethnic group. So partial a film cannot have the sweeping social message the media claims. For this film to have such a message, it should have explored the rage that motivates the people of Bensonhurst. (p. 187)

The rage and craziness Mazzocco refers to are a direct result of Italian Americans not being able to assimilate and not knowing how. While the movie may be criticized for its rendering of interracial relationships, Lee does a commendable job of showing the struggles Italian Americans face when they attempt to leave their neighborhoods. Angie and Paulie are silent, sympathetic, and tragic characters who have visions that are squelched by their friends and families.

MY COUSIN VINNY

Reminiscent of *Moonstruck*, *My Cousin Vinny* (1992) takes the former one step further by infusing the characters with unsolicited opinions, which in any other depiction might seem antagonistic. *My Cousin Vinny*, however, is a no-holds-barred comedic rendering of Italian Americans. In the film, Vinny (Joe Pesci) ventures to Alabama, along with his fiancée, Mona Lisa (Marisa Tomei), to defend his first lawsuit, a murder charge brought against his cousin. The comedic clash of cultures between the Brooklynese and the southerners parallels the clash between Vinny and Mona Lisa. These two cultural collisions are at the root of the comedy. The unsolicited opinions between Vinny and Mona Lisa are particularly humorous. The moment they arrive in town, we see this "crazy" exchange:

MONA LISA. What?

VINNY. Nothing. You stick out like a sore thumb around here.

MONA LISA. What about you?

VINNY. I fit in better than you. At least, I'm wearing cowboy boots.

MONA LISA. Oh yeah, you blend.

Shortly after Vinny's first court appearance, we see a continuation of this "intimate" exchange, which sets a communication precedent for the entire movie:

MONA LISA. You got one huge responsibility taking on this murder case. You screw up and those boys get fried.

VINNY. I know.

MONA LISA. So, you think you know what you're doing?

VINNY. Yeah, I think I know what I'm doing.

MONA LISA. Cause you didn't look like you knew what you were doing in that courtroom.

Most other depictions of such communication between a man and a woman would lead the audience to believe that the characters' relationship is in jeopardy. Instead the audience experiences a strong relationship with a unique Italian American twist—a twist that could be regarded as "crazy." Antagonism and supportiveness are two entirely separate emotions. To convey them as one can be confusing. When Vinny attempts to use a similar communication style in the courtroom, he infuriates the judge. Vinny's unwillingness to comply with the judge's courtroom rules embellishes the comedy while marginalizing Vinny as a working-class Italian American. In the end, Vinny's ability to walk between the two worlds of antagonism and support, or working-class Italian American and professional lawyer, allow him to win the case.

My Cousin Vinny represents the quintessence of the Italian American struggle with assimilation. The Italian American world has given Vinny an intuitive ability and worldview. The contradictory White Anglo-Saxon world encourages analysis and rationality. Being caught between the two worlds is a struggle I would term "crazy."

CONCLUSION

Through an examination of depictions of "crazy" Italian Americans in four mainstream films, I have attempted to show those dimensions of the Italian American character that are intriguing and can create compelling drama. As I stated earlier, dramatizations where ethnicity plays a key role in character motivation are fascinating to the American consciousness because the characters are not truly Americans, not truly assimilated. There is something comforting and sobering about these depictions of unassimilated Italian Americans. They are funny. They are tragic. But, at their very core, they are unique and culturally specific.

My overriding goal here is to assert that such depictions of Italian Americans can be viewed as negative because they encourage Italian Americans to maintain an unassimilated status quo that does not support education. Furthermore, they encourage acceptance of confining circumstances. While there is an intrigue in watching the characters manage a tightrope walk between emotions that are both tragic and comic and while an audience might enjoy the character who is never taken seriously, future images of Italian Americans must extend these "crazy" depictions into depictions that are multidimensional in their exploration of ethnicity and its impact.

REFERENCES

Ayella, M. (1990). "'They must be crazy': Some of the difficulties in researching cults." *The American Behavioral Scientist, 33,* 562–577.

Bach G. R., & Deutsch, R. M. (1979). *Stop! You're driving me crazy.* New York: Berkley Books.

Barolini, H. (Ed.). (1985). *The dream book: An anthology of writings by Italian American women.* New York: Schocken Books.

Birnbaum, L. C. (1993). *Black Madonnas.* Boston: Northeastern University Press.

Carilli, T. M. (1989). *An ethnography of creative writing: A study of the Sicilian-American culture through creative writing.* Unpublished doctoral dissertation, Southern Illinois University, Carbondale.

Carilli, T. M. (1990). *Italian-Americans as media scapegoats.* Paper presented at the National Association for Ethnic Studies, Fort Collins, CO.

Chaika, E. (1985). Crazy talk. *Psychology Today, 19,* 30–35.

Conforti, J. M. (1994). Italian Americans as "ethnics": Description or derogation? In J. Krase, & J. N. DeSena (Eds.), *Italian Americans in a multicultural society* (pp. 35–43). Stony Brook, NY: Forum Italicum.

Cornelisan, A. (1977). *Women of the shadows.* New York: Vintage Books.

Gambino, R. (1974). *Blood of my blood: The dilemma of the Italian-Americans.* New York: Doubleday.

Healey, J. F. (1995). *Race, ethnicity, gender and class*. Thousand Oaks, CA: Pine Forge Press.

Iorizzo, L .J., & Mondello, S. (1971). *The Italian Americans*. New York: Twayne.

Isaac, R. J., & Armat, V .C. (1990). The right to be crazy: The tragic results of a "progressive" crusade. *The American Enterprise, 1*, 34–42.

Mazzocco, A. (1995). Of Spike Lee's *Jungle Fever. Voices in Italian Americana, 6*, 186–188.

Monti, D. J., Jr. (1994). The working and reworking of Italian-American ethnicity in the United States. In J. Krase, & J .N. DeSena (Eds.), *Italian Americans in a multicultural society* (pp. 19–34). Stony Brook, NY: Forum Italicum.

Rolle, A. (1980). *The Italian Americans: Troubled roots*. Norman, OK: University of Oklahoma Press.

Stone, E. (1978, December 17). It's still hard to grow up Italian. *The New York Times*, pp. 42, 43, 86, 87, 88, 89, 90, 91, 101, 102, 103.

Talese, G. (1993, March 14). Where are the Italian-American novelists? *The New York Times*, pp. 1, 23, 25, 29.

Verdicchio, P. (1997). *Devils in Paradise: Writings in Post Immigrant Culture*. Toronto: Guernica Editions.

CHAPTER 10

Ethnic Humor and Ingroup/Outgroup Positioning: Eplicating Viewer Perceptions of All-American Girl

Mark P. Orbe, Ruth Seymour, and Mee-Eun Kang

ETHNIC HUMOR IN THE MASS MEDIA

Mass-marketed ethnic humor in the United States can be traced to the late 1700s, when comedic caricatures of non-White slaves appeared in theater presentations; European American performers in blackface first appeared on stage in the late 1820s (Moore, 1980). This tradition of minstrelsy continued for more than 100 years, with African Americans entering show business for the first time in the 1850s (Nelson, 1994; MacDonald, 1985). A century later, even after African Americans began to contribute to the formation of media images, some traditional minstrelsy images continue (Cooks & Orbe, 1993). These stereotypically inferior images provided mass audiences clear rationalizations for ongoing mistreatment of African Americans (Moore, 1980). African Americans, however, were not the only people of color subjected to this onslaught of negative imagery.

From as early as 1914 and into the 1980s, European Americans in "yellow face" have played Asian characters in film and television movies (Sing, 1989). In 1914, Mary Pickford was the first major non-Asian actor to portray an Asian person (*Madame Butterfly*). Since then, other well-known actors have applied "yellow face" to star in films, including Katherine Hepburn (*Dragon Seed*, 1940s), Shirley MacLaine

(*My Geisha* and *Gambit*, 1960s), Jerry Lewis (*Hardly Working*, 1981), Peter Sellers (*The Fiendish Plot of Dr. Fu Manchu*, 1932), and Joel Grey (Remo Williams: *The Adventure Begins*, 1985). In early film portrayals, Asian female characters were typically cast as "peasants, [subservient] geishas, dragon ladies, and exotic-erotics" (Sing, 1989, p. 23). Asian men, on the other hand, were characterized as "evil, sinister, diabolical, myopic, buck-toothed subhuman villains, or as passive and emasculated detectives" (Sing, 1989, p. 25). As television emerged as a primary source of entertainment, these formulaic images of Asian Americans traveled from the big screen into the homes of American viewers.

Representations of people of Asian descent on television increased in the 1960s. The premier of *Hong Kong* on ABC had a number of Asian characters and maintained the image of Chinese intrigue, sexy women, smuggling, and drug peddling (Wilson & Gutiérrez, 1985). The largest Asian presence on American television came with *Hawaii Five-O*, which aired from 1968 to 1980. At least three Asian actors fulfilled regular roles on the show, with more diverse but still stereotypical characters. After the mid-1980s, the number of Asian roles increased and included less confining portrayals. Television shows such as *Gung Ho*, *After Mash*, *St. Elsewhere*, *Tour of Duty*, *21 Jumpstreet*, and *Ohara* (which starred Pat Morita, the first Asian actor to have a network series in primetime) included Asian characters in a wide variety of more "realistic" roles (Sing, 1989, p. 28).

Still, these portrayals are exceptions to the general rule. Decades of "advances" in television programming have done little to lift media representations of Asian characters above stereotypical concoctions of mystery, crime, seduction, and subservience. In a country where the Asian population will increase an estimated 22% by the year 2000 (Henry, 1990), Asian Americans have been virtually invisible and largely marginalized on television. This ethnic group, like other non-Anglo groups, has been assigned negative codes in television that stereotype them as classic outgroups, and affirm the Anglo American status as culturally superior (Deming & Jenkins, 1991).

GROUP IDENTITY AND ETHNIC HUMOR

In interpersonal and intercultural communication theory (Brewer & Miller, 1984; Brewer, 1979; LeVine & Campbell, 1972), *ingroups* include those individuals a person has positive feelings about, interacts with frequently, and can depend upon in times of need (Brislin, 1993). They are often thought of as "similar to me" and their approval or disapproval of various behaviors is considered important. In contrast, *outgroups* contain individuals who are kept at a distance and viewed as "too different" to deserve a person's time, effort, and concern (Brislin, 1993).

Some humor scholars use this model to categorize ethnic humor (see, for example Nevo, 1991). *Ingroup* humor is an ethnic group's humor about itself and the world, through its own distinctive cultural prism and with its own cultural flavor, such as Jewish humor (Nevo, 1991) and African American humor (Cooks & Orbe, 1993). *Outgroup* humor is *about* a group rather than *of* a group and is designed by and for people *not* of that culture. Stupid Pole, greedy Jew, and lazy African American jokes are examples of derogatory outgroup humor. Like ingroup humor, outgroup humor has been widely studied and is characterized "as invective humor directed at racial and nationality groups, denigrating alleged attributes of those groups" (Schutz, 1989).

Audience interpretation of ethnic humor has been shown to rely heavily—but not entirely—on knowledge or presumed knowledge of the *source*. Multiple studies (see, for example, Cooks & Orbe, 1993) have shown the perceived funniness of humor to vary significantly according to identities of sources and receivers. For example, if a woman offers an antifemale joke, it is generally more acceptable to both male and female listeners than if a man offers the joke (Suls & Miller, 1976). Generally, members of a group are unlikely to appreciate disparaging humor about *their own* demographic or identity group. However, some listeners may laugh more freely at negative jokes about *other* groups if the source of the joke also is a member of the targeted group (Bourhis, Gadfield, Giles, & Tajfel, 1977) or if a video portrayal of the joke shows friendly, laughing reception by the targeted group (Suls & Miller, 1976).

Ethnic jokes categorizable as *outgroup* or *ingroup* also vary greatly in content. Outgroup humor tends to parody group characteristics that diverge from dominant norms: cultural differences in dress, physiognomy, social traditions, business practices, or religious customs. Ingroup humor has a more folksy tone; group members poke fun at themselves and create a richer, more intimate humor about themselves than outsiders are able to cartoon. Ingroup members draw on private slang, history, perspective and group "secrets." Their jokes about themselves can be sharp-tongued, even brutal, but are grounded in common group experience. Thus, the act of characterizing a joke *ingroup* or *outgroup* has some conceptual relation to its degree of perceived "cultural authenticity," especially as the characterization is made by members of the target group.

ALL-AMERICAN GIRL:
AN ASIAN AMERICAN TELEVISION FIRST

All-American Girl, a prime-time ABC sitcom that debuted in the fall of 1994, represented a first in television programming. This series, starring stand-up comedienne Margaret Cho, was the first prime-time television series to feature a family of Asian Americans. Celebrated as evidence of a growing cultural diversity on television, the show conceivably presented an instance where *ingroup* scripts—by and about Korean Americans—would be made available for millions of viewers (Korean and non-Korean). It soon appeared, however, that such would not be the case. Although *All-American Girl* initially was among the most watched programs (Kiska, 1994), reviews among Asian Americans, as well as non–Asian Americans, greatly varied.

Some non-Asian reviewers cited the show as "another sappy sitcom" (Kloer, 1994, p. D11) where "humor rises out of stereotypes" (Jarvis, 1994, p. 10). On the other hand, some Asian Americans were quick to offer praises for the show. "We're very optimistic about what we've seen, and we feel it's very significant that this is being tried," said Guy Aoki, head of Media Action Network for Asian Americans (quoted in Braxton, 1994, p. 1F). Some of the most positive responses came from younger Asian Americans. Paula Yoo, a 25-year-old Korean American (like Cho), readily identifies with the characters on the show (Yoo, 1994); others saw Cho as a spokesperson for Generation X Asian Americans. One of the most significant accolades for the show came when the Media Action Network for Asian Americans honored *All-American Girl* creator, Gary Jacobs, with a "Media Achievement Award" (Braxton, 1994).

However, amidst scattered praise for *All-American Girl*, several criticisms emerged about its portrayal of Korean American life (Lee, 1994; Yang, 1994). Some Asian American critics complained that the show presented a confused blend of various Asian cultures. Other critics were disturbed with stereotypical depictions of Korean Americans. Jeff Yang (1994), a writer for the *Village Voice*, honed in on the possible effect of these depictions:

> What's worse, the hilarious, hard-line cuts at casual racism that pepper her (stand-up) act, in the show, [have] crossed that ill-defined line between satire of stereotypes and representation of them. . . . Why not just go ahead and call it *Gooks 'R Us* ? (p. 47)

Yang goes on to predict, however, that many Asian Americans would continue to watch the show simply because "it's all we have" (p. 47).

The myriad of responses to *All-American Girl* prompted a series of research projects examining outgroup/ingroup perceptions of ethnic humor in the mass media (Seymour, Orbe, & Kang, 1996). Specifically, the research utilized a battery of methodological procedures (content analysis, questionnaires, and focus group discussions) to explore ingroup/outgroup perceptions of this situation comedy.

PERCEPTIONS OF ETHNIC HUMOR
ON *ALL-AMERICAN GIRL*

Prior to exploring the perceptions of "ethnic humor" on *All-American Girl*, Seymour et al. (1996) conducted a content analysis of the show's jokes. A total of 531 jokes from a sample of five selected shows were analyzed by a team of coders. Their analysis revealed that just over 17% included ethnic content, most often (75%) about Asian Pacific persons, cultures, or languages. A relatively smaller percentage of jokes (under 9%) focused on intergenerational differences between Margaret and her parents. As expected, Margaret Cho was most often the source of jokes (36%), followed by her grandmother (17%), mother (12%), older brother (12%), and father (4.5%).

However, one of the most significant findings of the content analysis revealed that most jokes *did not* contain ethnic content *or* intergenerational content. Of all the jokes analyzed, the vast majority of jokes (almost 77%) did not involve ethnic or intergenerational content. This finding is quite interesting, given that some television critics attributed the show's cancellation to its focus on "one-note ethnic humor" (Dorsey, 1995, p. C3).

In an extension to the work by Seymour et al. (1996), eight focus group discussions at three research sites in the Midwest were facilitated. Forty-four participants were divided into relatively small homogenous focus groups by ethnicity, nationality, and age. After watching a representative episode of *All-American Girl*, participants were asked to complete a brief questionnaire regarding the show, then researchers—utilizing an open-ended, general conversational interviewing approach (Orbe, 1994)—facilitated open discussions about general perceptions of the show. Although t-tests conducted on all questionnaire data among different groups (age, gender, nationality, and ethnicity) showed no significant differences, the focus group discussions produced a multitude of vividly rich descriptions that give insight into ingroup/outgroup perceptions of the show.

FOCUS GROUP THEMES

Following the process of a phenomenological inquiry (Orbe, 1994), Seymour et al. (1996) reviewed the information gathered and reduced the capta to twelve preliminary themes. Utilizing the notion of free imaginative variation (Lanigan, 1979), these initial themes, in turn, were reexamined in terms of their necessity to capture the essence of the information gathered. This reduction process yielded six essential themes:

1. Universality of an "All-American" comedy
2. Perceptions of authenticity
3. Treating Asian Americans as a monolithic group
4. Stereotypes: satire or caricature?
5. Generalizing effects of "edu-tainment television"
6. Important Asian American first

which appear to capture the essence of the focus group discussions.

Universality of an "All-American" Comedy

The most consistent perception among the diverse co-researchers was of *All-American Girl* as a typical American situation comedy that was "very clichéd," and "just happened [to include] some Asian American family." Both Koreans and non-Koreans depicted the show as a "facsimile" of many other American shows. *All-American Girl* seemed a fitting title, according to Korean and Korean American co-researchers, who described the show as more American than Korean.

It appeared that for many people, especially non-Korean Americans, the show's ethnic backdrop remained largely invisible, increasing the likelihood that viewers of different ethnicities could identify with the characters and their life experiences. It would appear that ABC and the producers of *All-American Girl* attempted to "Americanize" the lived experiences of a Korean American family to create a universal appeal to a mass audience. However, rating analyses reflect that the show did best in "big cities on both coasts [with notable Asian American populations] but found fewer takers in the part of the country between" (Dorsey, 1995, p. C3). This detail could imply that the "Americanization" of *All-American Girl* was insufficient to persuade some viewers to watch a show highlighting an all–Asian American cast.

Perceptions of Authenticity

During two non-Korean focus groups, not much attention was given to the cultural authenticity of *All-American Girl*. Although a few co-researchers commented on the "exaggeration of characters," most felt unqualified to make any substantial judgments. One European American participant acknowledged that he "didn't think it was a typical Korean family," but admitted, "it could be accurate. . . . I haven't had any exposure to Koreans or Korean Americans so I can't really tell." While non–Korean Americans felt unqualified to make any judgments on the accuracy of the show, Korean and Korean American focus groups devoted much discussion to the question of cultural authenticity. In addition to the problematic "blending of different Asian cultures," Korean and Korean Americans were also able to identify specific elements of the show that made it less-than-authentic: language/accent inaccuracies, mistaken aspects of Korean culture (i.e., crickets as pets), unfamiliar character attitudes and behaviors (especially of the Korean-born grandmother and parents), absence of typical Korean artifacts on the set (wall hangings, furniture, traditional rice cooker), and nontraditional interactions and relationships among family members. In fact, the show's lack of authenticity appeared to be a central issue to ingroup members. As one Korean American described, "We get bogged down with the inaccuracies, and so it disturbs us . . . it squelches all the humor that they're trying to attempt."

Treating Asian Americans as a Monolithic Group

Another concern involved how *All-American Girl*—in the words of one Korean American—"further promot[es] a stereotype that we're interchangeable." People of Korean descent took issue with the "blending" of Asian cultures on the show. The show's inclusion of a broad array of Asian characters, customs, and artifacts under the guise of presenting Korean American culture was problematic. "This fact turns me off . . . maybe Americans can't differentiate among Chinese, Korean, Japanese," said one Korean American. From the responses of some African American and European American co-researchers involved in this project, this concern appears to be valid.

Of the 13 non–Korean American focus group participants, only one European American man who had spent time in Asia while in the military was quick to point out the "confusion of different cultures." The remaining participants did not appear to question the cultural authenticity of the show and seemed to assume all characters, artifacts, and expressions as accurate representations of Korean culture.

The scripted tendency to treat Asian Americans as a monolithic group was also apparent in the way that the show portrayed the three different generations of the Kim family. In this regard, Korean-born characters (mother, father, grandmother) appeared to function within a similar "Americanized" wise-cracking style. This was something that both Korean and non–Korean Americans recognized as unrealistic.

Stereotypes: Satire or Caricature?

Much of the dialogue on the authenticity of *All-American Girl* specifically criticized character representations. Especially alarming to both Koreans and non-Koreans was the way in which the show used Korean [Asian] culture "as something not to be appreciated" but "made fun of." Although some participants described ethnic humor in the show as "kind of like a ribbing," others saw the characters as ethnic caricatures and linked the treatment of the Kims on *All-American Girl* with character representations in other ethnic comedies. One person of Korean descent went so far as to condemn the character representations as "cartoonlike." Some respondents described the "dilemma of a Korean American viewer"—finding the show funny, yet being offended by grossly exaggerated stereotypes.

The negative inclination of certain ethnic caricatures on the show emerged as especially distressing, given that many other Americans have little, if any, exposure to Korean Americans. One Korean American disclosed that "I chuckled at this show, but in the back of my mind, I can't help but worry." And, in fact, when asked about their perceptions on the accuracy of the show, European Americans involved in the study replied with great uncertainty.

Several European American co-researchers were quick to acknowledge the subjectivity of ingroup/outgroup positioning as consumers of ethnic humor. One European American woman explained that she "can't enjoy some of the ethnic sitcoms" because, as an outgroup member, she "can't laugh *with* [them] and . . . doesn't enjoy laughing *at* [them]." Another woman explained her sensitivity to how Korean viewers might feel while watching a show like *All-American Girl* in terms of her experiences when "women make jokes about women and men laugh."

Generalizing Effects of "Edu-tainment Television"

While co-researchers of Korean descent readily acknowledged that *All-American Girl* was a "sitcom, not a PBS documentary about Korean culture" and should be "watched for fun . . . not to gain cultural understanding," they expected that show would serve an educational role as well. One participant explained, "I thought it was great that there was a sitcom on Asian American families. . . . Exposure is really important— and what better way than to use prime time sitcoms?"

In fact, shows that highlight the experiences of underrepresented group members who are largely invisible or marginalized in television programming are especially important. *All-American Girl* "is the only comedy that shows [a] Korean family," explained one co-researcher.

"People might think that is [typical]; they don't have any other choice." Television shows featuring European Americans do not necessarily run the same consequential risks, since the media displays a greater variety of European American experiences.

Many co-researchers also described consequences that Korean Americans had experienced personally as related to the increased exposure of Margaret Cho and the popularity of *All-American Girl* (i.e., "You look just like Margaret Cho").

Important Asian American First

In spite of all of their criticism for *All-American Girl*, many participants called the show an "important first" for Asian Americans. Among Korean and Korean Americans, it was interesting to see a certain level of enthusiasm for the show, despite problematic concerns. One participant expressed a certain "obligation to watch the show as a Korean American," while others were "quick to watch" because "a Korean girl was playing the leading role." Even those who were critical of the show expressed a certain level of enthusiasm, as evidenced by one Korean American who disclosed that "it was kind of exciting. . . . I haven't seen so many Asians [on television] at one time."

Throughout the focus group discussions, *All-American Girl* invoked comparisons with other representations of ethnic families on television. The show was likened to earlier African American situation comedies, like *The Jeffersons*; many participants theorized that "improved" representations like those on *The Cosby Show* only occur with time. In this, Korean and Korean Americans appeared to look to the experiences of other ethnic minorities in television for consolation. Generally, they remained optimistic, recognizing the difficult and slow process by which change typically occurs—especially change within a system dominated by "non-minorities."

CONCLUSION

The combination of methods used in this research permitted more complex views to emerge regarding the nature of perceptions of cultural authenticity in mass media content. While a content analysis indicated a significant portion of ethnic humor in the show's script primarily articulated by Korean American characters, focus group discussions provided further insight regarding perceptions of the show.

Specific insight, for instance, was generated regarding the ingroup/outgroup positioning of viewers. While some might assume that ethnic comedies provide people of color an opportunity for mass-mediated ingroup positioning, such is not always the case. With *All-American Girl*, our findings indicate that ingroup/outgroup positioning was not simply a factor of being Asian American. Instead, many Korean American viewers assumed an outgroup stance since the show seemed to be Americanized to the point of being not identifiable as Korean American. The authentic "Koreanness" of the show became even more enigmatic given that several of the show's actors were non-Koreans performing humor written by non-Koreans. In this regard, the outgroup humor on the show suggests a return to the minstrel-like performance in which Korean and non-Korean actors perform humor written by non-Koreans.

Interestingly, some non–Korean Americans identified strongly with characters (ingroup stance) based on the strong "American" content of the show. Other non-Koreans automatically assumed an outgroup perspective based on the Asian American cast and typically had not watched the show. This blurred line between ingroup/outgroup status provides one explanation as to the lack of statistical significance between Korean and non-Korean responses to the show.

It is also interesting to note that one's subjective positioning did, in fact, appear to have some effect on specific perceptions of *All-American Girl*. For instance, non–Korean Americans interpreted the scripted tension between Margaret and her mother as a result of intergenerational differences. Korean and Korean Americans, on the other hand, appeared to view the source for this conflict as a tension between Americanization and traditional Korean values rather than from purely age-related factors. In this regard, age and ethnicity appear to be factors by which different cohorts adopted an ingroup or outgroup status position based on a distinct reading of the text. Existing literature on ingroup/outgroup positioning and ethnic humor does not seem to include a conceptual framework for discussing such a phenomenon.

These issues also reflect a larger consideration associated with mass-mediated images of underrepresented groups. Some respondents suggested that the show writers and producers assumed that blended, unauthentic images of Asians would appeal to the broader multi-ethnic audience. But does authenticity in cultural portrayals *necessarily* mean a smaller-sized audience? Is the American television audience only responsive to bland and blended cultural pluralism, or do scriptwriters offer only that fare to their viewers? The invisible assumption that market success requires cultural blandness cripples the ability of U.S. media to provide viewers with more authentic images of the cultures of all Americans. These images are vital given the high level of ethnic segregation in our society. The quality of cultural information in popular entertainment will continue to affect broader perceptions of people of color into the next century.

REFERENCES

Bourhis, R. Y., Gadfield, N. J., Giles, H., & Tajfel, H. (1977). Context and ethnic humour in intergroup relations. In A. J. Chapman & H. C. Foot (Eds.), *It's a funny thing, humour* (pp. 13–16). Oxford: Pergamon Press.

Braxton, G. (1994, September 14). It's all in the (ground-breaking) family. *The Los Angeles Times*, p. 1F.

Brewer, M. (1979). Ingroup bias in the minimal intergroup situation: A cognitive-motivational analysis. *Psychological Bulletin, 86*, 307–324.

Brewer, M., & Miller, N. (1984). Beyond the contact hypothesis: Theoretical perspective on desegregation. In N. Miller & M. Brewer (Eds.), *Groups in contact: The psychology of desegregation* (pp. 281–302). Orlando, FL: Academic Press.

Brislin, R. (1993). *Understanding culture's influence on behavior.* Fort Worth, TX: Harcourt Brace.

Cooks, L. M., & Orbe, M. (1993). Beyond the satire: Selective exposure and selective perception in "In Living Color." *Howard Journal of Communication, 4*(3), 217–233.

Dorsey, T. (1995, June 20). Many of the season's losers didn't deserve to be canceled. *Louisville Courier Journal*, p. C3.

George, N. (1994). *Blackface: Reflections on African Americans and the movies.* New York: HarperCollins.

Henry, W. A. (1990, April 9). Beyond the melting pot. *Time*, pp. 28–31.

Jarvis, J. (1994, November 5). The couch critic: All-American Girl. *TV Guide*, p. 10.

Kiska, T. (1994, September 21). Cho's show wins the debut ball, No. 5 overall. *The Detroit News*, p. 5C.

Kloer, P. (1994, September 14). "Girl": Cute premise but it doesn't follow through. *Atlanta Journal and Constitution*, p. D11.

Lanigan, R. (1979). The phenomenology of human communication. *Philosophy Today, 23*(i), 3–15.

Lee, E. (1994, November 19). Margaret Cho brings APA 20–somethings to television. *Asian Week*, p. 1.

LeVine, R., & Campbell, D. (1972). *Ethnocentrism.* New York: Wiley.

Luke, T. (1994, March 12). Asian Generation X member joking their way through life—and racism. *NW Asian Weekly*, p. 14.

Lynch, L. (1995, April 16). Who's news. *USA Weekend Magazine*, p. 1.

MacDonald, J. (1985). *Black and white TV: Afro-Americans in television since 1948.* Chicago: Nelson-Hall.

Moore, M. M. (1980). *Small voices & great trumpets: Minorities & the media.* New York: Praeger.

Nevo, O. (1991). What's in a Jewish joke? *Humor, 4*(2), 151–160.

Orbe, M. (1994). Remember, it's always whites' ball: Descriptions of African American male communication. *Communication Quarterly, 42*(3), 287–300.

Schutz, C. E. (1989). The sociability of ethnic jokes. *Humor, 2*(2), 165–177.

Seymour, R., Orbe, M., & Kang, M. (1996, November). *Asian families through an American prism: Ethnic humor, ingroup/outgroup perceptions and ABC's*

"All-American Girl." Paper presented at the annual convention of the Speech Communication Association, San Diego, CA.

Sing, E. (1989). *Asian Pacific Americans: A handbook on how to cover and portray our nation's fastest growing minority group.* Los Angeles: National Conference.

Wilson, C. C., & Gutierrez, F. (1985). *Minorities and media: Diversity and the end of mass communication.* Beverly Hills, CA: Sage.

Yang, J. (1994, October 4). Anything but the girl. *Village Voice*, p. 47.

Yoo, P. (1994, September 16). My so-called American life. *Detroit News*, p. 12C.

CHAPTER 11

Destroying the Past to Save the Present: Pastoral Voice and Native Identity

Richard Morris
and Mary E. Stuckey

What can be more melancholy than their history? By a law of
their nature, they seem destined to a slow, but sure extinction.
Everywhere, at the approach of a White man, they fade away. We
hear the rustling of their footsteps, like that of the withered leaves
of autumn, and they are gone forever. They pass mournfully by us,
and they return no more.

—B. Dippie, *The Vanishing American*

Among the forces that work against movement toward cultural diversity, few are as omnipresent and as consistently dehumanizing as stereotypes generated by the dominant society as a means of consuming the
identities of the "Other" (Phinney, Chivira, & Williamson, 1992; Rumbaut, 1994; Schmitz, 1992; Takaki, 1993; Todorov, 1992). And among
the stereotypes of Native Americans that members of the contemporary
hegemony in the United States seem to prefer is the "Indian" as "natural," as somehow more connected to and in tune with the environment
than are those who are more "civilized" and technologically advanced
(Bataille & Silet, 1980; Berkhofer, 1978; Cahn, 1969; Clifton, 1990;
Cornell, 1987; Friar, 1972; Hirschfelder, 1982; Kidwell, 1991; McBeth,
1983; O'Connor, 1980; Stedman, 1982). As both closer to nature and
more "primitive" than Euro-Americans, Native Americans are thus less
"corrupt" and at the same time less "advanced" than the members of
the dominant society; they retain their purity in the face of civilization
and thereby represent a glorified image of a past that it being swept

away before the onrush of societal change (Dippie, 1982). Here—as natural, primitive, less corrupt, less advanced, pure, unchanging—Native Americans become representative of pretechnological and "natural" life, ready for use by those who would advance arguments about the uncritical acceptance of technology as the keystone of progress (Mander, 1991).

One such use recently has emerged in the debate between advocates of technological progress as a means toward greater development of human potential and those more wary of technology's unambiguous benefits—a debate that is of particular interest because of the dehumanizing effect that the proponents of the "nature" side of the debate can have on those they ostensibly champion (see Barlow, 1995; Barlow, Birkeris, Kelly, & Slouka, 1995; Kadi, 1995; Sanders, 1995). What makes this strategic stereotype even more interesting is that it is advanced with seemingly benign, perhaps even kindly intentions aimed, one might suppose, at glorifying Native Americans, their cultures, their traditions, their modes of being. Therein lies the danger, for the creation and perpetuation of fictive images, even when generated from ostensibly "friendly" stances, challenge, displace, and render inchoate Native American identities and the cultures from which they emerge.

With that distinct possibility in mind, and borrowing from the insights of Stephen Browne and others, we argue here, first, that, combined with the pastoral voice, such depictions of Native Americans function to reconcile the apparent contradiction between traditional values and technological advances by reinterpreting and dissolving the past and, second, that the imposition of pastorally created identities serves to mask the consequences of a rhetorical strategy that has important negative consequences for Native American identities. Specifically, our essay proceeds in three parts. We begin with a brief explication of the pastoral voice. We then examine the consequences of pastoral voice for tribal identities through an examination of an article that appeared in *Audubon* magazine, as well as the consequences of pastoral voice for individual Native American identities through an examination of an article that appeared in *Harper's* magazine. Finally, we attend to the implications of this interpretive framework.

THE PASTORAL VOICE IN AMERICAN POLITICS

In an insightful essay, Stephen H. Browne (1990) argued that the pastoral voice can serve as a potent tool of political persuasion. Articulated as an ostensibly contemplative and philosophically objective stance, the pastoral voice creates for audience members a serene, "artistically created past, in which certain values and abiding principles are celebrated" (Brown, 1990, p. 46). The impulse to juxtapose the present with an idealized past is powerful, sometimes even overwhelming; it comes to us in uneasy voices that would speak to us of a time gone by—a time to which we would do well to return—when all was well, when the world was in harmony, when people had the "right" values. Those values move toward the audience through an explicitly moral vocabulary in which we find deeply embedded, normative claims that typically manifest a conservative bent through the advancement of the preservation of standards and values that this stance assumes to characterize as a past, golden age. This conservativism can be and often is "ambivalent," for, as Browne so well illustrates in the case of John Dickinson's "Letter from a farmer in Pennsylvania," the pastoral voice serves well the ends of advocating extensive changes in the structures of government and public policy:

> Pastoral . . . entails a reconfiguration of time and space, which takes the present and relocates author, text, and audience in a different realm. By abandoning the confusion of the near world, pastoral presents a world of clearer, simpler meanings. As a rhetorical strategy, however, pastoral must address current issues by redefining the terms of public action and rhetorical judgment. (Browne, 1990, p. 47)

Primary among the elements that constitute and reconstitute the pastoral voice are three that merit specific attention. First, the pastoral voice requires audience members to withdraw from the ordinary world, the here-and-now, so that they might imagine a place of deep serenity and contentment. Through this imaginative space the pastoral voice then provides a reconfiguration of time and place that enables audience members to bring forth imaginatively that fictive golden age in which seemingly forgotten values can stand alongside contrary values that are destroying the present. Finally, the juxtaposition of the golden age with the present enables audience members to move toward "appropriate" action. Not surprisingly, the pastoral voice tends to resonate most deeply during times of social dislocation, when public dilemmas and debates over what constitutes right action threaten the security of private spaces, when the applicability of old assumptions about the political world is in doubt, and when patterns of behavior, contingent as they are upon such assumptions, appear less unambiguously rewarding (Browne, 1990).

Potentially, there are numerous other uses to which one might put the pastoral voice. For instance, it is possible that the pastoral voice might serve less as a tool for continuing the argument between "nature" and "technology" and more as a means for rendering arguments irrelevant. Here, one might invoke the pastoral voice as a means of offering rhetorical reassurances. Through moral action, traditional values and the security they offer can coexist within a changed context brought about through technology. Uses of the pastoral voice, unlike uses of Hofstadter's (1979) paranoid style, therefore need not mark one as a querulous Luddite, afraid of technology and unable to program a VCR. Then, too, the pastoral voice might conceal conflicts between the past and the future, the preservation of the natural world and the embrace of technology, as well as between Native American cultures and Euro-American attempts to destroy those cultures.

NATIVE AMERICANS AND THE PASTORAL VOICE

The connection between Native Americans and the environment is now so prevalent as to be a cliché (recall, for instance, the famous advertisement of a Native American man crying as he looks upon the environmental devastation wrought by Euro-American practices). Native American characters in literature (*The Last of the Mohicans*, *Moby Dick*), in film (*Free Willy*, *Pocohontas*), and advertising ("Land O' Lakes" butter) thus serve as condensation symbols (Edelman, 1988, 1990) that speak for and about a time in the distant past when life supposedly was dependent on respect for nature and its attendant purity (Bataille & Silet, 1980; Berkhofer, 1978; Cahn, 1969; Clifton, 1990; Cornell, 1987; Friar, 1972; Hirschfelder, 1982; Kidwell, 1991; McBeth, 1983; Morris & Wander, 1990; O'Connor, 1980; Stedman, 1982). As condensation symbols, such depictions provide strong moral assertions regarding the importance of nature and purity.

Significantly, the "Indians" so depicted are not "savages," however noble; nor are they bloodthirsty and vicious opponents of westward expansion. They are, rather, the gentle and peaceful Indians whose simple and joyous life was supposedly consonant with the rhythms of the natural world; they are people who supposedly understood themselves as an intimate part of that world, not as hostile interlopers who endeavor to control and subdue it. These are also *supposedly* passive people—Indians who were the victims of imperialistic depredations, Indians whose lands were stolen and whose identities were destroyed by a culturally and militarily stronger people who now wish to "preserve" these poor creatures. As with the rest of the natural world, "Indians" supposedly have suffered as "civilization" has advanced, and their preservation (or, at least, preservation of their ways and wisdom), like that of the buffalo and the eagle, is now important within this framework to the spiritual and physical health of the larger society.

Along with the construction of Native Americans as relics of a past age, within this line of reasoning comes the responsibility to manage and preserve those relics so that future generations may continue to "benefit" from them. From this one may infer that "real" Indians are those who most closely match those worthy of preservation, those who are least like denizens of the modern world. We are to recognize them because they live in teepees, dine on venison, speak a peculiar form of English, and support themselves by trading wampum. "Preserving" Indians thus means limiting Native Americans to a specific time, a specific idyllic place, and a particularly exploitable mode of being—all of which renders Native Americans, historically, not only incapable of action, but also inappropriate *loci* for the actions of others. Native Americans live only to the extent that they occupy this pastoral past: their cause was long ago lost, and there is not now any cause demanding action. As victims, the survival of Native Americans and their cultures and achievements fade into a neglected *past*, where the present no longer can assist them. As victims forever caught in an idealized past, Native Americans are forever frozen, passive, forever acted on, now unable to initiate actions. This then folds back on the political construction of Native Americans as appropriate targets for the benevolence of the federal government, perpetuating their role as "wards of the state" who are incapable of making their own decisions or of managing their own resources. Through the pastoral voice, the imagined past destroys the potentialities of the present; for the Indians of imagination serve to legitimate both the ends and the means of the environmental movement, based as it is on the borrowed Native American belief that "In our every deliberation, we must consider the impact of our decisions on the next seven generations" (*Seventh Generation*, 1995).

These tendencies are well illustrated by issues of *Audubon* and *National Wildlife* magazines, issued within two months of one another, in which we find stories about the relationship between Native Americans and the environment. The *Audubon* article, for instance, details the efforts of the Kumeyaay Indians, "some of the earliest—and best—environmental managers in North America" (Maxwell, 1995, p. 100). Although we have no reason to believe that the Kumeyaay thought of themselves in such terms, they are here reconstructed as "environmental managers," as Indians who seemingly lived their life in explicitly Euro-American terms. Here motive emerges fully: in order to make the Kumeyaay "relevant" to issues of modern America, they must be understood in Euro-American terms that mutilate the people and their culture, that render them into terms already present within the dominant society.

The essayist further informs us that while the original Kumeyaay lands included the Pacific edge of California from the southwest portion of the state to what is now Mexicali, Mexico, "Some 2,500 descendants of the Kumeyaay now reside on a dozen reservations within San Diego County." Leaving aside the question of the destruction and fragmentation of Native American civilizations implied in this change, it is significant that contemporary Kumeyaay apparently are not Kumeyaay but are merely "descendants" of Kumeyaay. The pastoral voice—here already fully present—has defined Indians for us as people who, along with their land and language and customs, have passed into an idyllic past; all that remains are descendants of "real Indians," not "real Indians" in a changed context.

The pastoral voice, having disposed of contemporary Kumeyaay, preserves "tribal environmental management" as a product of "Native American leaders within the U.S. Environmental Protection Agency (EPA)" (Maxwell, 1995, p. 100). The essayist resolves the apparent conflict between the lack of "real Indians" and "Native American leaders" in the present tense by locating the present in the aegis of a spokesperson for the EPA who is a member of the "Tulapip Tribe of Washington State." Conflation of past with present thereby renders Native Americans interchangeable, for one need not be a resident of the San Diego community in question nor even a member of the tribe in question to speak with authority on the issues discussed in the article. One suspects that such an unmitigated transfer of authority would seem more blatant if the author had written about Euro-American inhabitants of Michigan as somehow speaking authoritatively about the politics of Black Mississippi, but such discontinuity here goes unremarked.

On the other hand, the essayist does provide readers with a spokesperson who ostensibly speaks for the Kumeyaay—Mike Connolly, who, "after a successful 12–year career as an aerospace engineer . . . moved in 1986 to the Campo Reservation, homeland of his mother, a full-blooded Campo Indian" (Maxwell, 1995, p. 101). Connolly's mother's "homeland," apparently, can be construed as all of San Diego County and part of Mexico rather than as a small reservation. Also notable is the notion that Indians have "homelands," not "homes" or "hometowns." The pastoral voice here objectifies for us the reservation, like the Native Americans who live on it, so that it might more easily become an easily identifiable symbol of serenity. The word "homeland" conjures up images of peaceful, rural experience, a place where people are from rather than where they remain.

Interestingly, we then find out that the author was accompanied on her "tour" of the Campo site by her seven-year old nephew; and it is through him—through the experience of childhood—that we learn the history of this particular tribe: "He suffered politely through Connolly's description of the original valleys . . . raised an eyebrow at the murderous activities of the forty-niners . . . then looked out the window with genuine relief when Connolly finally announced, 'Now we're on Campo'" (Maxwell, 1995, p. 102). The actual past—the history of a people—becomes here not simply a prologue, but a *dull* prologue that induces in a 7-year-old child merely a "raised eyebrow" in the midst of a retelling of actual atrocities, of blood and mayhem and suffering and injustice. Then, too, the original appearance of Native American land is unimportant; what matters is the "use" to which that land can be put in the present. Originally, in this frame, the land was "just" beautiful, a description that one must suffer through "politely." Just so, the technologically driven present—the management of Campo—is what is interesting and worth seeing. Pale alongside the conjured image of an idealized past created by the pastoral voice, the history of this place has little or no real relevance to the present, and the Native Americans of the present transform into an unreality insofar as they fail the test of relevance, unlike "real Indians" who are aerospace engineers, assimilated into and products of the dominant culture.

The destruction of the past as a necessary means of preserving the present is now fully in place. Actual land and people—both past and present—dissolve into a idyllic scene of tranquillity, where imagined "Indians" serve as a mechanism for social critique, where people become "environmental managers," where identity is reduced to an instrumentality ready for use. The possibility of considering Native American identities in relationship to the environment as an experience or set of experiences disappears through the fragmentation of experience into fictive history, fictive culture, and fictive "environmental management"—all of which serve to damage both experience and Native identity irretrievably.

The nature and extent of such damage is well illustrated by an essay titled "Saving Geese, Saving Himself," which appeared in *National Wildlife* within a month of the *Audubon* essay we have just examined. Here we encounter a tale of "How Eskimo Charles Hunt persuaded his people to restrict goose hunting—and resolved his own identity crisis in the process" (Kaye, 1995, p. 38). Unlike the Kumeyaay who needed to be idealized as wondrous environmental managers in order to serve specific ends of preserving the present, Hunt's people must confront their "selfishness" in order to be in harmony with their environment, and it is his job, as an employee of the Yukon Delta National Wildlife Refuge in Alaska, to convince his people that "Nowadays we must view the waterfowl differently. . . . Not as ours, but as a resource shared by people throughout the birds' range. Because if we don't work together, there aren't going to be birds for our children" (Kaye, 1995, p. 38). In other words, Hunt's people must come to the realization that rejecting their obviously selfish ways of the past and beginning to cooperate with the beneficent and wise White people will serve the good of all. Such cooperation, we are told, will end conflict between federal hunting regulations and the traditional practices of the Yup'ik, conflict that has existed since at least 1916. Nowhere are we reminded that "cooperation" of this sort requires the Yup'ik to renounce their traditional tribal claims, practices, and rituals so that the federal government can provide hunters with "an equitable, legal hunting opportunity" and a "carefully regulated" spring hunt (Kaye, 1995, p. 41). Thus, with limited resources the focal point of direct economic competition, the image of Native Americans as "environmental managers" here gives way to the need to promote their assimilation as a means of exploiting Native American resources.

The role of Native American identity here comes into focus as we are told that Hunt credits his job as Native American liaison with helping him to overcome "years of anger, alcoholism, violence and finally a prison sentence" (Kaye, 1995, p. 38). No longer struggling with whether he must live as Native American or White, Hunt's pastorally created identity beams with personal happiness and professional success so that his happiness and success stand as a signature of his transformation into a "productive" member of the dominant society. The lesson is clear: Those who transform themselves into such a pastoral identity experience personal happiness and professional success. The conditions that led to Hunt's "fall from grace," the possibility that his proselytizing might contribute to the destruction of the identities of others among his people, and the potential for dissolving alterity into sameness for the sake of preserving a peculiar ideal of homogeneity are singularly unimportant, as is Hunt, next to the images projected by the pastoral voice.

CONCLUSIONS

From one perspective it is important that the intensity of the conflict between traditional values and forms of social organization and technology be rendered irrelevant, for there is evidence that many Native American communities, as they are presently constituted, represent both an alternative and a threat to the burgeoning dominance of technology (Mander, 1991). As human societies increasingly embrace the virtual realities presented via television, video, and computer, the connection to the natural world is concomitantly diminished. To the extent that indigenous peoples have retained their traditional forms of social, political, and economic organization and have rejected the organizational forms that accompany the embrace of technology, they represent pockets of resistance to the dehumanizing effects of that embrace.

By focusing on Native American peoples, then, proponents of environmentalism would seem to be celebrating that resistance; arguing for a refusal of technology, for respecting the sanctity of the natural world. Through an emphasis on Native Americans as projected through the pastoral voice, however, it is clearly possible to argue for the possibility of a beneficent use of technology, for the development of a societal ethos that combines the acceptance of an "inevitable" technology (and its attendant social forms) with the preservation of traditional and life-affirming values.

If Native American communities and technologically driven forms of communal organization are indeed antithetical to one another, such rhetorical strategies announce the cessation of hostilities and declare technology the uncontested winner. Such a declaration, of course, depends on a specific depiction of Native Americans, a depiction that demands their pastoral presence as a ratifying symbol while also requiring their rhetorical extinction as separate communities with distinct forms of organization. For if Native Americans, as individuals or as collectivities, can reconcile the seeming contradiction between the demands of technological "advances" and their Native American identities, surely there is nothing to fear.

Any such "reconciliation," of course, demands the destruction of Native American selves, the articulation of Native Americans belonging solely and specifically to the past, and the relinquishment of religious and cultural practices, except as they may remain useful as spectacle. The "trappings" of Native American cultures are acceptable, so long as they are also trivial in the eyes of the dominant society. Native Americans may wear feathers as a Native American equivalent of the "Kiss Me, I'm Irish" buttons that surface every March 17th. As the Irish have become assimilated into the dominant society, such ethnic expressions have become emptied of content and consequently—and only thus—have been made welcome (Takaki, 1993).

When the identity of the Other is thus objectified, made into an object of voyeuristic interest, allowed a degree of uniqueness only insofar as it serves to pique the curiosity or serve the interests of the dominant society, the past out of which living, breathing individuals construct their lives and their identities must be destroyed to make room for images that serve the needs of a particular view of the present. Here and elsewhere, then, the pastoral voice, with its promise of a reconciliation of past values with present practices, masks the consequences of action, places identity at risk, and severely limits the constructive possibilities of cultural diversity.

REFERENCES

Barlow, D. (1995, March-April). Is there a there in cyberspace? *Utne Reader*, pp. 53–56.

Barlow, J. P., Birkeris, S., Kelly, K., & Slouka, M. (1995, August). What are we doing on-line? Heated debate about a hot medium. *Harper's*, pp. 35–39.

Bataille, G., & Silet, C. (1980). *The pretend Indians: Images of Native Americans in the movies*. Ames: Iowa State University Press.

Berkhofer, R. (1978). *The white man's Indian: Images of the American Indian from Columbus to the present*. New York: Knopf.

Browne, S. H. (1990). The pastoral voice in John Dickinson's first letter from a farmer in Pennsylvania. *Quarterly Journal of Speech*, 76:1, pp. 46–57.

Cahn, E. (Ed.). (1969). *Our brother's keeper: The Indian in White America*. New York: New Community Press.

Clifton, J. (1990). *The invented Indian: Cultural fictions and government policies*. New Brunswick, NJ: Transaction.

Cornell, S. (1987). *The return of the Native: American Indian political resurgence*. New York: Oxford University Press.

Dippie, B. (1982). *The vanishing American: White attitudes and U.S. policy*. Lawrence, KS: University Press of Kansas.

Edelman, M. (1988). *Constructing the political spectacle*. Chicago: University of Chicago Press.

Edelman, M. (1990). Introduction. In R. Morris & P. Ehrenhaus (Eds.), *Cultural Legacies of Vietnam: Uses of the past in the present*. Norwood, NJ: Ablex.

Friar, R. (1972). *The only good Indian: The Hollywood gospel*. New York: Drama Book Specialists.

Hirschfelder, A. (1982). *American Indian stereotypes in the world of children: A reader and bibliography*. Metuchen, NJ: Scarecrow.

Hofstadter, R. (1979 [1964]). The paranoid style in American politics. In R. Hofstadter, *The paranoid style in American politics and other essays*. Chicago: University of Chicago Press.

Kadi, M. (1995, March-April). Welcome to Cyberia. *Utne Reade*, pp. 57–59.

Kaye, R. (1995, June-July). Saving geese, saving himself. *National Wildlife, 33*, 38–42.

Kidwell, C. (1991, March-April). The vanishing Native reappears in the college curriculum. *Change*, pp. 19–23.

Mander, J. (1991). *In the absence of the sacred: The failure of technology and the survival of the Indian nations*. San Francisco: Sierra Club Books.

Maxwell, J. (1995, May-June). True nature. *Audubon, 97*, 100–105.

McBeth, S. (1983). *Ethnic identity and the boarding school experience of West-Central Oklahoma American Indians*. Washington, DC: University Press of America.

Morris, R., & Wander, P. (1990). Native American rhetoric: Dancing in the shadows of the ghost dance. *Quarterly Journal of Speech, 76*:2, pp. 164–191.

O'Connor, J. (1980). *The Hollywood Indian: Stereotypes of Native Americans in films*. Trenton: New Jersey State Museum.

Phinney, J. S., Chivira, V., & Williamson, L. (1992). Acculturation attitudes and self-esteem among high school and college students. *Youth and Society, 23,* 299–312.

Rumbaut, R. G. (1994). The crucible within: Ethnic identity, self-esteem and segmented assimilation among children of immigrants. *International Migration Review, 28,* 748–794.

Sander, S. (1995, March-April). The web of life. *Utne Reader,* pp. 69–71.

Schmitz, P. G. (1992). Immigrant mental and physical health. *Psychology and Developing Societies, 4,* 117–131.

Seventh Generation. (1995, early fall). *Catalogue.*

Stedman, R. (1982). *Shadows of the Indians: Stereotypes in American culture.* Norman: University of Oklahoma Press.

Takaki, R. (1993). *A different mirror: A history of multicultural America.* Boston: Little, Brown.

Todorov, T. (1992 [1982]). *The Conquest of America.* New York: Harper-Perennial.

CHAPTER 12

Ethnic Voices: Afrocentric Public Affairs Television Programming

Alice A. Tait

During the heat of civil rights protests in the 1960s, African American leadership focused on the mass media and singled out television as the prime offender for its lack of fair employment practices and failure to present accurate, credible representations of African Americans to the larger society.

The Federal Communications Commission received these complaints and ruled that stations must comply with the 1964 Civil Rights Act in their hiring practices. The FCC also issued a number of directives in the belief that increased employment might influence realistic and more favorable television representations of African Americans.

The incessant demand for programs demonstrating the African American culture resulted in a few recognizable efforts to remedy the dearth of African American television exposure. This paper examines these programs value to the African American community. In this work, Afrocentric theory is utilized to interpret how African Americans should be portrayed in the mass media. Afrocentricity involves a systematic exploration of relationships, social codes, cultural and commercial customs, mythoforms, oral traditions, and proverbs of the peoples of Africa, and the African Diaspora. Afrocentricity is the belief in the centrality of Africans in postmodern history.

Nommo, part of the Afrocentric doctrine, is especially relevant to an analysis of Afrocentric television programming. Nommo is an opportunity for the discussion of problems and the place where facts are disseminated. Historical, cultural, and political information can also be discussed during Nommo. An Afrocentric television program attempts to reflect all of these concepts in various forms. Afrocentric television programming is also a form of Nommo (Asante, 1988). *The Cosby Show*, although not explicating every avenue of African American life, represents the prototype Afrocentric television program as the images produced in the show were consistently reflective of African American culture. Conversely, the *Amos 'n' Andy* show was the antithesis of Afrocentrism (Tait & Perry, 1994).

In this section I explore several Nommo examples of African American–produced and directed programs. These programs were and are unique because they all sought to offer a diverse perspective of African Americans and Afrocentric programming. The goal of these programs was to document, explore, and articulate African American political, economic, and cultural issues. The programs themselves served as training programs by providing internships to African Americans so they might enter the broadcasting market.

Black Journal

Alvin Perlmutter, staff producer at National Education Television (the precursor of the Public Broadcasting Service public television system), conceived of the idea for *Black Journal*, the first national African American public affairs series, in April 1968 following Dr. Martin Luther King Jr.'s assassination. After meeting with African American community leaders and community members, a public affairs oriented magazine format was decided upon (Bourne, 1988). *Black Journal* documented, explained, and articulated African American political, economic, and cultural issues. Aired one hour each month, *Black Journal's* mission was to (1) define the African American reality of any potential film situation, (2) identify the causes of any problems in that situation, and (3) document attempts to resolve those problems, whether successful or not.

Black Journal premiered in June 1969 and received critical acclaim and an unprecedented (for public television) viewer response. The first show's segments consisted of an interview from an Oakland prison with Huey Newton on the future of the Black Panthers, a report on the Poor Peoples' Campaign in Washington, D.C., a satirical skit about the use of African Americans in advertisements, an essay on the view of the future by graduating African American seniors, a profile of a Harlem-based manufacturer of African-style clothing, a portrait of an African American jockey, and coverage of a Coretta King address at Harvard University (Bourne, 1988).

The process of making a *Black Journal* documentary usually involved selecting topics culled from personal contacts or from a library filled with various African American newspapers from around the country. This was discussed at the weekly editorial meeting. The producer, sometimes aided by an overworked staff researcher, then researched background and flew to continue this work on location, never for more than 4 to 5 days. Upon his or her return, a script was written and budgeted, and within approximately 2 weeks the producer and crew flew back to shoot. The editing process rarely took more than 2 or 3 weeks, and the documentary, which could range from 10 to 30 minutes, often aired on the next program.

Black Journal undertook several projects to improve African American participation in the media. The Black Journal Film Workshop was created to achieve this goal. It consisted of a 10–week crash course in basic film production and camera crew assignments. Instructors were both African American and Anglo-American technicians who volunteered their time to teach the new recruits.

As the production funds decreased, it became more difficult to maintain the high standard with which the program started, so, little by little, the staff began seeking other avenues for their ideas and talent. Tony Brown became the new executive producer and began experimenting with formats that would attract financial underwriting. After several format changes ranging from a game show to a *Carson*-type talk show to a variety entertainment show, Brown changed the name of the series to *Tony Brown's Journal*; he continued to serve as executive producer/host (Bourne, 1988).

In the fall of 1971, *Detroit Black Journal* was created and is now seen weekly on WTVS Tuesdays at 10 p.m. It reports events from the Black perspective and discusses ideas of concern in the community. A review of program topics and participants reveals a wide range of information and a wide choice of spokesmen. Without the treatment offered by *Detroit Black Journal* (*DBJ*), many topics might not have received airing. In many cases, much of the program content received little, if any, coverage in the major print media. Throughout its run, the program featured everything from panel discussions to performances by top-name Black entertainers. Past *DBJ* guests have included Rosa Parks, Stevie Wonder, Lena Horne, Ron Milner, Dick Gregory, Alex Haley Jr., Little Richard, Ossie Davis and Ruby Dee, and Nikki Giovanni. *DBJ* is now *American Black Journal*.

Profiles . . .

WWJ-TV (Detroit) filmed and broadcast *Profiles . . .* , a half-hour weekly television community service series, initially during prime time (Saturday, 8:30 p.m.) from November 1969 through December 1979.

Developed because of WWJ-TV's desire to operate more effectively in the public interest, and additionally, to employ increased numbers of African American, *Profiles* . . . became WWJ's response to the Kerner Commission Report.

Gilbert Maddox, host and producer of *Profiles* . . . , portrayed the African American community's hopes and frustrations and highlighted their accomplishments and achievements. One technique he employed was to interview guests in their homes with their families to display their degree of community involvement. Maddox presented African American professionals, politically active persons such as retired Congressman George Crockett (a former judge) and Mayor Coleman Young; significant events such as the NAACP Freedom Fund dinner, that organization's annual fund-raiser, usually featuring some nationally renowned speaker; the historical contributions of Paul Robeson and Malcolm X; contributions of the working class; Detroit's African American and African American–controlled institutions such as Homes for Black Children: and the community's dissident voices, including those of the Minister of the Nation of Islam. These stories appealed to youths, adults, Caucasians, African Americans, female, and male audiences, and also showed alternative role models available in the African American community.

Prior to producing, hosting, and directing *Profiles* . . . , Maddox was responsible for a number of other programs with similar objectives, most notably: *Black and Unknown Bards, Negro History Series, Office of Economic Opportunity, Mayor's Development Team Report,* and *C.P.T. (Colored* People's Time) *Television Program.* Maddox's work as chronicled in this discussion revealed that he was deeply grounded in the applied aspects of Afrocentricity before *Profiles* . . . , and was conversant with the work of such scholars as M. Karenga (Kawaida theory) and M. Asante (Afrocentricity). *Profiles* . . . reflected Afrocentric programming (Tait & Perry, 1994).

For My People

One response to the inequities in the media was initiated by Project BAIT (Black Awareness in Television) with the show *For My People.* Television was viewed as a way to serve "The Struggle," that is, the Black Power struggle. The resulting television show, *For My People,* was planned as a continuation of the Black Power movement. David Rambeau is the executive producer/director and interviewer of *For My People,* the longest-running program dedicated to the news and public affairs information needs of African Americans in Detroit. *For My People* airs weekly on Detroit FOX network affiliate WKBD Channel 50.

Airing for the first time in 1970, the overall programming focus is community-based public affairs information. In 1971, *For My People* also began a 10–year run on WDET, Detroit's public radio station. *For My People* airs on WKBD Channel 50 on Saturday mornings between 6 a.m. and 7 a.m., and at present is a one-hour show but began as a half-hour show. Channel 50 maintains records regarding issues discussed on *For My People*, and guests who appeared on the show.

For My People also airs 7-days-a-week on a Detroit-based independent cable station, Barden Cable, on a rotating schedule. *For My People* airs on Barden Cable channel 67 to a possible audience of 119,000 subscribers in the city of Detroit only. Topics for discussion focus primarily on economics/finance, politics, education, and social struggle. *For My People* interviews consist of an African American Project BAIT interviewer and an African American guest. Guests are ordinarily from an African American organization, and discuss a topic from the African American perspective that is of basic interest to the survival of prosperity of the African American community. Essentially, Afrocentrism is a conscious effort to use African Americans as sources and references on any subject, and to seek only the expertise of African Americans. Whenever guests are solicited from any organization for the show, African Americans are explicitly requested, so local African American political and economic leaders are accountable for the issues discussed. Rambeau hopes the interview format transmits Afrocentrism by directing the audience to view the discussion within the context of Afrocentrism. The production staff of *For My People* consists of Project BAIT workshop members who view Project BAIT as a "school" of art and communication. It offers hands-on training and experience in video production among other activities that encourage faculty and students to become actively involved in their community. To demonstrate the Afrocentric focus, the host of the interview wears a traditional African dashiki. As expressed by the producer/host/founder, David Rambeau, the Project BAIT Afrocentric ideals are:

- That African Americans are the focal point of any and all concerns.
- That any issue is validated with respect to its impact on the African American community.
- That the discussion format of *For My People* is not accountable to represent, nor is it interested in, the Eurocentric viewpoint.

Black Nationalist and Pan-Africanist ideology (referred to here as Afrocentrism) as outlined in the Project BAIT membership training manual of 1982 is as follows:

BAIT is a Black Nationalist or/and Pan-Africanist organization. Study of either or both of these political positions can and must be done. We don't push this ideology on members but it should be clear to everyone that this is our position. Most folk enter without any kind of conscious position. Within the group we ask people to do certain tasks that if they possessed a nationalist philosophy they would do automatically. This is perhaps best since people generally don't [want] ideology, they want skills, jobs, etc. The leadership merely gives them assignments or tasks that fulfill a nationlist's ideology and ordinarily folk will be along simply because it is in their own best interest anyway. However, there must be some consciousness raising in the group about our relationship to each other, to our community (that's why among other reasons we request that members bank at the Black bank) and to the other communities that we come in contact with. Thus, when there are differences of position on a particular question, we don't make our decision on an arbitrary basis[;] we attempt to make our decisions in congruence with our philosophy of life and that is Black nationalism. (Rambo, 1982, p. 7).

According to Rambeau, *For My People* is still on the air because it serves Channel 50 as a cover against complaints concerning equal representation within the African American community. *For My People* covers news and public affairs programming by, for, and about African Americans.

WGPR-TV *and Black Ownership*

The relationship between Afrocentricity and ownership can best be understood by reviewing the work of Fife (1979). She found that African American ownership does impact images in the news; such images are influenced by philosophies of ownership and philosophies of ownership are in turn influenced by community characteristics. WGPR-TV debuted September 1974, and holds the distinction of being the first Black-owned and operated TV station in the United States. WPGR's philosophy was that African Americans living in Detroit deserve a television station attuned to their community in the same way that the "mainstream" media are attuned to the White community. WGPR's stated purpose was to provide African Americans the opportunity to have experiences with the broadcast industry, so they stress training and community access, emphasizing a Black perspective to the largest degree possible. WGPR aired several hours daily of locally produced programming, including *Big City News*, discontinued in 1992, a 30–minute, Monday through Friday newscast. Both the management and ownership viewed *Big City News* (BCN) as focusing on the African American community, while complementing mainstream media with alternative perspectives on current events. *Big City News* used the same newscast format as larger operations. Crews were sent out on assignment to general news events as well as to specific events in the African American community not covered by the mainstream media. Management stressed that a *Big City News* viewer would see news from an African American perspective. By "African American perspective," management meant that (1) the implications of issues for minorities are discussed, and (2) the participation of African American leaders in area events is fairly and fully covered. *Big City News* saw itself as "commitment coverage" to represent the African American community.

To that end, WGPR monitored their syndicated news sources for stories about African American issues to supplement local coverage. They sometimes contacted syndication services to complain about the dearth of African American issues to supplement their local coverage. They included as many visible minorities in stories as possible, including neighborhood leaders as well as citywide or national leaders. They especially tried to showcase "success stories" of African Americans. Results from a content analysis of WPGR-TV programming showed that the programming reflected the station's philosophy.

Thus, the essence of WGPR's television programming philosophy was Afrocentric because it placed African ideals at the center of its programming philosophy and the ownership did not separate itself from the community.

CONCLUSION

All programs were products of the African American movement. These pioneering programs were created as a response to an admitted deficiency: to serve an audience that had never been adequately addressed directly before. These pioneering programs performed a necessary function quite effectively by documenting, exploring, and articulating African American political, economic, and cultural issues.

REFERENCES

Angelo, F. (1974, February 8). Gilbert Maddox: TV host, *"profiles"* breaks Black stereotypes. *Detroit Free Press*, pp. 7–8.

Asante, M. K. (1988). *Afrocentricity*. Trenton, NJ: Africa World Press.

Bourne, S. (1988, May). Bright moments. *The Independent*, pp. 10–11.

Fife, M. D. (1979, September). The impact of minority ownership on broadcast program content: A case study of WGPR-TV's local news content. *Report to the National Association of Broadcasting*. Office of Research and Planning.

Judge, F. (1969, November 27). Channel 4 to launch *Black Profiles*. *The Detroit News*.

Rambo, D. (1982, December). BAIT notes on practice. A brochure published by BAIT.

Tait, A. A. (1989). Profiles portrayal of African-Americans, 1969–1979: Detroit's direct response to negative stereotypes. *Michigan Academician,* 21(4), 313–322.

Tait, A. A., & Perry, R. L. (1994). African-Americans in television media: An Afrocentric analysis. *Western Journal of Black Studies,* 18(4), 195–200.

Tait, A. A., & Perry, R. L. (1987). The sociological implications of the civil rights movement for black character development and generic programming within the television medium: 1955–1985. *The Negro Educational Review,* 38, 224–237.

Winkfield, J. (1995). The agenda setting and uses and gratifications: Implications of Afrocentricity in public affairs television programming. Unpublished master's thesis. Michigan State University.

CHAPTER 13

The Representation of Arabs in U.S. Electronic Media

Rebecca Ann Lind
and James A. Danowski

The study of media representation of various social and cultural groups is vital for several reasons. Chief among these is the realization that the media do not merely "report" events—the reports themselves are representations of reality that are inextricably linked to the reporter's perceptions (Kern, 1981; Mowlana, 1984; Said, 1981). As Trew (1979) argues, "all perception involves theory or ideology and there are no 'raw,' uninterpreted, theory-free facts" (p. 95). And to report one's perceptions requires they be encoded—another value-laden process, according to Roeh (1981): "no author or speaker is free of the necessity to choose words, syntax, and order of presentation" (p. 78).

Further, any representations of social or cultural groups that may be based on racial stereotypes are worthy of examination. Stereotypes are not merely descriptive; they exist within a historical context and contain both descriptive and evaluative aspects (Gorham, 1995; Seiter, 1986). Stereotypes exist only because people construct them. Gorham's (1995) definition of racial stereotypes—"the operationalization of racial myths as social reality beliefs concerning members of racial groups based on perceived group affiliations" (p. 6)—emphasizes their social construction. As shown below, past representations of Arabs in Western media have relied heavily on racial myths and stereotypes. Has this pattern continued into the mid-1990s, or have things improved?

This chapter analyzes the representation of Arabs in U.S. electronic media by studying the transcripts of approximately 35,000 hours (nearly 136 million words) of television and radio content aired on ABC, CNN,

PBS, and NPR[1] from February 1993 to February 1996. This study improves upon previous research (which is sorely in need of an update, since most studies were published in the 1970s to mid-1980s) by analyzing a much larger body of text, by analyzing the universe of programs rather than a sample thereof, and by relying on a more rigorous methodology than is typical of much content analysis. This research utilizes a form of computerized network analysis that, according to Danowski (1993), provides qualitative analysis by using quantitative procedures. Danowski's Wordlink program allows us to (1) discover and map the relationships among words within messages; (2) interpret the underlying themes and structures present in mediated representations of Arabs; (3) discern the frequency with which certain words, terms, concepts, attitudes, and values are associated with Arabs; and (4) do something Terry advocated 25 years ago (1971, p. 96): "A word tabulation would be an extremely informative study and would provide more concrete verification" of patterns evident in the portrayal of Arabs in the U.S. press.

This investigation becomes even more important when considering the primacy of electronic media as an information source—most Americans cite TV as their most important source of news (Roper, 1985)—and the cultivation research of Gerbner and others, which argues that by viewing television, people assimilate values and feel they understand what is going on in the world. Several studies have shown links between Arab portrayal in the media and public opinion about relevant issues (Adams & Heyl, 1981; Belkaoui, 1978; Kressel, 1987; Suleiman, 1984).

As noted, much attention has been paid to Arab portrayal in the Western press. The wide-ranging work has focused on newspapers and newsmagazines (Belkaoui, 1978; Barranco & Shyles, 1988; Mishra, 1979; Suleiman, 1965; Terry, 1971; Terry, 1974; Whitehead, 1987), editorials (Piety, 1983), political cartoons (Lendenmann, 1983), television news (Adams & Heyl, 1981; Roeh, 1981), entertainment and doc-

---

1. All segments of these programs aired between May 1993 and January 1996 were analyzed. ABC: "Breaking News," "Good Morning America," "News Special," "Nightline," "Prime Time Live," "This Week with David Brinkley," "Turning Point," "World News Saturday," "World News Sunday," "World News Tonight," "20/20." CNN: "Both Sides with Jesse Jackson," "Capital Gang," "Crossfire," "Diplomatic License," "Evans & Novak," "Future Watch," "Health Week," "Health Works," "Inside Business," "Inside Politics," "Larry King Live," "Moneyline," "Moneyweek," "News," "Newsmaker Saturday," "Pinnacle," "Reliable Sources," "Science and Technology Week," "Showbiz Today," "Special Assignment," "Talkback Live," "Your Money." NPR: "All Things Considered," "Morning Edition," "Weekend Edition." PBS: "American Experience," "Charlie Rose," "Frontline," "Nova," "Wall Street Journal Report," "Washington Week in Review."

umentary television (Shaheen, 1984), popular fiction (Sabbagh, 1990; Terry, 1983; van Teeffelen, 1994), and textbooks (Jarrar, 1983). The general consensus seems to be that Arabs have—with some exceptions and with some improvement over time—been fairly consistently portrayed in a racist, stereotypical, and negative fashion.

According to Shaheen (1984), four myths are evident in televised portrayals of Arabs: Arabs are fabulously wealthy; Arabs are barbaric and uncultured; Arabs are sex maniacs with a penchant for White slavery; and Arabs revel in terrorism (p. 4). These myths seem to mesh well with the findings of other researchers, although not all myths are equally evident in all types of content. Additionally, previous research found that Arabs and Muslims are often lumped together—yet, according to Ghareeb (1983), "the Arabs do not number more than 12% of the world's Muslims" (p. 161).

Past studies have concluded that Arabs are associated with violence and terrorism and are often seen as the aggressors in the conflict with Israel. So strong are these associations that, according to Bazzi (1995) and Alter (1995), the media are quick to blame Arabs for terrorist acts such as the 1995 Oklahoma City bombing, even without any evidence.

The media content analyzed in the present study includes coverage of the Oklahoma City bombing, but does not focus on it. Rather, this study investigates the full range of 3 years' worth of news and public affairs content on ABC, CNN, NPR, and PBS, so we can determine precisely how Arabs are portrayed in the electronic media—in a global sense, not just in times of crisis.

METHOD

"You shall know the meaning of a word by the company it keeps" (Baker & Hacker, 1980) is a quote often cited by scholars of computational linguistics who study statistical patterns in large text collections. These scholars acknowledge that people vary in the meanings they have for words. Some meanings are idiosyncratic, while others (macro-level meanings) are widely shared and may be linked with membership in particular social, ethnic, or language communities. Wittgenstein's work provides the theoretical basis for making use of statistical text analysis to identify societal or macro-level meanings for words.

The macro-level meanings of words can be estimated by looking at the extent to which words frequently appear in close proximity; that is, we can infer words' meanings from the statistical distributions of their co-occurrences. We can be relatively confident that the language community (e.g., the audience of news and public affairs programs on ABC,

CNN, PBS, and NPR) has a high degree of agreement about the meanings of those words. We therefore are able to infer the meanings of particular words (e.g., "Arab" and "Arabs") by investigating their surrounding word context.

A method that is increasingly popular is to take large sets of content, called *corpora*, and perform statistical analysis of word co-occurrences. The basic unit of analysis is the word pair—two words that are used together. For this study we filtered 3 years' worth of transcripts of news and public affairs programs, using computer programs that function like an information refinery. Our software was set to slide a window through the text and find all words that appeared seven words before and seven words after the words "Arab," "Arabs," "Arabic," and "Arabian." The program recorded and counted the windowed word pairs. Because of the focus of this study we expected there would be relatively high use of formal names of organizations, countries, and so on, therefore we used a seven-word window radius so these formal words would not limit our sight through the window. We could then see some of the more common words associated with our target "Arab" words.

RESULTS

We searched through a total of 135,759,087 words, looking for word pairs that previous studies of Arabs' representation in the media led us to assume would be associated with Arabs. We were particularly interested in investigating whether Arabs were portrayed as wealthy, barbaric, terrorists, and aggressors. We also investigated the extent to which Arabs are linked with Islam, and the extent to which Arabs are portrayed in association with Israel. We didn't focus on the stereotype of the Arab as sex maniacs, because we assume that image relates to entertainment content rather than news.

Overall, Arabs seem to be relatively absent from U.S. news and public affairs programs. We found a total of 7,801 references to Arabs in the nearly 136 million words analyzed—only 0.00575% of all words. Thus, an Arab reference appeared only about once every 17,000 words. This analysis didn't employ a drop list (words such as *a, an, be, but, could*, etc., which are sometimes excluded by computational linguistics scholars), but even if half of the words would have been dropped, the proportion of references to Arabs would still be only about one hundredth of one percent. The electronic media are not extensively focusing on Arabs. However, it remains important to determine whether even limited coverage reflects the stereotypes discovered in previous research.

Wealth

Our investigation of the depiction of Arabs as "fabulously wealthy" found that words such as "money," "rich," "economic," "wealthy," and additional synonyms for wealth were included in the same window as "Arab" or "Arabs" a total of 134 times. The most frequent word pair (36 occurrences) was "economic-Arab/s." The word pair "wealthy-Arab/s" occurred 13 times, while "rich-Arab/s" occurred 14 times. There was even some indication of relative wealth among Arabs, with the word pair "richer-Arabs" occurring 10 times. The discovery of only 134 relevant word pairs seems to indicate that this stereotype is not particularly evident in news and public affairs programs. Indeed, of the 7,081 total references to Arabs, only 1.7% addressed issues of wealth.

Terrorism

The corpus was examined for the co-occurrence of the word "Arab/s" with lexical variations of the word "terror." We found a total of 169 such co-occurrences. The most frequently appearing word pair was "terror-Arab/s" (71 occurrences), followed by "terrorist/s-Arab/s" (51 occurrences) and "terrorism-Arab/s" (43 occurrences). These 169 word co-occurrences reflect only 2.2% of the total references to Arabs; however, we are not ready to conclude that Arabs are no longer portrayed in the media as terrorists. We will return to this point later.

Barbarism

Operationally defining *barbarism* in modern terms is not an easy task. The "barbarians" have been referred to mainly by classical scholars of the Roman Empire and its fall. For our study, we consulted *Roget's Thesaurus* and liberally included in our analysis words that seemed to capture the sense of barbarism. The literal word pair "barbaric-Arab" appeared only once in the entire corpus, but we found diverse other words that are associated with classic notions of barbaric behavior. These include "massacre," "enemies," "violence," "hate," "victims," "hostility," "hysteria," "bloodshed," "extermination," "slaughter," "lunatic," "dismembering," "treacherous," and many others. Since we are analyzing "aggression" in addition to "barbarism," and there is some similarity between these concepts, we were careful not to duplicate the words included in the analyses.

The words "Arab/s" or "Arabian" co-occurred with words associated with barbarism a total of 1,164 times. The most commonly occurring word pair was "Arab/s-massacre/d" (70 instances). "Arab/s-hate/red" appeared 49 times, and "Arab/s-violence" appeared 38 times.

"Arab-fear" appeared 26 times, while "Arab-threat" and "Arab-enemies" each appeared 19 times. In all, 14.9% of Arab references contained some allusion to "barbarism," which indicates the continued presence of the "Arab as barbarian" stereotype.

Relations With Israel

With the many centuries of conflict between Semitic peoples in the Middle East—and the intensifying of this conflict in the past 50 years with the creation of the modern state of Israel—we would be surprised if our analysis did not contain frequent word pairs linking Arabs and Israelis. In fact, such word pairs were the most frequent in the corpus. There were 2,611 co-occurrences of "Arab/s," "Arabic," or "Arabian" with "Israel" or "Israeli/s," which represents 33.5% of all Arab mentions.

Even though we anticipated a large number of these word co-occurrences, we were surprised at the magnitude, and wondered to what extent Arabs are linked with countries other than Israel. To investigate this, we analyzed the corpus for word pairs linking Arabs with America, Europe, England, Japan, and other countries. We found very few instances of such linkages, other than between "Arab/s" and "America/n," which had 588 co-occurrences. Given the media analyzed for this study are American, and the position of the United States as a world power, we expected a significant number of references linking Arabs to America or Americans. Yet at 588 co-occurrences, the connection between Arabs and the United States is made less than one quarter as often as that between Arabs and Israel. Other countries were linked with Arabs far less frequently. For example, Arabs were linked with England/Britain 52 times, Russia/Soviets 33 times, Europe 32 times, and Japan 22 times. All other countries—Spain, Sweden, Cuba, France, Germany, Italy, and so on—were linked with Arabs fewer than 20 times (and in some cases only once.)

While the Arab-Israeli relationship is not a stereotype per se, the preponderance of presentations of Arabs in terms of their involvement with Israel indicates at the very least that "Arabs" are defined in terms of "Israel." This becomes even more evident in our investigation of religion, below.

Aggression

The contemporary hostilities between Israel and the Arab countries that occurred during the time of this study is evident in the word pairs analyzed for depiction of Arabs as aggressors. As noted above, there is conceptual overlap between "barbarism" and "aggression," so we included in the study of aggression only those words we associated with modern states of hostility and open conflict between peoples. These include direct conflict words such as "war," "conflict," "kill/ed," "fighting," "attack," "bombing," and so on. We found a total of 864 word pairs linking Arabs and aggressive behavior, with "Arab/s/ian-war/s" occurring 243 times, "Arab/s/ic-kill/ed/ings" occurring 179 times, and "Arab/s-attack/s/ed" occurring 124 times. Thus, Arabs were linked with aggressive behavior in 11.1% of all mentions. Again it seems the stereotype of "Arab as aggressor" is alive and well, particularly when seen as part of a greater picture including barbarism and terrorism.

Peace

Prior research claims that Arabs have been portrayed as aggressors. However, we looked not only for evidence of aggression, but also for evidence of Arabs' association with peace. We found a total of 633 word pairs linking "Arab/s" and "peace/ful" or "peacemaking/keeping/loving," which reflects 8.1% of all Arab mentions. While the connection between Arabs and peace is not as strong as that between Arabs and hostility, there are significant co-occurrences of words linking Arabs with peace.

Religion

Others have claimed that the unrelated entities of "Arabs" and "Islam" are often lumped together indiscriminately. To investigate this, we analyzed co-occurrences of "Arab/s" and words associated with Islam, Judaism, and Christianity. Given the conflict in the region, we expected a high number of co-occurrences of "Arab/s" and words such as "Jew/ish." A total of 632 such word pairs were found, with "Arab/s/ic-Jew/s/ish" accounting for all but ten. This reinforces our earlier finding of a very strong Arab-Israeli relationship.

Words linking Arabs and Islam occurred less frequently than did words linking Arabs and Judaism, but were much more prominent than words linking Arabs to Christianity or to religious practices not associated with one specific religion. Word pairs such as "Arab/s-Muslim/s" and "Arab/s-Islam/ic" occurred 426 times. Only 45 word pairs linked Arabs to Christianity; all but 7 of these took the form of "Arab/s-Christian/s." A total of 51 word pairs linked Arabs to general religious concepts: The words "Arab/ic-god" co-occurred 20 times, "Arab/s/ic-religion/ious" co-occurred 17 times, and "Arab/s-holy" co-occurred 14 times.

All told, 1,154 word pairs linking Arabs to religion were discovered in the corpus, representing 14.8% of all Arab references. Most of these linked Arabs to Judaism (8.1% of all Arab mentions), and it is reasonable to consider these part of the greater relationship between Arabs and Israel, discussed earlier. Arabs are clearly associated with Islam (5.5% of all mentions), and clearly not associated with Christianity (0.8% of all mentions). Thus it does seem as though Arabs are linked with Islam in the media, but that link does not seem to predominate.

Culture

Given the focus of this book, we thought it interesting to extract all word pairs associating Arabs with lexical variants of "culture." Throughout the entire corpus of nearly 136 million words, "culture" variants were paired with "Arab/s/ic" only 20 times (0.3% of all Arab references). The most common co-occurrence was "Arab-culture," which appeared 13 times.

Summary by Topic

Table 13.1 shows the summary counts for all word pair frequencies by topic area, along with the percentage value, based on the 7,801 total occurrences of the words "Arab/s," "Arabic," and "Arabian" within the corpus.

DISCUSSIONS AND CONCLUSIONS

Overall, this study found very little coverage of Arabs and even less coverage of Arab culture in the U.S. electronic media. It appears reasonable

TABLE 13.1
Summary of Arab Representation by Topic Area

Topic	Freq.	Percent*
Israel	2,611	33.5
Barbarism	1,164	14.9
Religion (Total 1,154)		
Judaism	632	8.1
Islam	426	5.5
Christianity	45	0.6
Nonspecific	51	0.7
Aggression	864	11.1
Peace	633	8.1
Terrorism	169	2.2
Wealth	134	1.7
Culture	20	0.3

* Percent of the 7,801 total references to Arabs contained in the corpus.

to assume that if a people and their culture are ignored, this leaves a fertile field for negative stereotyping. The picture that emerges by the lack of attention to Arabs and Arab cultures is that these countries, these peoples, and their cultures are neither significant nor important. If the American public counts on television for its news, it is not learning much about Arabs. Arabs and Arab cultures thus are marginalized.

What depictions there were of Arabs served mostly to reinforce the predominant stereotypes delineated in prior research. However, one improvement of prior stereotypes seems clear—at least in news and public affairs programming, the Arab is not portrayed in a manner that reinforces the "Arab as fabulously wealthy" stereotype. Arab wealth is not a frequent subject of the media content we analyzed.

Yet there is an overwhelming association in the media between Arabs and violence, threats, and war, which serves to foster the stereotypes of "Arab as barbarian/aggressor/terrorist." While there were fairly few word pairs directly linking Arabs and terrorism, we must interpret that in conjunction with our separate investigations of aggression and barbarism. The concepts of aggression, barbarism, and terrorism are closely related, and to a certain extent our findings reflect our decision to include a set of words in one category rather than another. Thus, if we consider the big picture created by layering all three of these concepts, we are left with an image that overwhelmingly reinforces the perception of Arabs as threatening, frightening, terrible, unreasonable warmongers. This seems little changed from the conclusions of prior research.

Our finding of a fairly clear association between Arabs and peace reflects a positive depiction of Arabs, which presents an alternative to the "Arabs as aggressive/barbaric/terrorist" depiction. The appearance of this positive image is reassuring, but it occurs much less frequently than does its negative counterpart.

Another of our major findings is that Arabs are defined most strongly in terms of their relations with Israel. Such Israeli-oriented coverage of Arabs reflects a subordination of Arabs and Arab cultures, and reinforces the already-evident marginalization of Arabs and Arab cultures discussed above. Arabs and Arab cultures are not defined and do not exist as entities unto themselves; they exist primarily in terms of Israel. Again, the ground remains fertile for continued racism and stereotyping.

We believe this investigation of these electronic media transcripts—nearly 136 million words over a 3-year period—has resulted in rich quantitative information about the qualitative representation of Arabs on ABC, CNN, NPR, and PBS. The validity of this study—internal and particularly external—reinforces a clear picture of how Arabs are represented in some of the largest U.S. news and public affairs program sources on television and radio.

REFERENCES

Adams, W. C., & Heyl, P. (1981). From Cairo to Kabul with the networks, 1972–1980. In W. C. Adams (Ed.), *Television coverage of the Middle East* (pp. 1–39). Norwood, NJ: Ablex.

Alter, J. (1995, May 1). Jumping to conclusions: Many in the press and public were quick to assume the crime had Mideast origins. But "John Doe" is one of us. *Newsweek, 125,* p. 55.

Baker, G. P., & Hacker, P. M. S. (1980). *Wittgenstein, understanding and meaning: An analytical commentary on the philosophical investigations.* Chicago: University of Chicago Press.

Barranco, D. A., & Shyles, L. (1988). Arab vs. Israeli news coverage in the *New York Times,* 1976 and 1984. *Journalism Quarterly, 65*(1), 178–181, 255.

Bazzi, M. (1995, August). The Arab menace. *The Progressive, 59,* 40.

Belkaoui, J. M. (1978). Images of Arabs and Israelis in the prestige press, 1966–1974. *Journalism Quarterly, 55*(4), 732–738, 799.

Danowski, J. A. (1993). Network analysis of message content. In W. D. Richards Jr. & G. A. Barnett (Eds.), *Progress in communication sciences* (vol. 12, pp. 197–221). Norwood, NJ: Ablex.

Ghareeb, E. (1983). A Renewed look at American coverage of the Arabs: Toward a better understanding? In E. Ghareeb (Ed.), *Split vision: The portrayal of Arabs in the American media* (pp. 157–194). Washington, DC: American-Arab Affairs Council.

Gorham, B. (1995, August). *Stereotypes in the media: So what?* Paper presented to the Association for Education in Journalism and Mass Communication, Washington, DC.

Jarrar, S. A. (1983). The treatment of Arabs in U.S. social studies textbooks: Research findings and recommendations. In E. Ghareeb (Ed.), *Split vision: The portrayal of Arabs in the American media* (pp. 369–380). Washington, DC: American-Arab Affairs Council.

Kern, M. (1981). The invasion of Afghanistan: Domestic vs. foreign stories. In W. C. Adams (Ed.), *Television coverage of the Middle East* (pp. 106–127). Norwood, NJ: Ablex.

Kressel, N. J. (1987). Elite editorial favorability and American public opinion: A case study of the Arab-Israeli conflict. *Psychological Reports, 61*(1), 303–313.

Lendenmann, G. N. (1983). Arab stereotyping in contemporary American political cartoons. In E. Ghareeb (Ed.), *Split vision: The portrayal of Arabs in the American media* (pp. 345–353). Washington, DC: American-Arab Affairs Council.

Mishra, V. M. (1979). News from the Middle East in five U.S. media. *Journalism Quarterly, 56*(2), 374–378.

Mowlana, H. (1984). The role of the media in the US-Iranian conflict. In A. Arno & W. Dissanayake (Eds.), *The news media in national and international conflict* (pp. 71–99). Boulder, CO: Westview Press.

Piety, H. (1983). Bias on American editorial pages. In E. Ghareeb (Ed.), *Split vision: The portrayal of Arabs in the American media* (pp. 125–142). Washington, DC: American-Arab Affairs Council.

Roeh, I. (1981). Israel in Lebanon Language and images of storytelling. In W. C. Adams (Ed.), *Television coverage of the Middle East* (pp. 76–88). Norwood, NJ: Ablex.

Roper, B. (1985). *Public attitudes toward television and other media in a time of change.* New York: Television Information Office.

Sabbagh, S. J. (1990). *Sex, lies & stereotypes: The image of Arabs in American popular fiction.* ADC Issue Paper #23. Washington, DC: ADC Research Institute.

Said, E. W. (1981). *Covering Islam: How the media and the experts determine how we see the rest of the world.* New York: Pantheon Books.

Seiter, E. (1986). Stereotypes and the media: A re-evaluation. *Journal of Communication, 36*(2), 14–26.

Shaheen, J. (1984). *The TV Arab.* Bowling Green, OH: Bowling Green State University Popular Press.

Suleiman, M. W. (1984). Development of public opinion on the Palestine question. *Journal of Palestine Studies, 13*(3), 87–116.

Suleiman, M. W. (1965). An evaluation of Middle East news coverage in seven American news magazines, July–December 1956. *Middle East Forum, 41(2),* 9–30.

Terry, J. (1983). Images of the Middle East in contemporary fiction. In E. Ghareeb (Ed.), *Split vision: The portrayal of Arabs in the American media* (pp. 315–325). Washington, DC: American-Arab Affairs Council.

Terry, J. (1974, Autumn). 1973 US press coverage on the Middle East. *Journal of Palestine Studies, 4,* 120–133.

Terry, J. (1971). A content analysis of American newspapers. In A. Jabara & J. Terry (Eds.), *The Arab world: From nationalism to revolution* (pp. 94–113). Wilmette, IL: The Medina University Press International.

Trew, T. (1979). Theory and ideology at work. In R. Fowler, B. Hodge, G. Kress, & T. Trew (Eds.), *Language and control* (pp. 117–156). London: Routledge & Kegan Paul.

van Teeffelen, T. (1994). Racism & metaphor: The Palestinian-Israeli conflict in popular literature. *Discourse and Society, 5*(3), 381–405.

Whitehead, S. (1987). *Arab portrayals in U.S. & British newsmagazines: A comparative analysis.* (Eric Documentation Reproduction Service, #ED 283223)

CHAPTER 14

Moving Beyond the Screen: Hollywood and Mexican American Stereotypes

Fernando Delgado

Over the last twenty years the media representations of Mexican Americans have evolved from stereotyped "Other" into opportunities for self-representation. Though stereotyping of Mexican Americans continues, a "boom" in Mexican American media self-expression has complicated matters and produced more complex articulations of identity and culture. Mexican Americans must still struggle with relatively few opportunities in the mass media, yet there have been increases in the Mexican American (and Latino) presence on the screen and behind the scenes.

Hadley-Garcia (1990) and Keller (1994) have noted that there has been a Latino and/or Mexican American presence since the beginning of Hollywood. The post–Chicano Movement era, however, has encouraged a brighter focus on the politics of representation and the role of Mexican Americans in front of and behind the cameras. The shift, among intellectuals and performers, has been to recognize and articulate how an influential entertainment industry effectively fuses the ideological with the cultural. As Mexican American media stereotypes have been critiqued, a parallel development has occurred among academics who assess the breadth and historical depth of these representations. Entertainers and critics have increasingly asked questions, and voiced concerns, about the roles, plots, and characters that are designated Mexican American as well as the producers, directors, writers, and actors who make and execute the production and programming decisions. List (1992), noting the parallel between Hollywood's representations of the female and the Latino, explains that "Anglo representations of the

Latino control the image of the ethnic in a similar way, coding him/her as Other through spectacle and stereotype" (p. 25).

This essay deals with the relationship between media representation and criticism as they circulate around Mexican Americans, and the challenges facing media activists and academics alike. I begin where many others have, with the long history of Mexican American representation by the U.S. entertainment industries (television and film). The foundational work of others, most notably Keller (1985), Woll (1977), Pettit (1982), and Cortés (1983), have clearly delineated the historical and archival evidence regarding Mexican American (and, broadly, Latino) representations and stereotypes (see also Ramírez Berg, 1990, and Keller, 1994). I will differ from these important contributions by emphasizing the meaning and potential of Mexican American representation and self-representations in the circulation of film and television to wider audiences. I will suggest that as the entertainment industries have complicated Mexican American representations by creating spaces for Mexican Americans to write, direct, and act in films and television productions, critics and academics must also complicate their theories and perspectives on the mass media, stereotypes, and Mexican Americans.

MEXICAN AMERICAN REPRESENTATIONS: HISTORY, CRITICISM, AND THE TEXT

The foundational works in the criticism of Mexican American representations have tended to follow three lines of inquiry: (1) a focus on the historical (archival) presence of Mexican Americans in Hollywood (Hadley-Garcia, 1990; Keller, 1994); (2) textual and historical analyses of cinematic texts to examine the persistence of limiting and negative stereotypes of Mexican Americans (Ramírez Berg, 1990; Pettit, 1980; Cortés, 1983); and (3) polemical essays that challenge a perceived dominant paradigm of media, especially film, production (Treviño, 1982; Ramírez Berg, 1993). Each of these lines of inquiry ultimately center on the text.

Noriega explains why the text (in his words the "image") is central to Chicano criticism:

> But the strategic importance "image" analysis cannot be overstated because other film scholars are not likely to consider the issue of "Chicanos and film" until the Chicano "image" has been extracted from and shown to exist within the "specifically cinematic dimensions" that are the object of current scholarship. (1992b, p. xii)

Noriega's observation is important; it suggests that an intellectual and political imperative for a dominant media criticism paradigm to emerge.

The foregrounding of the text among a community of scholars, infused by the ethic of Chicano ideology, has informed how critics and historians have examined the relationship between Mexican Americans and the U.S. media industries.

However, beginning in the 1980s a series of mainstream films crafted by Mexican American and Latino artists have positively complicated matters and opened other lines of inquiry. Keller (1994) observes that as a result several criteria should be used to characterize Chicano films:

> One is control over the material, whether or not that material is produced within Hollywood. The Hollywood Chicano films *Born in East L.A., Zoot Suit, La Bamba,* and *American Me* qualify as such because they were mostly controlled by Chicanos. The other criterion, an admittedly subjective and ambiguous one that requires analysis and argumentation on the part of the film scholar, is the authenticity and relevancy of the material itself, including the ability of the film to transcend formulas and box-office exploitativeness. (p. 208)

The development of these new media products encouraged critics, still text (or image) bound, to analyze the aesthetic, political, and cultural dimensions of a body of mainstream Mexican American (and Latino) films (*Zoot Suit, La Bamba, Born in East L.A., Ballad of Gregorio Cortez, El Norte, The Milagro Beanfield War, Stand and Deliver, American Me,* and *Mi Familia*). Simultaneously, scholars were developing the intellectual and critical sensibilities that were current in the fields of media, cinema, and cultural studies. Noriega (1992b), himself one of the new breed of scholars, supports this view. He argues that "Chicano scholars have likewise entered into a *renacimiento* that has ushered in new archival materials and research as well as diverse critical approaches" (p. xi). As a result of the parallel developments in the entertainment and academic fields, critics could be both critical and celebratory in examining their own culture's media products (albeit mediated through an industry still largely devoid of Latinos) and still aware of the continuing trend of stereotypical representations (evidenced in such films of the 1980s as *8 Million Ways to Die, Colors,* and *Extreme Prejudice*).

The presence of contemporary films, created with the presence and influence of Mexican Americans and Latinos, has generated a boom in criticism (Fregoso, 1990, 1993a, 1993b, 1993c; Canfield, 1994; Noriega, 1995; Tafoya, 1993; see also the section on Chicano Cinema in Noriega, 1992a). These critiques, borrowing from the literary and textual traditions found in cinema and cultural studies, have tended to locate Mexican American self-representations within the historical context of Hollywood's history of negative representations. As Fregoso (1993a) notes, "Chicano and Chicana cultural politics has been, and continues to be, an oppositional politics" (p. xvii).

Yet, the articulations of Mexican American culture, in the aesthetic and political dimensions, have received considerable analysis. As well, the impulse to affirm certain dimensions that constitute Chicano cinema have been featured in several textual analyses (see Tafoya, 1993; Fregoso, 1990). Noriega (1992c), perhaps anticipating Keller's call for criteria regarding the constitution of Chicano cinema, explains that "four elements of Chicano thought and artistic expression—resistance, affirmation, maintenance, and mestizaje—provide the basis for a culture-specific analysis" (p. 169).

Maintaining the critical focus on the cinematic, and to a lesser extent the televisual text, other critics have continued to locate Mexican American identity within the ideological framework of Chicanismo, though a more complex version than was deployed by activists during the Movement. Fregoso (1993a), echoing an earlier generation of Chicano scholarship, contextualizes contemporary Mexican American cinema within the model of internal colonialism—replete with oppression and marginalization. In the instance of *Born in East L.A.*, Fregoso (pp. 62–64), supporting Noriega, argues that the historical marginalization of Mexican Americans suggests that resistance and the politics of representation come together at the site of commodified popular culture (mainstream films).

The work of Chicano critics relocates Mexican American media production within the sociopolitical and sociocultural realms. Consistent with the cultural studies tradition of examining culture as social practice (Hall, 1980) as well as producing an "interrogation of society's structure of domination" (Turner, 1992, p. 5), Chicano film critics, particularly Noriega and Fregoso, have been able to affirm the cultural, political, and aesthetic value of Mexican American films. They have also been able to suggest that Mexican American artists are aware that their products are created in an institutional and social context that has often been antagonistic toward Mexican Americans and their culture. Critics, it follows, should then find the politics of Mexican American films to be multilayered; both explicitly ideological and implicitly subversive.

However, when we acknowledge that mainstream films are commodities designed to capture wider, possibly heterogeneous audiences, there are ruptures in Noriega's and Fregoso's cultural studies approaches. Fregoso, referencing Noriega and Keller's work, has noted a "by, for, about" logic in Mexican American cinema. However, given the economics of mainstream Hollywood, Mexican American films cannot simply be by, for, or about Mexican Americans. The fact that film and television production are still mediated by individuals—who with them talents, visions, and dollars—possessing alternative perspectives and cultural experiences suggests that it is difficult to have a singularly authentic Mexican American media expression. Yet, while the "by" is mitigated by producers, directors, editors, and actors coming from Anglo-American, African American, even international communities, the "about" in Mexican American films continues to foreground Mexican American individual and communal experiences. Noriega (1992c) observes that "most Chicano feature films are based on true stories or historical events" (p. 171), no doubt coming from the range of experiences discernible in Mexican American history.

The development of a Mexican American cinema has occurred simultaneously with an evolving intellectual and critical community. Mexican American critics can pursue their Chicano ideology as well as incorporating a growing tradition of critical theory and cultural studies approaches to media criticism. Yet the critical and analytical work is still largely focused on the text. True, there is always a recognition of the social as it contextualizes, even overdetermines, the production of Mexican American films. What remains largely untouched, and certainly undertheorized, is the "for," the other problematic that cultural studies suggests—the role of the audience in the making of social meaning.

MEXICAN AMERICANS, THE MEDIA, AND AUDIENCES

Turner (1992), in his examination of the development British Cultural Studies, delineates the textual and interpretive strands of the interdisciplinary project that is commonly called cultural studies. Cultural studies, in its British formulation and American idiom, is an interdisciplinary project that can "be seen as an open-ended and ongoing theoretical struggle to understand and intervene into the existing organizations of active domination and subordination with the formations of culture" (Grossberg, 1989, p. 114). Given the media industries' influence on culture and society and the contestations regarding how the media represents Mexican Americans, cultural studies attention to the text and the audience's relation to, and reading of, it (Morley, 1992; Fiske, 1986; Fiske, 1987; Condit, 1989) would appear to be a useful strategy to explore Mexican American (self-)representations and the reception of these by multiple audiences.

CULTURAL STUDIES AND AUDIENCES

There has been a veritable explosion, on both sides of the Atlantic, of cultural studies of the media. Several scholars, following Hall (1981), have focused on the relationship between media text and audience, suggesting that there are multiple ways and positions of interpreting the text or making meaning. Following Morley (1992), one way to conceive of the media is as a cultural phenomenon that should not be decontextualized from its social and material foundations. Audiences and their tension relationship to the media text should also be grounded in social and material conditions.

At the farther end of continuum that began with a linear effects model, passed through a middle point of uses and gratifications research, and now tending to audience based ethnographies of meaning-making, cultural studies have generated a theoretical and methodological language rife with interpretation, polysemy, consumption, and decoding. The sum of these is suggestive of a privileging of the audience. As well there is willingness to investigate the tensions and oppositions that audiences might bring to their role in the communication of meanings and images. According to Seiter et al. (1991) "central to most of these [cultural] studies is the question how (specific) audiences make meanings and pleasures in their engagement with television programs in the context of everyday life" (p. 3).

In this essay the issue is how various Mexican American and non–Mexican American audiences make sense of images of Mexican Americans, regardless of who has produced (or encoded) these images and representations. In short, it is to move beyond the text centered approach to the study of Mexican American media self-representations as well as other representations.

MEXICAN AMERICAN AUDIENCES

Because of space limitations I will focus on Mexican American audiences. Little is known about Mexican American relations to the media. Unlike other communities, Mexican American audiences have been largely undervalued by researchers working in any number of media research traditions. Before moving on to the specific analysis of Mexican American (and Anglo-American) responses to self-representations, I will highlight findings regarding Mexican American audiences.

Greenberg et al. (1983) have produced the most systematic work on Mexican Americans and the media. Greenberg et al.'s study is a useful, though dated, survey with compelling facts and figures regarding the content of U.S. mass media and its relationship to Mexican Americans. It contributes to our understanding of the stereotyping and exclusion of Mexican Americans across media.

Others have comparatively studied Latinos' perceptions of media representations (Tan, 1980; Faber, O'Guinn, & Meyer, 1987). Recent studies have also focused attention on the relationship between media, particularly television, and cultural factors including language, assimilation, and self-concept (Faber, O'Guinn, & Meyer, 1986; Subervi-Velez, 1986; Subervi-Velez & Necochea, 1990).

The relatively few studies, coming out of textual and uses and gratifications traditions, assist in our basic understanding of how Mexican Americans function and operate as audiences, but they are not as complex or focused as they might be. Fregoso (1993a) goes so far as to observe that "Chicano films inscribed Chicanos as their ideal audiences. Stated another way, in the early period Chicano films were made by Chicanos, about Chicanos, and fundamentally for Chicanos who were inscribed in the film text as the intended audience/spectators" (p. 129). However, given the economics of the mainstream media, whatever the primary or intended audience, media products—Mexican American or other—are accessible to a broad array of audiences who can and do read media texts in various and often unpredictable ways. Not critically attending to these audience-text relationships misses the point of studying identity articulations, stereotypes, even the communication (as social) process itself. There appears, however, to be a movement toward studying Mexican American audiences' relationship to representations and self-representations (Ríos, 1992; 1996; Delgado, 1994).

MEXICAN AMERICAN AUDIENCES AND TEXTS

I have consciously pointed toward the development of research strategies that account for analyses of representation, self-representation, and, finally interpretation (by audiences). It is in the circulation of images and narratives, the cultural and ideological situatedness of producers and audiences, that critics will find greater theoretical and political complexity. To this end I have examined how diverse audiences have decoded films that Keller, Fregoso, and Noriega categorize as Chicano or Mexican American. Here I will focus on one—*American Me*—and how audiences interpreted what they saw on the screen.

American Me, superficially the story of gang life in and out of prison and the consequences of pursuing "la vida loca," presents a powerful depiction of Mexican American family and community. Noting the family and community narrative, Gutierrez-Jones (1995), in a more complex interpretation, argues that

> *American Me* may thus be read as a narrative about coming to terms with the grieving which attends the mythic original consensual viola-

tion and with the subsequent incorporation by certain groups of Chicanos of yet another homosocial economy built on the fallacy of the shamed and guilty victim. (p. 149)

For Fregoso (1993a), "the film is about the depraved and ruined Chicano *familia*" (p. 123). For both critics *American Me* is ultimately a Chicano film.

Once we move beyond semiotic or historical analyses of the politics of the text or its production, the circulation of media images and narratives may render any judgments regarding a Chicano cinema irrelevant. In my own study (Delgado, 1994) the male audience members who observed *American Me*—both Anglo and Mexican American—were focused on what the film meant to them—given their cultural and ideological positions outside of Chicano politics or intellectualism. What mattered to them were their own interpretive resources and understanding of a narrative that was more or less removed from their cultural or ethnic experiences (all had difficulties relating to or identifying with the gang component).

Gutierrez-Jones and Fregoso, in their critiques of *American Me*, demonstrate their own positionality (informed by their cultural, ideological, and intellectual commitments and perspectives). The participants in my study produced responses based on the social structures that have circumscribed their subjectivities. *American Me*, despite the intentions of its creator(s), comes to mean something to audiences based on how they have been interpolated. For example, one Anglo male noted that Santana (*American Me*'s protagonist) "sort of seemed real . . . he was like a lot of characters I've run across [on television]." A second Anglo male offered that people like Santana "are always in the [Chicago] *Sun-Times* and *Trib* . . . you know, your typical gang member or pusher." While Fregoso might note that Santana does seem real, her judgment will has a different trajectory based on her unmediated cultural experiences. The Anglo interpretants have a decidedly mediated, hence stereotypical, understanding of Mexican American maleness. They register none of the shock or sadness that marks Fregoso's analysis (1993a, pp. 122–130).

Mexican American interpretants were neither surprised nor shocked by the figure of Santana or his actions. One noted that "we've got gangs along the river, there are guys like that around that I know." But, he also notes, "yeah, you know they [gangsters] are out there. . . . TV just it makes seem like there are more of them." A second Mexican American male differed, "I never ran across them. Guys like these gang bangers, [I] see them on television, movies but they are like cartoon characters. But that stuff about family, hard times, man, that's true—that stuff is real."

Even such small fragments suggest that audiences can vary across a range of subject positions and identities. The communicative meaning of *American Me*, of all media, should be investigated as a social process that involves the interpretive potential of audiences. Text-centrism produces too partial an analysis. Chicano critics should continue to analyze texts, but, if they wish to more completely investigate the meaning of these films, they should also go beyond the screen to ways of "showing how members of different groups and classes, sharing different cultural codes, will interpret a given message differently, not just at the personal/idiosyncratic level, but in a way systematically related to their socio-economic position" (Morley, 1992, p. 88).

Mexican American films should be examined in the social context, especially as they enter mainstream media industries. As commodities available for widespread and repeated consumption simple and didactic judgments regarding the Mexican American text are difficult to sustain. The challenge for Mexican American critics is to move toward ways of dealing with complicated texts presented to complex and divergent audiences. It is in these interactions that meaning is made meaningful and the effects of stereotypes can be more accurately assessed and deconstructed.

REFERENCES

Canfield, R. (1994). Orale, Joaquin: Arresting the dissemination of violence in *American Me*. *Journal of Popular Film and Television, 22*(2), 60–68.

Condit, C. M. (1989). The rhetorical limits of polysemy. *Critical Studies in Mass Communication, 6*, 103–112.

Cortés, C. (1983). *The Greaser's Revenge* to *Boulevard Nights*: The mass media curriculum on Chicanos. In M. T. Garcia (Ed.), *History, culture and society: Chicano studies in the 1980s*. Ypsilanti, MI: Bilingual Review Press.

Delgado, F. P. (1994). A necessary amalgamation: Integrating intercultural communication and cultural studies (Doctoral dissertation, University of Iowa, 1994). *Dissertation Abstracts International, 55*, 08A.

Faber, R. J., O'Guinn, T. C., & Meyer, T. P. (1986). Diversity in the ethnic media audience. *International Journal of Intercultural Relations, 10*, 347–359.

Faber, R. J., O'Guinn, T. C., & Meyer, T. P. (1987). Televised portrayals of Hispanics: A comparison of ethnic perceptions. *Intercultural Journal of Intercultural Relations, 11*, 155–169.

Fiske, J. (1986). Television: polysemy and popularity. *Critical Studies in Mass Communication, 3*, 392–408.

Fiske, J. (1987). *Television culture*. London: Methuen.

Fregoso, R. L. (1990). *Born in East L.A.* and the politics of representation. *Cultural Studies, 4*, 264–280.

Fregoso, R. (1993a). *The bronze screen: Chicana and Chicano film culture*. Minneapolis, MN: University of Minnesota Press.

Fregoso, R. L. (1993b). *Zoot Suit*: The "return to the beginning." In J. King, A. M. López, & M. Alvarado (Eds.), *Mediating two worlds* (pp. 269–278). London: BFI.

Fregoso, R. L. (1993c). The representation of cultural identity in *Zoot Suit*. *Theory and Society, 22,* 659–672.

Greenberg, B. et al. (1983). *Mexican Americans and the mass media.* Norwood, NJ: Ablex.

Grossberg, L. (1989). The formations of cultural studies: An American in Birmingham. *Strategies, 2,* 114–149.

Gutierrez-Jones, C. (1995). *Rethinking the borderlands: Between Chicano culture and legal discourse.* Berkeley and Los Angeles: University of California Press.

Hadley-García, G. (1990). *Hispanic Hollywood: The Latins in motion pictures.* New York: The Citadel Press.

Hall, S. (1980). Cultural studies: Two paradigms. *Media, Culture and Society, 2,* 57–72.

Hall, S. (1981). Encoding/decoding in television discourse. In S. Hall et al. (Eds.), *Culture, media, language.* London: Hutchinson.

Keller, G. D. (1994). *Hispanics and United States film: An overview and handbook.* Tempe, AZ: Bilingual Review/Press.

Keller, G. D. (Ed.). (1985). *Chicano cinema: Research, reviews & resources.* Tempe, AZ: Bilingual Review Press.

List, C. (1992). Chicano images: Strategies for ethnic self-representation in mainstream cinema (Doctoral dissertation, Northwestern University, 1992). *Dissertation Abstracts International, 53,* 06A.

Morley, D. (1992). *Television audiences and cultural studies.* London: Routledge.

Noriega, C. A. (1995). "Waas sappening?" Narrative structure and iconography in *Born in East L.A. Studies in Latin American Popular Culture, 14,* 107–128.

Noriega, C. (Ed.). (1992a). *Chicanos and film: Essays on Chicano representation and resistance.* New York: Garland.

Noriega, C. A. (1992b). Introduction. In C. A. Noriega (Ed.), *Chicanos and film: Essays on Chicano representation and resistance* (pp. xi–xxv). New York: Garland.

Noriega, C. A. (1992c). Between a weapon and a formula: Chicano cinema and its contexts. In C. A. Noriega (Ed.), *Chicanos and film: Essays on Chicano representation and resistance* (pp. 159–189). New York: Garland.

Pettit, A. G. (1982). *Images of the Mexican American in fiction and film.* College Station, TX: Texas A & M Press.

Ramírez Berg, C. (1990). Stereotyping in films in general and of the Hispanic in general. *Howard Journal of Communications, 2,* 286–300.

Ramírez Berg, C. (1993). Ya basta con the Hollywood paradigm! *Jump Cut, 38,* 96–104.

Ríos, D. I. (1993). Mexican-American audiences: A qualitative and quantitative study of ethnic uses for mass media (Doctoral dissertation, University of Texas, 1993). *Dissertation Abstracts International, 54,* 048A.

Ríos, D. I. (1996). Chicano cultural resistance with mass media. In R. M. De Anda (Ed.), *Chicanos and Chicanos in contemporary society* (pp, 127–142). Boston: Allyn & Bacon.

Seiter, E. et al. (Eds.). (1991). *Remote control: Television, audiences & cultural power.* London: Routledge.

Subervi-Velez, F. (1986). The mass media and ethnic assimilation and pluralism. *Communication Research, 13,* 71–96.

Subervi-Velez, F., & Necochea, J. (1990). Television viewing and self-concept among Hispanic American children—A pilot study. *Howard Journal of Communications, 2,* 315–329.

Tan, A. (1978). Evaluation of newspapers and television by blacks and Mexican Americans. *Journalism Quarterly, 55,* 673–681.

Tafoya, E. (1993). *Born in East L.A.:* Cheech as the Chicano Moses. *Journal of Popular Culture, 26,* 123–129.

Treviño, J. S. (1982). Chicano cinema. *New Scholar, 8*(1–2), 167–180.

Turner, G. (1992). *British cultural studies: An introduction.* New York: Routledge.

Woll, A. L. (1977). *The Latin image in American film.* Los Angeles: Latin American Center, UCLA.

PART III

Mass Media
and Conflicts

CHAPTER 15

O. J. Live:
Raced Ways of Seeing
Innocence and Guilt

Darnell Montez Hunt

Despite an abundance of twists and turns, the road paved with literature on mass media continues to lead to one of two places: to a place where media are assumed to be powerful relative to audience members, or to a place where the opposite view is held to be true. At the former place, scholars argue that media are successful at injecting hegemonic ideas directly into the minds of rather passive audience members (cf. Adorno, 1991), or that any audience opposition to specific ideas is in the long run overwhelmed by constant media exposure (cf. Althusser, 1971; Foster, 1985). At the latter place, scholars counter that audience members are active interpreters who often overlook or consciously subvert the meanings intended by the creators of media (cf. Klapper, 1960; Blumler and Katz, 1974; Fiske, 1987). At stake in this debate, of course, is the very "construction" of reality (cf. Berger and Luckmann, 1966). In the United States context, as the following case suggests, race plays a pivotal role in the process.

During the early morning hours of June 13, 1994, two slashed and mangled bodies—a White woman and man—were discovered lying in pools of their own blood in one of Los Angeles's most fashionable neighborhoods. Within hours, news media learned of the grisly scene and went to work digging out key who's, when's, why's, and how's that would prove so central to the emerging case. Shortly thereafter, electronic networks around the world were buzzing with news of the murders of Nicole Brown-Simpson and Ronald Goldman and of evidence pointing toward the guilt of Black football legend O. J. Simpson. Here, it seems, "reality" ended and a clash of social realities began.

Opinion polls taken shortly after the murders and throughout the trial depicted a major and enduring rift between White and Black Americans regarding their beliefs about Simpson's innocence or guilt (Clarinet Electronic News Service). Indeed, it appeared as if different ways of seeing—"raced ways of seeing"—shaped how most people within these groups understood the evidence emerging from the heavily mediated case. In what ways might these differences have shaped the media-audience encounter? Moreover, what are the implications for media-powerful and audience-powerful understandings of this encounter?

What follows is *not* a study of O. J. Simpson's innocence or guilt, but rather a study of people's *knowledge* about and *investment* in Simpson's innocence or guilt. In this study, I reject the rather common premise that the media frenzy surrounding the double murder case was mere journalistic sensationalism (e.g., *Los Angeles Times*, January 25, 1995, p. A13). It was much more. Beyond media desires for ratings, beyond audience appetites for titillation, this frenzy stemmed from a clash of cultures in the United States—from divergent ways of seeing, from implicit and explicit efforts to privilege a particular social reality. Indeed, the Simpson case provides us with a unique opportunity to trace the interdependence between knowledge and ways of seeing, to explore the intersections where competing positions collide, diverge, or coalesce. Mass media texts constitute one such intersection, while audience activity defines another. Below I present an analysis of a prominent media text concerning the case in order to explore the manner in which its depiction of "reality" relied upon raced ways of seeing. Similarly, I explore how raced ways of seeing defined "reality" for two small Los Angeles groups—one composed of White women and men, the other of Black women and men—who viewed the text and discussed their perceptions. As a prelude to these analyses, however, I briefly sketch the meteoric rise of the trial in the public consciousness and the emergence of a hegemonic perspective on Simpson's innocence and guilt.

THE SOCIAL CONSTRUCTION OF THE "TRIAL OF THE CENTURY"

From the very beginning, the "trial of the century"—as the upcoming court case would be dubbed in the media—captured the imagination of viewers around the nation (and globe) as few events before or since. It seemed to have all of the necessary elements:

- Celebrity—A Black football legend; his glamorous lifestyle and wealthy circle of friends; high-profile and high-priced attorneys.

- Tragedy—Two victims struck down in the prime of their lives; domestic abuse out of control; a fallen American "hero."

- Conflict—A (Black) defendant versus the champions of (White) victims' rights; a defense "dream team" versus the resources of a district attorney who must win at all costs.

- Drama—Poignant reflections on the victims; tearful families; devoted fans.

- Mystery—Blood drops; footprints; fingerprints; gloves; socks; time-frames; demeanor; drug-hit theories.

- Scandal—Secret sexual liaisons; evidence contamination; evidence planting; racially incendiary tapes; defense misconduct; prosecution misconduct; juror misconduct; a police officer testifying for the prosecution takes the 5th.

- Spectacle—A low-speed Bronco chase, cheering fans and curious on-lookers; Mafia informants take the stand for the defense.

- Controversy—The defense compares a policeman involved in the case to Hitler; the family of one of the victims, and members of the Jewish community, are outraged.

- Suspense—Will damning evidence against Simpson be revealed? Will Simpson take the stand? Will the jury be able to reach a verdict? Will enough jurors remain? Will Simpson spend the rest of his life in jail, or will he be set free? What will the public reaction be?

- Resolution—The jury deliberates for less than four hours and finds Simpson not guilty of two counts of murder; trial postmortems fill the airwaves as participants and analysts put their own spin on what it all meant.

These narrative elements all worked together to set up a classic story line, complete with plotting and pacing, heroes and villains (cf. Kozloff, 1987). But the allure of these elements did not simply emerge from a vacuum, it was *constructed* out of the concerns, fears, beliefs, and expectations associated with particular social contexts. That is, the events surrounding the trial acquired their meanings only as actors from varying social locations interacted with one another, only as they debated and negotiated what was put before them by police/prosecution and defense leaks to the media, live coverage of the proceedings, and the resulting media framings. The events acquired their meanings only as actors processed this data through the filter of their own experiences with and understandings of the social structures in which they found themselves embedded. And these meanings, of course, were fed back into the construction cycle as actors took issue with one another's understandings and acted accordingly.

For example, many trial observers charged the Simpson defense with "playing the race card" because of its suggestion that a racist policeman planted evidence in an attempt to seal Simpson's conviction. Fallout over this issue—despite the actions of those who claim that "race" had nothing to do with the case—only worked to increase the profile of race *as representation* in the trial, to raise the stakes involved with any outcome. In this sense, raced ways of seeing worked to shape what was seen by observers, and, ultimately, worked to construct the event as-the-trial-of-the-century.

The result: The trial's grip on audience interest was tightened, with many observers comparing the trial to a riveting soap opera (*Los Angeles Times*, October 9, 1995, p. S3). Indeed, the murder case was the top story covered on U.S. network news programs for most of 1995 (*Los Angeles Times*, October 9, 1995, p. S4). High levels of audience interest continued throughout the trial, leading members to change their viewing routines, which decimated the ratings for syndicated programming unfortunate enough to be pitted against the live coverage (*Variety*, February 27, 1995, p. 53). Many local stations in Los Angeles saw their ratings soar as a result of gavel-to-gavel coverage (*Los Angeles Times*, February 11, 1995, p. A16). Finally, when the verdicts were read, 91% of all television sets in operation were tuned into the coverage; only the first U.S. moon landing and the funeral of John F. Kennedy garnered a larger share of the audience (*Los Angeles Times*, October 5, 1995, p. A7).

In short, the Simpson murder case became a "media event" of the first order, a society-wide forum where values, norms, and social structures are scrutinized, challenged, and celebrated (Dayan & Katz, 1992; Fiske, 1994). Gavel-to-gavel, live coverage on Los Angeles television, Cable News Network (CNN), and radio stations around the nation preempted regularly scheduled programming and signaled an important departure from the routine. Although organized outside the media, namely by the state, coverage of this ongoing event was preplanned, announced, and then advertised by the media in advance. This "trial of the century" became a "high holiday" from the routine (Dayan & Katz, 1992, p. 32), an unprecedented "contest" where the media framed daily developments in terms of "winners" and "losers" (p. 33). And as many media commentators (as well as the judge in the case) noted, the American legal system—with its notion of a "fair" trial, its litany of rules and procedures, its belief in the ability of jurors to ferret out truth beyond a "reasonable doubt"—was also on trial. In this larger trial, the media audience constituted the jurors, and a favorable outcome meant that they would affirm the system and celebrate it.

But the trial, as media event, also necessarily tapped into enduring cleavages in U.S. society, namely race, class, gender, and sexuality (Fiske, 1994). These "cultural currents" flow through some of the narrative elements diagrammed above and shed light on the salience of different "social realities" in the United States.

Feminists, for example (much as they had done in the wake of the Anita Hill/Clarence Thomas media event), used the case to focus attention on a particular cause, this time domestic violence and abuse (e.g., see *Los Angeles Times*, October 4, 1995, p. A18). These activists thus framed the events surrounding the trial as a wake-up call to do something about society's failure to recognize and address the problem of battered women. By default, Simpson became an icon for male-domestic-abuser and, by implication (before the trial began), guilty of murder as well (e.g., Weller, 1995).

Others saw the case as a test of the justice system, whether or not a wealthy defendant is able to buy an acquittal by hiring a "dream team" of slick attorneys who know how to exploit legal loopholes, muddy evidence, and plant doubt in jurors' minds. This perspective also seemed to imply that Simpson was guilty, or at least that the evidence against him was overwhelming (e.g., *Time*, April 17, 1995, pp. 32–34).

In contrast, others seemed to latch on to the case as an opportunity to expose police corruption, to draw attention to the mechanisms by which the justice system has disproportionately placed Black males behind bars (Marable, 1983). Indeed, in a television interview during the height of the prosecution's case, lead defense attorney Johnnie Cochran proclaimed that many Black observers considered him a modern-day Joe Louis in the case, a "great Black hope" of the courtroom rather than the boxing ring (KCAL-TV interview with Cochran, February 26, 1995, 10:30–11:00 p.m.).

Despite these conflicting projects, a dominant or "hegemonic" perspective eventually emerged concerning the case: O. J. Simpson, an enraged, jealous, sociopath committed the final act of an obsessed wife-abuser by murdering his ex-wife and her male friend. Indeed, anecdotal evidence suggests that newsworkers—especially White newsworkers—overwhelmingly held this view (*Los Angeles Times*, October 9, 1995, p. S7–8). I maintain that this perspective was "hegemonic" in the sense that it was dependent upon an uncritical acceptance of the police/prosecution's presentation of "fact" and, by default, worked to legitimate a key component of a racist criminal justice system. While some scholars have argued that media frames worked to "exculpate" Simpson and "exonerate Simpson's individual acts of violence against his former wife" (e.g., McKay and Smith 1995, pp. 62–63), their analyses seem to be primarily descriptive of the period shortly after the murders. Indeed, well before the start of the trial, the hegemonic perspective described

above—which would be carefully articulated by the Simpson prosecution team in its opening statements—already enjoyed a privileged status
in the mainstream media. And it would enjoy this status throughout the
course of the trial. Some examples:

* *Newsweek* magazine, June 27, 1994. "It will likely be months
  before a trial, but the *bizarre* swing of public sympathy toward
  Simpson worries officials [emphasis added]."
* *Saturday Night Live*, NBC, April 15, 1995. White male newscaster:
  "Dismissed juror Jeanette Harris revealed this week that the jury is
  mired in dissension, divided into two groups—those who believe
  Simpson is guilty, and those who are just plain stupid." Crowd
  cheers at the punchline.
* *Vanity Fair* magazine, June 1995. In his column on the trial,
  Dominick Dunne refers in passing to the defense claim of police
  conspiracy/cover-up as a "preposterous theory."
* *Los Angeles* magazine, July 1995. The cover presents a darkened
  image of Simpson and labels it "the Othello syndrome," referring to
  a psychological condition named for Shakespeare's Black protago-
  nist who is obsessed with and murders a White lover. Inside, the
  story's headline continues the comparison to this tragic character:
  "Don Juan in Hell. They stalk. They publicly humiliate. They murder. And afterward, they don't feel very bad. Welcome to the Othello Syndrome."
* *Time* magazine, October 9, 1995. The introduction to the issue's
  cover story, "O. J. and Race: Will the Verdict Split America,"
  implies, as the prosecution argued in closing, that the defense used
  race as a smoke screen to cloud overwhelming evidence against him.
  The last two sentences sum up the article's position: "The defense's
  evocations of race in the trial *may have been only an inflaming
  diversion.* But on the subject of race, America is tinder dry this season [emphasis added]."

Predictably, perhaps, this hegemonic perspective on innocence and
guilt was echoed in the short video screened for study informants.

BREAKING THE ICE: *PRIMETIME* AND THE 911 TAPES

The video segment screened for study informants was produced for
Primetime Live, an ABC news magazine that aired at 10:00 p.m. on
March 29, 1995. This program bills itself as a "blend of hard-hitting

investigative reports, newsmaker interviews and compelling human interest and feature stories" (1995–96 *Primetime* press release). As a "news" program and a product of the ABC news operation, *Primetime* is beholden to a litany of journalistic values, ideals, and routines—not the least of which include the reliance upon "facticity" (Fishman, 1980; Tuchman, 1987), and the closely related "strategic ritual" known as "objectivity" (Schudson, 1978; Fishman, 1980; Tuchman, 1987).

The segment opens with a dramatic summary of events surrounding "the night she [Nicole Brown-Simpson] called for help." *Primetime* anchor Diane Sawyer (White female) hosts this 17–minute video and interviews three police officers who responded to Brown-Simpson's infamous 911 call in October of 1993. All of the officers—Officer Lerner (White male), Officer Lally (White male), and Officer Kent (White female)—describe their assessment of the situation and their conversations with Simpson and/or Brown-Simpson. The segment presents these assessments both through on-camera interviews and voice-over narration. It intersperses these assessments with the voices of Simpson and Brown-Simpson, courtesy of a secret police tape recording made that evening of officer conversations with the disputing couple.

The segment begins with a brief sound bite from the 911 tape. This is followed by a sound bite from court testimony in which prosecutor Officer Lerner testifies that Brown-Simpson was "visibly shaken" that evening. From here, the segment moves to Brown-Simpson's Gretna Green home, where Sergeant Lally describes the events of the evening to Sawyer and points out where they occurred. The audiotape of Simpson explains that he and Brown-Simpson had gotten into an argument that evening. Sawyer reveals that the argument revolved around one of Brown-Simpson's ex-boyfriends, of whom Simpson was jealous. The segment then introduces Officer Kent as the female officer who "stayed with Nicole Brown as the other officers calmed Simpson down."

Officer Kent describes Simpson as full of rage and says she could tell by "just the look in his face" that "she [Brown-Simpson] was in danger." The segment juxtaposes this depiction to sound bites from the tape in which Brown-Simpson explains her history of disputes with Simpson and how she had managed these conflicts in the past. But her methods, it seems, were not successful in this incident: Simpson arrives at her home and, according to Officer Lally, splinters her door. Sound bites from the tape feature Simpson denying responsibility for the broken door. But Officer Lally tells Sawyer that Simpson "had a problem with, ah, admitting mistakes."

The segment continues with sound bites from Brown-Simpson noting that Simpson had not hit her that evening, or in the last 4 years, but that she had been frightened by him that evening. But Simpson sound bites claim that the argument was caused by Brown-Simpson. Police officers comment on both perspectives, supporting Brown-Simpson's and discounting Simpson's. Indeed, Sawyer notes that Simpson agreed to pay for the door. Officer Lally then explains to Sawyer that Simpson had not been arrested because the incident constituted just "a trespass and a vandalism." The balance of the segment focuses on the officers' warnings to Brown-Simpson about the dangers of escalating violence in domestic conflicts. The segment concludes with a sound-bite preview of the next day of testimony in the murder trial. This sound bite features prosecutor Christopher Darden (Black male) sparring with defense attorney Johnnie Cochran (Black male) over upcoming evidence in the case.

One way of analyzing the above narrative is as *text*. That is, the *Primetime* segment may be understood as *constructed* out of narrative elements (images, sound bites, narration, and so) by someone, with a particular perspective, for some purpose. But this analysis would tell us little about how real viewers might make sense of the segment at any given point in time. Audience research suggests that different viewers— within limits (cf. Hall, 1973)—may interpret the same text in strikingly different ways (Fiske, 1987). In this sense, the text constructed by *Primetime* newsworkers might best be viewed as a kind of raw material that study informants had to work with the evening of the interviews, as they fashioned their understandings of the 911 incident and murder trial. I present such a textual analysis of the *Primetime* segment below in order to explore how raced ways of seeing may have contributed to the construction and slant of this raw material. Later, I explore how raced ways of seeing may have prompted study informants to arrive at conflicting understandings of this text.

Primetime newsworkers, consistent with the logic of journalistic practice (Altheide & Snow, 1979), *frame* and *package* the text from the onset. That is, newsworkers use the preview of the piece like a headline or lead to privilege certain textual elements over others, to establish a slant for the segment consistent with certain concerns (cf. Brunsdon & Morley, 1978; van Dijk, 1993). Amidst dissolves between a photo of Simpson and Brown-Simpson smiling together at a reception, a police car with lights flashing, and the Gretna Green location of the incident, the segment is previewed:

> SAWYER. Tonight, a *Primetime* exclusive. A tape of Nicole Brown-Simpson recorded in her home on the night she made that 911 call. For the first time, O. J. Simpson and Nicole in their voices telling what happened.
>
> BROWN-SIMPSON. He gets a very animalistic look in his . . . all his veins pop out, his eyes are black . . . it's just black cold. . . . And when I see him it just scares me.

SAWYER. Two of the police who were there that night tell the story—a minute by minute account that sheds new light on the troubled relationship the state says led to murder.

OFFICER. And I told her, just by looking at him, that she needs to get away from him, that he was going to end up killing her one of these days. (*dissolve to preview of second segment*)

Despite journalistic nods at objectivity (e.g., "the troubled relationship *the state says* lead to murder"), this opening establishes a particular tone for the piece, framing the narrative that follows in accordance with the hegemonic perspective (especially the domestic violence perspective). This framing, of course, depends as much on what is *not* shown/said as what is (cf. Brunsdon & Morley, 1978; Hunt, 1997). For example, Sawyer notes that "for the first time" both Simpson and Brown-Simpson will tell "in their own voices" what happened that evening. But the preview then proceeds to present only the voices of Brown-Simpson, who describes Simpson's "animalistic look," and a Officer Kent, who says she warned Brown-Simpson that Simpson "was going to end up killing her one of these days." The preview concludes on this note, *without* the voice of Simpson explaining his own behavior during the incident. The newsworkers who edited the *Primetime* preview obviously had access to Simpson's voice (i.e., it appears later on in the segment) and could have used it in the preview. The fact that they chose not to is indicative of the particular frame that organizes the entire text.

This frame, in short, identifies Brown-Simpson as an innocent victim of domestic abuse, and Simpson as a guilty, out-of-control, "animalistic" batterer. Indeed, throughout the text, Sawyer carefully depicts Brown-Simpson as a sympathetic character (i.e., the vulnerable female), her demeanor and actions described in sexist and/or stereotypical ways that work to elicit compassion:

SAWYER. . . . In the aftermath of the troubled night the estranged couple each tells a separate story as a *frightened woman lets down her guard* to the policeman who answered her call [emphasis added].

SAWYER. In a tired voice, Nicole Brown, *wearing a tee-shirt, gym shorts and barefoot*, told police how she dealt with Simpson and how she felt about it [emphasis added].

SAWYER. She seemed *so tired, so deeply weary* [emphasis added].

SAWYER. Finally, it was time for Sergeant Lally to go. His last memory was of Nicole Brown *in her kitchen*, apologizing for the trouble she had caused the police [emphasis added].

Sawyer and the officers interviewed in the segment also work to forge a sympathetic image of Simpson-Brown with their references to her name. Sawyer and the officers routinely refer to Brown-Simpson as "Nicole"—someone we all know on a first-name basis—and/or "Nicole Brown"—someone who, despite her legal adoption of Simpson's name, is somehow distant from him. This treatment works to reaffirm Brown-Simpson's purity as an innocent victim.

In contrast, the text's naming of Simpson portrays him rather unsympathetically. He is "O. J. Simpson" in first reference, and "Simpson" thereafter. Never is he just "O. J. " Similarly, his defense attorneys are referred to twice as the "dream team" (once by Sawyer and once by prosecutor Darden), echoing economic/class arguments that Simpson can unfairly afford to buy his way out of the murder charges.

The text also works to counter Simpson's depiction of the incident. That is, when newsworkers opt to use his voice from the police tape, and his words offer an explanation for his behavior, an alternative perspective immediately follows to counter this explanation. As media scholars have noted, this technique allows newsworkers to make important narrative points without actually saying it themselves, without jeopardizing their veneer of objectivity (cf. Fishman, 1980). In the following exchange, Officer Lerner confronts Simpson about damage to a door at the Gretna Green home of Brown-Simpson. Simpson denies responsibility for the damage, but the issue concludes with Sergeant Lally telling Sawyer that Simpson had a "problem" with "admitting mistakes":

LERNER. You did a hell of a job on that door, I got to tell ya.

SIMPSON. That door was already broke, you know. The bottom part was already broke.

LERNER. . . . Have you got any objection to paying for repair?

SIMPSON. I don't object to paying, but I can't believe that she can't tell them that this door was already broke! And the door—my kids broke the door!

SAWYER. The split is still there.

LALLY. Yeah, the split, the whole thing's still split. Apparently this is the same door.

SAWYER. So when they're talking about the bottom part being broken already, they're really talking about this still?

LALLY. That's what the kids broke. Yeah.

SAWYER. Just this part?

LALLY. That's what Nicole told me. Yeah, just that little bottom part. And, ah, but this thing was split all the way up this side.

SAWYER. Because the door was locked?

LALLY. Right, exactly. He blamed the kids for breaking the door. That thing was split all the way up the top. *And, ah, I think he had a problem with, ah, admitting mistakes* [emphasis added].

Newsworkers also rely upon repetition to reinforce the hegemonic frame. For example, the description of Simpson's "animalistic look" and Brown-Simpson's fear of him is repeated throughout the text—once in the preview portion (see above) and throughout the remainder of the text—to support the notion that Simpson had an "other side." Indeed, "animal(istic)" appears in the text three times to describe Simpson; "black" and "frighten(ed)(ing)" appear four and three times, respectively, as Brown-Simpson describes elements of his countenance. Moreover, Sawyer and the officers use "scare(s)(ed)" eight times in the text to describe Brown-Simpson's reaction to Simpson. As all of these descriptions visibly come from the mouths of White speakers to describe a Black subject (or Brown-Simpson's reaction to him), they combine in the text to activate potent racial stereotypes. These stereotypes, of course, have long been used in the West to establish the superiority and innocence of Whites, the inferiority and guilt of Blacks (Fanon, 1967; Dates & Barlow, 1990). This broader binary opposition nicely parallels the differing depictions of Brown-Simpson (i.e., "idealized blonde beauty") and Simpson (i.e., "essential Black savage") found elsewhere in the text.

For example, newsworkers reinforce the notion of Simpson's "other side" by the use of juxtaposition in the text: a domesticated, smiling Simpson from the preview (one consistent with his celebrity image) sharply contrasts with a shouting Simpson on the police tape. Newsworkers punctuate this juxtaposition later in the text with Officer Kent's poignant memory of her warning to Brown-Simpson:

> KENT. Well, I told, um, Nicole about these domestic situations—that they usually escalate to where somebody really gets hurt or even killed. And I told her *just by looking at him* that she really needs to get away from him because he was going to end up killing her one of these days [emphasis added].

In short, as Dyson (1996, p. 30) puts it, "The unspoken, perhaps unconscious belief of many Whites is that if he's guilty, if this could happen to O. J.—the spotless embodiment of domesticated Black masculinity—it could happen to any Black man. This translates into 'no Black male can really be trusted'."

The techniques/devices described above all work together to present Simpson as a frightening figure, one who is obsessed with Brown-Simpson and violently jealous of her attraction to other men. That he had not hit Brown-Simpson that evening, or in the previous 4 years, is mentioned only in passing, buried between descriptions of his "other side" and Sergeant Lally's memory of Brown-Simpson's "prophetic" words:

> SAWYER. It is important for the defense, though, sections of this tape. For instance, when she says, he hadn't hit her that night, right?

LALLY. That's correct, he didn't.

SAWYER. What did you as a veteran of a number of these calls over the years think is the most important thing on that tape?

LALLY. First of all, if you listen to the tape, um, ah, she Nicole Brown describes this, ah, *other side* of Mr. Simpson—this rage that he gets into on occasion.

NICOLE. He gets a very animalistic look in him. All his veins pop out . . . his eyes are black, just black, cold, like an animal. I mean, very, very, weird. And at the end it just scared me.

LALLY. At some point, ah, she said, "Well, I, I'm not afraid of him hitting me again because he hasn't hit me in the last 4 years. Ah, he had to do a lot of community service."

NICOLE. . . . he had to do a lot of community service and stuff like that for it. I just always believed that if it happened one more time that I don't totally think I believe it would happen, but I was just scared. I think if it happened once more it would be the last time.

LALLY. I thought that was very *prophetic* when she said that to me [emphasis added].

In short, the *Primetime* text works to (re)produce a particular perspective on Simpson's innocence or guilt. Through its focus on domestic violence—the establishment of Brown-Simpson as an innocent victim and Simpson as a guilty batterer—the text produces a binary opposition that invokes powerful racial (and gendered) meanings, meanings that connect with the hegemonic perspective emerging from the trial. "Just by looking at him," as Officer Kent put it, Simpson appears to be guilty of murder as well. An interesting empirical question, it seems, is whether White and/or Black viewers might read this text differently? In other words, how might raced ways of seeing influence viewers' reception of this text and the trial?

READING *PRIMETIME*: RACED WAYS OF SEEING "THE TRIAL OF THE CENTURY"

Given the findings of opinion polls surrounding the case, one might expect to observe significant differences in how Black and White study informants made sense of the *Primetime* text. This is exactly what I found when I analyzed the discussions of two study groups, one "White" and one "Black." Both groups were interviewed the same evening, March 30, 1995, at a focus group facility on Los Angeles's Westside. This location was only a few miles away from the infamous Bundy Drive murder scene. Both group discussions were prompted by screenings of the 17–minute segment from *Primetime Live* analyzed above. This segment had aired the previous evening. Following group screenings, same-race moderators (e.g., see Bradburn, 1983) prompted both groups to discuss how they would explain "what they just saw" to a family member or friend. Moderators then removed themselves from the discussions, allowing group members to set the discussion agenda. Near the end of the hour-long discussions, moderators returned to the discussion with a series of four standard questions. The discussions were videotaped and transcribed. Following works in the audience ethnography tradition (c.f., Morley, 1974, 1980, 1992; Fiske, 1989), my goal was to trace the contours of the meaning-making process as it *emerged* in both groups.

All informants identified themselves as either "White" or "Black." The White group was convened at 6:00 p.m.; it consisted of six males and four females. The Black group was convened at 8:00 p.m.; it consisted of five males and five females. Groups were selected to simulate naturally occurring meaning-negotiation processes. That is, the informants in each group were friends and/or relatives who routinely interacted with one another prior to the interview. Moreover, informants reported that they had followed the trial closely, most reporting that they had regularly discussed developments with other group members since the murders.

While I do not claim that the groups are representative of the Black and White populations in the U.S., they were selected to reflect a range of different statuses within each population. For example, men and women were represented nearly equally in both groups. Members of both groups were also mixed in terms of socioeconomic status. Annual family income ranged from $14,000 to $100,000 in the White group (mean about $45,000), and from $14,000 to $50,000 in the Black group (mean about $29,000). Roughly half of the White group members were college graduates, while only two of the Black group members had obtained at least a college degree. All informants had obtained at least a high school degree. Informants ranged from 28 to 63 years of age in the White group (mean = 48.2), and from 28 to 59 in the Black group (mean = 46.3). Names were changed to protect informants' anonymity.

Informants in the White group generally accepted the text in a *referential mode* (cf. Liebes & Katz, 1993), discussing the most important news in the text in terms of the presented narrative or their own experiences, failing to consider its construction *as text* (unless specifically prompted to do so). That is, their reflections tended to echo and uncritically affirm key ideological positions embedded in the text. Accordingly, most informants regarded Simpson's jealous rage, Brown-Simpson's fear, or the good job done by the police on the scene as the most significant news in the segment:

GREG. Well, I think Nicole thought she was gonna be killed by this guy. I think the rage that he had.

BOB. I think the whole idea of the video was to show that the police had done a good job . . .

NANCY. Yeah, that's what I picked up.

BOB. I think everybody knew that O.J. had a bad temper, and everybody knew that Nicole had . . . I mean we heard the 911 a long time before this came out.

JIM. Yeah!

BOB. I thought the 911 was more informative.

PAUL. I don't think that O.J. just had a bad temper, I think O.J. had a disease of jealousy. You know it's just like a person having a disease with alcoholism or a person having a disease with drugs. O.J. had a disease with jealousy. And you know, people can be cured, you know, there's a lot of people in prison that have killed their wives over jealousy and finding their wives with different lovers, stuff like that.

Nonetheless, as discussion continued in this group, one of the informants, Greg, challenged the emerging consensus and described the *Primetime* text as "totally slanted," as "PR for the LAPD." Another informant, Elaine, quickly supported his view by noting that Simpson could be heard talking "like a regular person" on the secret tape recording, not the enraged and jealous lunatic the text portrayed him to be. But this comment—like others she offered—was essentially ignored by the rest of the group. Instead, attention remained focused on Greg, who was clearly seen as a threat to the dominant view in the group. Group members took turns dismissing and/or explaining away his observations, sanctioning him for transgressing the emerging group consensus. He was clearly just "down on the police":

NANCY. We all knew it [the 911 incident] . . . we had heard it before.

GREG. It [the *Primetime* segment] was totally slanted.

ELAINE. I only heard O. J. on the background talking like a regular person.

BOB. How was it slanted? (*shouting/loud talking*)

GREG. The one woman cop saying, the one woman cop going like, "I told her, I told her, he is gonna kill you." You know?

BOB. But she didn't know the tape was going either, remember?

GREG. She wasn't on the tape. She was being interviewed and said she had told her that.

NANCY. Yeah, but they go through counseling. The police knew what they were talking about. They confront this situation every, almost every day.

GREG. Sure!

MARILYN. Every day!

NANCY. They know what's gonna happen. And like Paul said there are thousands of people in prison.

JIM. The purpose of the tape was to show, like Bob said, that the police are doing a good job. They've been taking a bashing in the press and everything. So, this is their opportunity to go show that they do a good job.

GREG. Of course, this is PR for the LAPD.

MARILYN. You are really down on the police.

Instead of echoing ideological stances privileged in the text, informants in the Black group read the text in a *metalinguistic mode* (Liebes & Katz, 1993), questioning the techniques, devices, and interests that undergird its construction. Accordingly, these informants frequently honed in on points that were either buried in the text or mentioned only in passing. For example, one informant, Margo, described the report that Simpson had not physically hit Brown-Simpson in 4 years as "the most important news" in the segment. Other informants pointed to news of the officer's secret taping of the incident, questioning whether it marked the beginning of the LAPD "planning this whole thing" (i.e., the "conspiracy") against Simpson:

MARGO. The part that she said that . . . that he didn't hit her in 4 years . . .

CHERYL. In 4 years.

BARBARA. Well, I hadn't heard that before . . .

JAMAL. What to me was most important . . . was that that officer was taping . . . that was. . . .

DARYL. That's against the law . . .

JAMAL. Well, they say it was legal . . .

BARBARA. They said it was legal.

JAMAL. Well, for some reason he at that time choose to tape . . .

MICHAEL. But, wait a minute . . . I thought, when you tape somebody you have to let them know they're being taped.

DENISE. Well, the FBI don't . . . *(laughter)*

BARBARA. The police could do what ever they want to do, I mean they go on your property, they rummage through your house . . . go through your things . . .

MARGO. Okay, why did he have a tape recorder in his pocket?

DENISE. He went there to tape . . .

LEROY. Because based on the fact that . . . on how many times they had been there . . .

BARBARA. So they went prepared for whatever . . .

LEROY. They went prepared . . .

BARBARA. Well, he did make the point . . . that he said. . . . Well, if you're going to nail O. J. Simpson, you needed to have your facts, you need to have everything together . . . so

LEROY. Because now he's going. . . .

CHERYL. That might have been the beginning of them planning this whole thing.

In many respects, Black informants' identification of "the most important news" in the *Primetime* text was consistent with the *mode* in which they talked about the segment. While informants in the White group (with the exception of Greg and Elaine) discussed the *Primetime* text in a strictly referential mode, informants in this group understood the text largely in metalinguistic terms. That is, informants' openness to the possibility of conspiracy prompted them to discuss the text *as construction*, as the product of newsworkers who relied upon certain techniques to fashion a coherent narrative, a "one-sided" narrative:

CHERYL. You know what you have to remember about this whole program? (*shouting/loud talking*)

CHERYL. I don't know when they taped this program, but all this was done after the fact. So, the policewoman could have been saying that just to make . . . to try to put on for points.

BARBARA. Right.

CHERYL. It may not have been like that at all.

DENISE. She might be . . . to cash in to . . .

CHERYL. Well, I think she would cash in but she's tried to make it look one way.

BARBARA. One sided.

CHERYL. The whole tape is one sided.

In short, informants in the Black group "worked very hard" to read the *Primetime* text and maintain their initial perspectives on the Simpson murder case (cf. Condit 1994, p. 432). These informants were suspicious of the prosecution's case against Simpson, and considered it likely that Mark Fuhrman—the White officer who allegedly found a bloody glove at Simpson's home—was guilty of planting evidence in the case. Moreover, they attributed these suspicions to a "plot" on the part of Whites to "keep Blacks down." Their difficulty with the text, of course, is a testament to how well newsworkers framed the *Primetime* narrative to convey Simpson's guilt. Consequently, these informants were openly critical of the text, opting to amplify understated points and question the ones emphasized by newsworkers.

In contrast, most informants in the White group did not have to engage in such labor. For them, the text was a clear window onto the 911 incident and the unfolding trial. When Greg and Elaine challenged the emerging group consensus, they were promptly sanctioned by other members for questioning what appeared to them as incontrovertible "evidence" in the case. This "evidence," of course, clearly indicated that Simpson was guilty of murder and that Fuhrman was innocent of planting the glove. Indeed, the framing that shaped the *Primetime* narrative was so consistent with these informants' initial perspectives that it was invisible to them.

In the end, I could discern no clear patterns along class or gender lines in informant understandings of the case—despite the wealthy defendant and domestic abuse projects. Raced status, it seems, was clearly the prominent variable separating the groups' readings of the text and case. Nonetheless, while Black informants openly talked about themselves as raced subjects, White informants rarely referred to themselves in racial terms. That is, Black informants frequently used pronouns of solidarity (e.g., we, us, our) when referring to "Blacks" or "African Americans." White informants rarely used these pronouns when "Whites" was the referent (cf. Cramer & Schuman, 1975; Hunt, in press).

CONCLUSIONS

To the scholar of U.S. culture, it should come as no big surprise that informants' "ways of seeing" the text and case clearly diverged along racial lines. Race exerts its force in the United States as a powerful *representation*—as a commonsense, irresistible, and self-reproducing framework for explaining (and justifying) inequality in society (Prager, 1982; Farr & Moscovici, 1984; Omi & Winant, 1994; Hunt, 1997). Socially constructed and fluid, this framework consists of tenets that continually adjust to the maneuvers of competing social groups. Indeed, individual actors helplessly rely upon this framework, despite its shortcomings, to make sense of their own experiences, their relationship to various social groups (i.e., their identity). Actors also depend upon this framework for sizing up others, for interpreting their actions, and for-mulating responses to them. In this sense, actors and the others they endeavor to understand are "raced."

Accordingly, throughout the history of the nation, the structures of inequality that arose out of social interaction were also raced. These structures generally worked to push White-raced Americans toward the top of the status hierarchy and Black-raced Americans toward the bottom (Franklin, 1965; Farley & Allen, 1989; Omi & Winant, 1994). The

U.S. criminal justice system, for example, has been stacked against Black-raced Americans from the beginning. From landmark Supreme Court cases that affirmed the subordinate status of "Blacks" (Berry, 1994), to the unbridled use of police force against "Blacks" (Blauner, 1972), to the contemporary overrepresentation of Black-raced males in U.S. prisons (Marable, 1983; Hacker, 1992), this system in the minds of many Black-raced observers has always been against "just-us." White-raced Americans who have benefited from this system, either directly (e.g., lawbreakers who escape prosecution or who receive lighter punishments) or indirectly (e.g., "safe" neighborhoods), often have a very different understanding of this particular social structure and their relationship to it (Hacker, 1992). This observation may be particularly true in Los Angeles, a city plagued in recent years with a string of high-profile, raced conflicts (e.g., see Bullock, 1969; Johnson, Jones, Farrell & Oliver, 1992; Horne, 1995; Hunt, in press).

As I argued above, the *Primetime Live* text incorporated, amplified, and recirculated many of these racial meanings vis-à-vis the Simpson media event. Regardless of Simpson's actual innocence or guilt, the text is hegemonic in the sense that it works to buttress the prosecution case, and by default, legitimate a racist criminal justice system. But for Black-raced informants, this text seemed to trigger memories of their own past experiences and *suspicions* (cf. Turner, 1993) about the workings of a racist society. Consequently, these informants were prompted to challenge the ideologies embedded in the text and to question the prosecution's case that the text worked to support. The study encounter became a forum for informants to openly talk about themselves as Black-raced subjects, to affirm their own raced subjectivities, to "do-being" Black in America (cf. Garfinkel, 1967).

In contrast, White-raced informants largely accepted the ideologies embedded in the text and treated the screening as a clear window onto the world. Occupying privileged positions in the racial hierarchy, most of these informants found it easy to embrace the hegemonic perspective on the case, to have faith in the criminal justice system. When this faith was challenged by Greg and Elaine, the group moved to punish the transgressors, to blunt their attacks, to restore order. Moreover, these informants exercised their option of talking about themselves in non-racial terms (e.g., see Waters, 1990; and Hunt, 1997), as if their ways of seeing constituted some normative perspective outside race, as if their faith in the system was based on some objective reality rather than subjective interest.

In the final analysis, these informant readings say much about the media-powerful/audience-powerful debate alluded to at the onset of this paper. That is, these readings ultimately underscore the futility of the debate and suggest that the balance of power may often lie somewhere in the middle. While the readings of White-raced informants demonstrated the power of media to reinforce hegemonic views of reality in the minds of some audience members, the readings of their Black-raced counterparts demonstrated the ability/tendency of others to resist. Although these readings were patterned by informants' locations in social structure (i.e., the racial hierarchy), dissident voices emerged from time to time as informants in both groups collectively negotiated the meanings of the text and case. In short, the outcome of the struggle between texts and viewers—the contest by which "reality" is affirmed— is always an open, empirical question. In the U.S. context, raced meanings and status are likely to play prominent roles in this ongoing struggle.

REFERENCES

Adorno, T. (1991). The schema of mass culture. In J. M. Bernstein (Ed.), *The culture industry: Selected essays in mass culture*. London: Routledge.

Altheide, D. L., & Snow, R. P. (1979). *Media logic*. Beverly Hills, CA: Sage.

Althusser, L. (1971). Ideology and ideological state apparatuses. In *Lenin and philosophy and other essays*. New York: Monthly Review Press.

Berger, P. L., & Luckmann, T. (1966). *The social construction of reality: A treatise in the sociology of knowledge*. New York: Anchor Books.

Berry, M. F. (1994). *Black resistance, white law: A history of constitutional racism in America*. New York: Penguin.

Blauner, R. (1972). *Racial oppression in America*. New York: Harper & Row.

Blumler, J., & Katz, E. (1974). *The uses of mass communication*. Beverly Hills, CA: Sage.

Bradburn, N. M. (1983). Response effects. In P. Rossi, J. Wright, & A. Anderson (Eds.), *Handbook of survey research*. San Diego, CA: Academic Press.

Brunsdon, C., & Morley, D. (1978). *Everyday television: 'Nationwide.'* London: British Film Institute.

Bullock, P. (1969). *Watts: The aftermath. An inside view of the ghetto by the people of Watts*. New York: Grove Press.

Condit, C. M. (1994). The rhetorical limits of polysemy. In H. Newcomb (Ed.), *Television: The critical view*. New York: Oxford University Press.

Cramer, M. R., & Schuman, H. (1975). We and they: Pronouns as measures of political identification and estrangement. *Social Science Research, 4,* 231–240.

Dates, J., & Barlow, W. (1990). *Split image: African-Americans in the mass media*. Washington, DC: Howard University Press.

Dayan, D., & Katz, E. (1992). *Media events: The live broadcasting of history*. Cambridge, MA: Harvard University Press.

Dyson, M. E. (1996). *Between God and gangsta rap: Bearing witness to black culture*. New York: Oxford University Press.

Fanon, F. (1967). *Black skin, white masks.* New York: Grove Press.

Farley, R., & Allen, W. R. (1989). *The color line and the quality of life in America.* New York: Oxford University Press.

Farr, R. M., & Moscovici, S. (1984). *Social representations.* Cambridge: Cambridge University Press.

Fishman, M. (1980). *Manufacturing the news.* Austin, TX: University of Texas Press.

Fiske, J. (1987). *Television culture.* London: Routledge.

Fiske, J. (1989). Moments of television: Neither the text nor the audience. In E. Seiter, H. Borchers, G. Kreutzner, & E. Warth (Eds.), *Remote control: television, audiences, and cultural power.* London: Routledge.

Fiske, J. (1994). *Media matters: Everyday culture and political change.* Minneapolis, MN: University of Minnesota Press.

Foster, H. (1985). *Recodings: Art, spectacle, cultural politics.* Port Townsend, WA: Bay Press.

Franklin, J. H. (1965). The two worlds of race: A historical view. In T. Parsons & K. Clark (Eds.), *The Negro American.* Boston: Beacon Press.

Garfinkel, H. (1967). *Studies in ethnomethodology.* New York: Polity Press.

Hacker, A. (1992). *Two nations: Black and white, separate, hostile and unequal.* NewYork: Ballantine.

Horne, G. (1995). *Fire this time: the Watts uprising and the 1960s.* Charlottesville, VA: University of Virginia Press.

Hunt, D. M. (1997). *Screening the Los Angeles "riots:" Race, seeing, and resistance.* Cambridge, U.K.: Cambridge University Press.

Johnson, J. H., Jones, C. K., Farrell, W. C., Jr., & Oliver, M. L. (1992). *The Los Angeles rebellion,1992: A preliminary assessment from ground zero.* Los Angeles: UCLA Center for the Study of Urban Poverty Occasional Working Paper Series, UCLA Institute for Social Science Research.

Klapper, J. (1960). *The effects of mass communication.* New York: Free Press.

Kozloff, S. R. (1987). Narrative theory and television. In R. C. Allen (Ed.), *Channels of discourse.* Chapel Hill, NC: University of North Carolina Press.

Liebes, T., & Katz, E. (1993). *The export of meaning: Cross-cultural readings of "Dallas."* Cambridge, MA: Polity Press.

Marable, M. (1983). *How capitalism underdeveloped black America.* Boston: South End Press.

McKay, J., & Smith, P. (1995, February). Exonerating the hero: Frames and narratives in media coverage of the O. J. Simpson story. *Media Information Australia, 75,* 57–66.

Morley, D. (1974). Reconceptualizing the media audience: Towards an ethnography of audiences. Birmingham, UK: Centre for Contemporary Cultural Studies.

Morley, D. (1980). *The nationwide audience.* London: British Film Institute.

Morley, D. (1992). *Television, audiences and cultural studies.* London: Routledge.

Omi, M., & Winant, H. (1994). *Racial formation in the United States from the 1960s to the 1990s.* New York: Routledge.

Prager, J. (1982). American racial ideology as collective representation. *Ethnic and racial studies 5,* 99–119.

Schudson, M. (1978). *Discovering the news: A social history of American newspapers.* New York: Basic Books.

Tuchman, G. (1987). Representation and the news narrative: The web of facticity. In D. Lazere (Ed.), *American media and mass culture: Left perspectives.* Berkeley, CA: University of California Press.

Turner, P. A. (1993). *I heard it through the grapevine: Rumor in African-American culture.* Berkeley, CA: University of California Press.

van Dijk, T. A. (1993). *Elite discourse and racism.* Newbury Park, CA: Sage.

Waters, M. C. (1990). *Ethnic options: Choosing identities in America.* Berkeley, CA: University of California Press.

Weller, S. (1995). *Raging heart.* New York: Pocket Books.

CHAPTER 16

Mass-Mediated Realities and the Persian Gulf War: Inventing the Arab Enemy

Marouf Hasian, Jr.

We have before us the opportunity to forge for ourselves and for future generations a new world order, a world where the rule of law, not the law of the jungle, governs the conduct of nations.
—George Bush, 1991

Although the Gulf War is over, the conflict, its characters, and its cultural memory are still very much a part of the American imagination. Men and women with little remembrance of Vietnam or Korea will use this war as one of the emblematic markers of their life, a defining moment of patriotism and honor. This was a war that "we" hesitated to engage in, dreaded, prepared for, and won. A hyperreal media kept the world enthralled in the details of a campaign that witnessed the transfer of half a million troops to the exotic "Orient" and the spending of billions of dollars in the name of Kuwaiti independence and the maintenance of the new world order. America's exceptionalism and its power were present for the rest of the globe to simultaneously appreciate, envy, and curse.

For some, the Gulf War was a vindication of the Bush administration's contention that a just war could be won as long as the people's will was not thwarted by a liberal press or an irrational minority. With a minimal loss of allied life, a technically advanced United States had reestablished itself as a military and economic power that had fully recovered its moral capital. By leading the entire world against an isolated and barbaric Iraqi leader, it had shown its dedication to the tenets of international law while at the same time husbanding precious resources for future generations.

Yet for other academicians and members of the public, the rhetorical significance of the Gulf campaign continues to be source of debate. Press analysts who once acquiesced in the formation of press pools now provide us with tales of censorship, while military experts deliberate over the efficiency of the Coalition forces. Other commentators now contend that perhaps short-term political and economic considerations triumphed over the long-term solutions of negotiation and regional settlements. Lucaites and Taylor (1993), for example, lament the ways in which many members of the 102nd U.S. Congress helped to create discursive constructions of prudence based on military "necessity" that triumphed over other possible courses of action. One commentator complained that the war brought "wanton destruction of Baghdad and the ongoing bullying of numerous small states around the globe" (Ahmad, 1994, p. 94). Some critics go even farther, and argue that this Middle East engagement was "less a 'victory' to be 'celebrated' than a catastrophe to be mourned" (Stam, 1992, p. 101).

Although there are many illuminating ways of looking at the Gulf War, this essay will focus on one small part of this discursive tapestry, the Western media's portrayal of the Arab "Other" in mobilizing support for war. The decision to get involved in any war is often a complex undertaking, but there is little doubt that in order to justify any substantial loss of life you need to rhetorically magnify your enemies. With the balkanization of what once was the "Soviet Union," Americans have needed to invent a new evil empire with which to spar. The U.S. gaze turned to the "Orient," that mythic land of the "Other." As Said (1979) once observed, the "Orient" has been crafted by the academy, by museum displays, colonial offices, and countless numbers of anthropological, biological, linguistic, racial, and historical theses (p. 7).

This appropriation of the Oriental "Other" for purposes of war has manifested itself in a variety of historical situations, including the reconfiguration of the Japanese during World War II. Today, we have different characterizations that we can add to our growing collection of fabrications as we look toward the Near East. As Collier (1994) explains, Islamic "fundamentalism" has come to "replace communism as the principal perceived threat to Western reason and democracy" (p. 395). Pulcini (1993) similarly points out that the recent conflict has "once again focused the world's attention on the Arab people" (p. 27). This attention has not been an unmixed blessing.

In order to illuminate the complexities of this situation, this essay is divided into four sections. In the first part of the project, I provide a brief summary of some of historical and cultural prefigurations of the

"Arab" that existed prior to the Gulf War. In the second section, I look at the selective coverage of the military confrontation by the media. In the third segment I review the domestic politics that reconfigured the Arab within. In the last section I discuss the heuristic value of this type of investigation.

ARAB PREFIGURATIONS IN THE
ANGLO-AMERICAN IMAGINATION: 1890–1990

At least since the time of the Crusades and Saladin (1138–93), Anglo-Americans have been both fascinated and repulsed by the figure of the "Arab." During the Middle Ages, Arabs were considered to be exotic creatures, whose religion and manners symbolized the antithesis of what it meant to be Christian and civilized. Anglo-Saxon histories taught millions of European and American schoolchildren that Arabs were a nomadic race that hindered the progress of the Occidental races. In some encyclopedia entries, the very name "Arab" has been associated with deviance and degeneration (Shaheen, 1985, p. 165). In the dichotomous conceptualization of Western rationality, these Oriental "Others" represented the *absence* of reason and history. As Aswad recently opined:

> The Mid-East was competitive with Europe and was eventually conquered by Europe. It is a Third World region that historically has not been liked very well. When you review many of the textbooks, you notice that even the way we learn history chronologically is wrong. When we study the passing of civilization up to the West, we go from the Roman Empire and the Byzantine Empire right up to Europe. We don't acknowledge that in the Middle East there were the centers of learning for about 400 years. (quoted in Wiley, 1991, p. 5)

During colonial times, nations like England had commissions that dismissed the "entire body of Arabic and Sanskritic learning as worthless" (Ahmed, 1991, p. 30). Moslems and Arabs thus appeared only as the negative mirror images of what was absent in the West.

In the American press, Arabs first gained national attention in the late 1890s and early 1900s when immigrants began to appear in mainstream publications (Pulcini, 1993, p. 28). Initially characterized as peddlers and beggars, these Arabs soon became the "villains of choice" (Shaheen, 1985) with the advent of the motion picture industry. The discovery of oil in the Arabian peninsula now allowed new stereotypes to be added to existing templates and perceptions. In countless movies, novels, and cartoons, Arabs were now portrayed as creatures who were terrorists, polygamists, and radicals. As Moghrabi observed, the "stereotypes of Arabs as terrorists or as rich sheiks" was born out of the "frustration American people find in giving identity to Arab people" (Wiley, 1991, p. 5).

For decades, Arab-Americans organized in an effort to fight these stereotypes, but the dense tapestry of fabrications continued to be a part of Western perceptions of the "Other." On a daily basis these prejudices are harmful enough, but with the advent of war, they become even deadlier.

CULTURAL AMNESIA AND THE ARAB "OTHER" IN THE MASS-MEDIATED GULF WAR

During the many months the mass media's coverage of the Iraqi war (1990–1991), Americans and other Westerners learned little about the Arab people, their customs, their accomplishments, or their desires. Just as politicians and military experts gradually pushed aside the option of negotiated settlements in the region, the media chose not to engage in any lengthy discussion of the belief structures of the communities that they would soon occupy. In place of dialogue and mutual construction of relationships, we had mass-mediated simulations that positioned Arabs as belonging to good or bad "nations"—depending on their *response* to Western coalition initiatives. Within these new narratives, an Arab was accepted if that person acquiesced in the activities of the Coalition or cried out against the tyrannies of Islamic fundamentalism. These Arabs were now no longer the "Other"—as long as they took on the personae of the Westerners.

On the surface this bifurcation between good and bad Arabs appears to be an illustration that the dominant American press and the military was nonracist and fair in its conduct of a just war. Don't all Arabs now have the chance to become democratic? Weren't the Western powers simply defending the rights of moderate Arabs against their more passionate and reactionary neighbors? Yet a closer reading reveals that these constructions of the good and bad Arab were still pernicious reconfigurations of the "Other," mass-mediated constructions that explained more about the anxieties of the West than they did about the denizens in the region. From within Western motifs and lexicons, civilization and culture are the possessions of those who are stable and militarily secure, and this was a region that was out of control. The discussions of the heat and desert during the war perpetuated the notion that this was a land unfit for habitation, further extending earlier prefigurations that only deviants would choose to live in this region. The existence of oil supplies in the desert appeared to be a cruel irony, in that the deserving nations of the world were dependent on foreigners of the area. Within these mythic fabrications, regardless of whether a person was characterized as either a good Arab (Kuwaiti, Saudi, etc.) or a bad Arab (Iraqi or Palestinian), they were still in need of Western leadership.

These selective readings allowed the Bush administration, its allies, and supportive audiences to characterize themselves as reluctant interventionists, members of a unified community that had exhausted all other remedies. Ostensibly, this was a war for Kuwaiti independence, a preventive act that would stop future confrontations. This was also a war that supposedly would bring stability to an area that was filled with occupants who threatened the world with their constantly squabbling, chaotic policies, and fratricidal wars.

Miles away, in America, millions of citizens who may have never heard of Kuwait now found themselves asked to send their sons and daughters to war in order to preserve the American way of life. All that many of these social actors focused on was the chance to get rid of the Vietnam syndrome, an opportunity to show what American technical ability could do with a public behind them and a press that could no longer play the role of interloper. Within these imaginative fantasies, former Vietnam veterans and their families could engage in a form of cultural amnesia that forgot that the Middle East was a place that had its own citizens, its own religions, and its own stock of values and desires. These seemed to weigh little in a cultural calculus that allowed neighbors to once again tie yellow ribbons around trees in support of a great act of redemption. Children who should have had the chance of learning about the life of other persons thousands of miles away were instead exposed to thousands of exhortations that reminded them that America's former setbacks were no longer manifestations of national or community divisions. Any troubles that accompanied earlier interventions were now considered to be simply brief interludes in a much longer protracted engagement with a prefigured American enemy—the Arab. This selective punctuation of American and world history could not be built on just any martial cultural memory, for this is a war that would commit hundreds of thousands of troops for a potentially long-term engagement. Rhetors needed to sift through the sands of time in order to find the best rationale for war.

Within America's collective cultural memory, the most righteous war that had ever been fought was World War II. Here was a war that America had also reluctantly entered, where the rational world of the Allied powers had also been assembled against the forces of darkness. Like the Crusaders before them, the forces of Christianity rallied around new flags and new faiths in a war with a new infidel. Historically distance is effaced as new mass-mediated texts helped officials relive the glories of the past as they mobilized for war. Coming up with plausible excuses for war is not always an easy task, and in the early stages of the confrontation America's executive leadership filled the newspapers and airwaves with a plethora of explanations of why the nation needed to send its troops. As one *Washington Post* noted on November 15, 1990:

> Since Bush first sent U.S. forces to the gulf to counter Iraq's August 2 invasion of Kuwait, he and other administration officials have had trouble articulating clearly the reasons for their actions. They have cited various rationales, from protecting U.S. oil supplies and avoiding economic damage to countering unprovoked aggression and confronting a modern-day Hitler. By all accounts, the administration's words and actions so far have failed either to convince Saddam that the United States is serious about going to war against him or to make Americans understand clearly why they might have to fight. (Hoffman, 1990, p. A1)

Hoffman was perhaps correct in his analysis of the ineffectiveness of some of these rationales, but he underestimated the power of vilification. Anxious Kuwaiti and U.S. officials soon found that opinion polls in the months following the Iraqi invasion showed that the American public did not seem to be mobilizing around the themes of democracy and human rights in Kuwait, but the image of Saddam Hussein as the enemy was evoking much more response (Sigelman et al., 1993, p. 364).

Advocates of military solutions to the Gulf crisis concluded that Americans would go to war, but they needed the right reasons. Consciously or unconsciously, public officials and other commentators on the war found themselves contributing to new constructions of the Arab "Other." Once considered to be a dependable counterweight to Khomeini's Iran, now Hussein found himself depicted as the world's next Hitler. Within these Occidental narratives, the Iraqi leader became the living embodiment of fascism.

Rhetorically, focusing on the demonization of Hussein and reviving the story of World War II accomplished several tasks. It allowed the advocates of military intervention an opportunity to trivialize the efforts of those who were opposed to the war. These critics could now be characterized as Chamberlain-like figures whose policies of appeasement would do nothing to placate a modern dictator. At the same time, the vilification of Hussein could built on the stereotypes and prejudices that already circulated about Arabs and Moslems, placing the Iraqi leader in the well-known position of irrationally leading a nation against the collective forces of civilization. Simultaneously, the focus on Hussein meant diverting attention away from rationalizations that clearly did not have great appeal for many audiences—maintaining the oil supply or sustaining a military balance in the Gulf region.

More importantly, the focus of attention on Saddam deflected attention away from more troubling questions, such as the issue of why

Arab regional initiatives were failing or the impact of economic sanctions. In the absence of any discussion of the views of any other Iraqi men and women, Hussein becomes the synecdochical figure who represented any Arab or Moslem who held views that could be considered hostile to Western interests. The mythic Islamic fundamentalist is now a capacious enough figure to include anyone who might object to American intervention.

On the surface, these images and descriptions of the Arabs of the Gulf may seem to be innocuous and entertaining, but in volatile situations these iconographic images can be deployed by influential rhetors who advance particular policy considerations. Perhaps the best example of this media blitz came in the form of the "Nayirah" story, where a witness testified before a Congressional caucus that Iraqi soldiers were throwing out babies from their hospital incubators in Kuwait City (MacArthur, 1992). This tale was told countless times in the Western press, and Americans now had before them graphic evidence of the barbarism of the region. Journalistic investigators would later point out that "Nayirah" was none other than the daughter of one of Kuwaiti ambassadors to the United States, but in the meantime both the public and their representatives were deliberating about the exigencies of the situation. Within many of these fabricated tales, immediate military intervention seemed to be the only viable option. Funded largely by the Citizens of a Free Kuwait and promoted by the powerful public relations firm of Hill and Knowlton (Roschwalb, 1994, p. 268), Nayirah's performance helped mobilize support for the advocates of war, while at the same time allowing the citizens of Kuwait to portray themselves as victims who were interested only in promoting democracy.

Before the discovery of these atrocities, many Americans may have been skeptical about the president's characterization of Hussein as another Hitler, but this quickly changed. For the advocates of war, allowing more time for other solutions meant that the West was shirking its responsibilities. The Nayirah controversy represented more than simply a publicity ploy. The incubator tale seemed to fit Western notions of Islamic fundamentalism and recalcitrance. These media accounts now pitted not one but at least two stereotypical depictions of Arabs against each in the discursive war between some members of the press and the defenders of Hill & Knowlton. On one side of the controversy, we have the Iraqi invaders, but on the other side, we now have portraits of desperate Kuwaitis who are willing to violate Western ethical norms in order to dupe the American Congress into believing that Hussein would invade Saudi Arabia or stay in their own nation permanently. These are mirror-images of the same "Other," that hapless Arab who needs Western guidance and rationality.

This problem is exacerbated when critics review the ways in which the media discussed the death tolls and other casualties in the aftermath of war. One of the most persuasive techniques used by the supporters of the Coalition intervention in the Gulf war involved the use of distancing techniques that trivialized the loss of life during the conflict. In other wars like Korea and Vietnam, public support for presidential interventions declined within weeks after the reporting of heavy casualties (Umberson & Henderson, 1992, p. 3), but during the Gulf War many officials could proudly report that there were relatively few American deaths. In one of his speeches, President Bush reminded his listeners that "we mourn the loss of every single one of our armed forces and coalition forces" (*New York Times*, December 12, 1991, p. A6). At the same time, the Pentagon decided to suspend the traditional public ceremonies that usually accompanied the return of soldiers coffins. Many Coalition leaders used linguistic devices that treated the war deaths as tragic and yet necessary sacrifices made in the name of a just conflict.

This type of rhetoric can be sharply contrasted to discussions of the Iraqi casualties. In the first few months of 1991, newspaper reporters who were a part of the privileged press pool system euphemistically described civilian deaths and injuries as "collateral damage," a military term that gives the impression that any loss of life has little to do with human agency, volition, or activity (Umberson & Henderson, 1992, p. 7). Any damage to the Iraqi Arabs still needs to be calibrated, but now we have no discussion of coffins or sacrifice but rather a count of the number of tanks destroyed or airfields cratered. By focusing on American technical expertise and bombing precision, leaders could de-emphasize the damage that was being done by massive bombing missions. When U.S. air raids mistakenly hit one shelter that contained hundreds of Iraqi civilians, the Pentagon responded with claims that Hussein was responsible for this damage by hiding his military forces behind the innocent (Umberson & Henderson, 1992, p. 11).

If these strategies failed, there was still one more strategic argument that could be employed that helped maintain the fragile line between the humane supporter of the Coalition forces and the inhuman creature that stood behind the tyrant Hussein. Employing traditional notions of military "necessity," political leaders could still admit that the air campaigns had taken a large number of lives, but these could now be justified as part of an effort to reduce "Iraq's armed forces by 50 to 60 percent, a level that many military leaders" viewed as "an important threshold to make ground combat less costly" (Umberson & Henderson, 1992, p. 11). While individual American soldiers who lost their lives were treated as reluctant warriors that had done their duty, the Arabs who supported Saddam were characterized as Moslem fanatics who were parts of the menacing "Republican Guard" or "tank units." These were "Saddam's Henchmen" (Bush) who were willing to follow their leader into a defenseless nation like Kuwait. While various estimates placed the losses of the Iraqi "Other" at between 85,000 and 150,000, what remains painfully obvious is that the attention of the American public was focused on the quick completion of the war—at minimal cost to the allies. Unlike Vietnam, this would be an iconographically aesthetic war, and the nation could return to business as usual now that they had conquered the latest manifestation of the Oriental "Other."

COPING WITH THE ENEMY WITHIN: SURVEILLANCE AND THE POLITICS OF SUSPICION IN THE WEST

While thousands of troops battled abroad, millions at home maintained a different kind of surveillance. Having been exposed in previous decades to countless movies that depicted Arabs as terrorists, many citizens of the Coalition forces now began to worry about the enemy within. Like Japanese Americans before them, Arab Americans now found themselves having to cope with several different tensions. On the one hand, they wanted to prove their loyalty to their country in condemning Hussein's invasion of Kuwait. On the other hand, many Arabs believed that the conflict needed a Pan-Arab solution, and that the Bush administration was simply participating in a conspiracy to promote the military solution. The confluence of these factors meant that now Arab Americans had to be careful how they articulated their own values. They were now living within a culture that contained such xenophobic fears that in January of 1991 the FBI announced that it would single out Arab Americans for questioning about terrorist activities (Wiley, p. 5).

Thankfully a plethora of organizations came to Arab Americans' aid, but the characterizations remained. As Stam (1992) recently opined:

> The Gulf War media coverage consistently channeled empathy according to clear hierarchies of human value. At the apex, Americans and Europeans, then Israelis, then Arab allies, and lowest on the ladder, Arab enemies. Even the oil-suffocating cormorants in the Persian Gulf and the animals in the Kuwait City Zoo, some commentators noted, garnered more sympathy than the Iraqis. The zealous citizens who sported "Nuke Iraq" T-shirts or who patriotically roughed up Arab-Americans in the streets (even those from countries allied with the United States) intuitively understood the subliminal message sent by the media and the administration: Arab life has no value. (pp. 114–115)

For many Americans, all that mattered was getting the troops home safely. The "Other" was an afterthought.

ASSESSMENT: THE POLITICAL POWER THAT COMES
WITH THE ABILITY TO DEFINE THE ARAB "OTHER"

For rhetorical critics who are interested in explicating the links between ideology, discourse, and politics, the characterization of the Arab "Other" during the Gulf War provides us with an interesting case study of how prefigurations can influence purportedly objective accounts of conflicts in distant lands. The media coverage of the Persian Gulf War combined the genres of docudramas with news reports in order to create a new means of communication (Kenney, 1994, p. 100). In spite of occasional criticisms of the handling of the Persian Gulf War, some polls indicated that more than 80% of the American public thought that the news coverage of the war was either good or excellent (Jensen, 1992, p. 120). Yet in the process of crafting this "new" means of communication, we have defined and described the war as a battle between recognizable foes, where foreign creatures combat the forces of the Enlightenment.

To be sure, these mass-mediated constructions that demonized Hussein may have been powerful and effective, but they were not simply crafted by the Bush administration alone. If communication is a dynamic relationship, then the power of any symbolic image involves rhetors, audiences, and their observers. The pride and prejudices of millions of Westerns were taken into account in textual constructions that humanized some Arabs while at the same time dehumanizing others. The believability of these figurations does not simply come from the deployment of one salient characterization in an isolated point in time. Rather, the reconstruction of the Arab "Other" is an edifice manufactured over a lengthy period of time.

Years after the end of the so-called Coalition war against Iraq, we find ourselves again listening to tales about the growing power of Hussein, and lamentations that we have been too lenient on tyrants in the past. How we choose to interpret those tales, and the amount of cultural amnesia that we are willing to tolerate, will alter the way we think about the coming New World Order.

REFERENCES

Ahmad, A. (1994). Reconciling Derrida: "Spectres of Marx" and deconstructive politics. *New Left Review, 208,* 88–106.

Ahmed, A. (1991). Islam—the roots of misperception. *History Today, 41,* 29–31.

Collier, J. F. (1994). Intertwining histories: Islamic law and Western imperialism. *Law & Society Review, 28,* 395–408.

Hoffman, D. (1990, January 15). Messages as mixed as audiences. *Washington Post,* pp. A1, A28.

Jensen, R. (1992). Fighting objectivity: The illusion of journalistic neutrality in coverage of the Persian Gulf War. *Journal of Communication Inquiry, 16,* 20–32.

Kenney, K. (1994). Review essay: (Mostly) critical views of Gulf War TV. *Journal of Communication, 44,* 100–105.

Lucaites, J. L., & Taylor, C. A. (1993). Theorizing the grounds of rhetorical judgment. *Informal Logic, 15,* 31–40.

MacArthur, J. (1992). *Second front: Censorship and propaganda in the Gulf War.* New York: Hill & Wang.

Pulcini, T. (1993). Trends in research on Arab Americans. *Journal of American Ethnic History, 12,* 27–60.

Roschwalb, S. A. (1994). The Hill & Knowlton Cases: A brief on the controversy. *Public Relations Review, 20,* 267–276.

Said, E. (1979). *Orientalism.* New York: Vintage Books, 1979.

Shaheen, J. G. (1985). Media coverage of the Middle East: Perception and foreign policy. *The Annals of the American Academy of Political and Social Science, 482,* 160–175.

Sigelman, L., Lebovic, J., Wilcox, C., & Allsop, D. (1993). As time goes by: Daily opinion change during the Persian Gulf crisis. *Political Communication Quarterly, 10,* 353–367.

Stam, R. (1992). Mobilizing fictions: The Gulf War, the media, and the recruitment of the spectator. *Public Culture, 4,* 101–126.

Umberson, D., & Henderson, K. (1992). The social construction of death in the Gulf War. *Omega, 25,* 1–15.

Wiley, Ed, III. (1991, March 14). Gulf War a perfect backdrop for hate crimes against Arab-Americans. *Black Issues in Higher Education, 5.*

CHAPTER 17

Who's the Victim? Intercultural Perceptions Between African American and Korean American Business People in Dallas

Meta G. Carstarphen and Tae Guk Kim

In 1992, Los Angeles exploded in violent riots that lead to a reported $1 billion in damages and contributed to over 50 deaths (Mydans, 1994). Much of the destruction and loss was concentrated in commercial communities where a substantial number of the merchant/owners were Korean and the consumers were African American. Media accounts that followed the violence made much of long-simmering tension between African American and Korean American communities.

In many large cities where Korean American businesses operate in predominately African American communities, similar tensions can exist and be potentially explosive. One incident involving members of the two communities can touch off a widespread disturbance that may result in the destruction of properties and even human lives.

Like Los Angeles, Dallas hosts neighborhoods that are predominately African American, but whose businesses are owned by a large number of Korean Americans. Since 1993, three highly publicized incidents that involved Korean American merchants and the African American community occurred, including a 1994 slaying of a 42–year-old African American male by a Korean merchant in neighboring Fort Worth (Davidson, 1995) . Consequently, reportage on these incidents touted underlying racial motives as causation for these incidents, a recurring theme in press coverage throughout the country, including the Dallas media.

However, media identification of "racial tensions" between these two communities give no more than ambiguous clarification of the key cultural and communication issues at stake. Moreover, if press coverage of Korean and African Americans is limited to highly publicized incidents of violence, then the global view of these communities may be fractured.

In exploring these two communities' responses to each other, as well as their patterns of reliance upon majority media, this paper hopes to more clearly define where media information may be supplanting actual experiences. Connections between such media habits and specific perceptions held by Korean Americans and African Americans about each other will be probed.

LITERATURE REVIEW

Many communication theories about the interaction among groups look at social aspects between majority and minority communities, and how those power relationships are reflected in the communication among these groups. Framing such discourse within a social context lends critical perspectives. As one researcher argues, we can only know part of a story if we attempt to examine only the surface text, without consideration of how it serves "a function in the creation, the maintenance, or the change of such contextual constraints as the dominance, the power, the status, or the ethnocentrism of one of the participants" (van Dijk, 1985, p. 19). More recent research has probed the special social circumstances that affect intergroup communication among communities outside the majority. Specific attention focuses on the role of the media as conduits of widely dispersed and influential forms of social discourse.

Perhaps nowhere is the social impact and social influence of media discourse more hotly debated than in the area of race and ethnicity. The media reflect perceptions of deep social divisions along color lines, and merely report these same deep fissures as different audiences view them. These differences—openly explored during findings from the 1968 *Kerner Commission Report on Civil Unrest*—remain constants, certainly for African Americans: "To their eyes, the mainstream media speak for a White nation" (Hacker, 1994) .

Moreover, research findings consistently indicate that African Americans have a strong belief that the mainstream media is "White," because composite television news images "feed racial stereotypes, encouraging White hostility and fear of African Americans" (Entman, 1994). Frequently absent from the mass media is the examination of issues from the viewpoints of African Americans. Other research notes that print media fare just as poorly, particularly when it comes to establishing "frames" for data, suggesting that "the press prefers to present differences between the fortunes of Whites and Blacks in terms of the high probability of Black loss—bad news for and about Blacks" (Gandy, 1994, p. 47).

For Korean immigrants and Korean Americans, their perception of the majority media rests within a different set of experiences. Traditionally, Asian Americans "simply remain invisible" or the press covers them in "shallow, stereotypical ways" (Wong, 1994). Even the grouping of many different Asian ethnicities under the umbrella of "Asian American" is inherently problematic, ignoring cultural differences among peoples of Asian descent.

But in what ways do the larger social contexts of media interaction shape the ways in which ethnic groups see each other? Are there cultural patterns that can influence how such groups respond to and use the media? What happens when minority cultures collide within these media structures? Ella Stewart's study of communication between African Americans and Korean Americans in Los Angeles since 1988 provides insight into patterns established there. In her analysis of these perceptions and attitudes, she noted:

> While part of this economic disparity between African Americans and other ethnic minority groups can be attributed to a poor educational system and low income, part of the disparity can be attributed to racial discrimination. . . . The civil unrest that followed the verdict in the Rodney King case on April 29, 1992 also underscored the differing perceptions that Koreans and African Americans had toward each other, and the difficulty of communication between the two groups. (Stewart, 1993, p. 25)

Survey results from the 58 African American and 21 Korean American respondents challenged at least one persistent media myth: that African Americans resented Korean merchants' operations in their neighborhoods because of jealousy or resentment. Rather, Stewart explains that the differing communication styles and expectations between the two groups contributed to their strife:

> African Americans do not consciously single out Korean American businesses as targets for attack. However, African Americans did reveal that those Korean proprietors who were rude and consistently showed disrespect toward African Americans may unwittingly set themselves up for retaliation, especially during a civil disturbance. (Stewart, 1993, p. 45)

Mary Louise Pratt describes the phenomenon of communication and interaction between two hostile groups as a process of transversing "contact zones," a term she uses to "refer to social spaces where cultures meet, clash, and grapple with each other, often in highly asymmetrical relations of power" (Pratt, 1991, p. 34). Intercultural relations between African Americans and Korean Americans seem to reflect this process of social negotiation. This transaction is heightened by the prevalence of Korean American merchants whose presence of economic authority sets up a dominant power relationship between them and their African American customers. Life in the "contact zone," as Pratt suggests, involves a necessary set of social transactions between two cultures in opposition: "Along with rage, incomprehension, and pain, there were exhilarating moments of wonder and revelation, mutual understanding, and new wisdom—the joys of the contact zone" (Pratt, 1991, p. 39). What part of this transaction are the media capturing?

METHODOLOGY

Eighty-eight African American business people and 84 Korean American business people responded to our survey. Each of those queried was asked to either fill out a 60–question survey or respond to these questions by student interviewers. Potential respondents were canvassed in specific geographic neighborhoods within the southern area of Dallas, where there are predominately African American neighborhoods with a high concentration of both Korean American and African American business owners.

Subjects were questioned over a period of 6 months, during interviews conducted from March through August 1994. We preceded this investigation with the development of two survey instruments—one in English, one in Korean—with which our target populations would be comfortable. All together, we generated 10,320 individual responses.

STUDY RESULTS

Characteristics of Respondents

According to the 1990 Census, there were 296,994 African Americans and 2,459 Koreans residing in Dallas. The median, or average, household income was $19,224 for African Americans; for Koreans, $24,317 (Showalter, 1995).

Interesting characteristics emerged from a review of the demographic portion of our surveys (Questions 1–3, and 52–60). Of the total African Americans (88), 29 identified themselves as business owners, compared to 66 (out of 84) Koreans. Fifty-three African Americans said they were managers, as opposed to only 12 Koreans, with six who failed to identify themselves either way. This indicates that more Korean stores are managed by owners than in African American businesses.

The mean number of years in operation for African American businesses is 4.8 years, with 35% of the 71 respondents saying that their stores had been operation for only 1 year, and 37% saying that they had been in business from 2 to 5 years. The oldest African American business had been operating for 16 years.

For Korean-owned businesses, the mean number of years was 4.1 years. Thirty-three percent had been operating for only 1 year, and 44 percent (43.5) indicated they had been operating for 2 to 5 years. The oldest Korean business had been in the area for 17 years. Thus, the business experiences of both groups were roughly equivalent, showing that each had virtually equal stakes in this community.

All businesses indicated representation in retail, wholesale, and service areas. One major difference between the two groups, however, was the much stronger showing of African American businesses in the service area—23%—compared with only 8% of the Korean businesses. On the other hand, 80% of the Korean businesses surveyed were retail, with an additional 11% both retail and wholesale. In contrast, 61% of the African American stores were strictly retail, with 8% both retail and wholesale operations.

Only 12% of the Korean shops employ nonfamily members, compared to 48% of the African American shops who do. Seventy-four percent of Korean stores were managed by the store owner and the spouse, contrasting with 32% for the African American shops.

Evaluating the Other

Our respondents had exposure to others outside of their own cultural groups through very specific ways: either as customers, competitors, or employees. Questions that specifically focused on the interactions between these store owners and their employees, as well as their interactions with customers, gave some specific contexts in which they could evaluate others. More general questions that simply asked how each group perceived each other amplified these views.

Korean store owners overwhelmingly employ their own family members, yet there was some experience with "outsiders" working with them. In evaluating the performance of their employees, 13% of the Koreans placed African American employees in the category of "good performance," while 45% placed them in the category of "poor performance." They tend to rate Korean American employees the highest, with

76% of them rated as good performers, compared to only 2% in the poor performance category.

On the other hand, 75% of the African Americans surveyed rated their African American employees in the category of "good performance," with only 2% rating them as poor performers. Seventy percent think highly of their Mexican American employees as well, with 73% of them rating them as good performers, and only 12% in disagreement. There was no data suggesting that African Americans had hired any Korean employees.

Interestingly, despite Koreans' low evaluation of the performance of their non-Korean employees, they report that they get along well with all of them. Fifty-four percent of the Korean owners report that they get along well with their African American employees (with only 5% disagreeing) and 72% said they get along well with their Mexican American employees. By contrast, 83% of the African Americans report good relationships with their African American employees, while 76% say they get along with their Mexican American workers.

These two groups differ in their perceptions of experiences with their customers, as well. Only 35% of the African American respondents felt their customers took advantage of them by stealing merchandise or refusing to pay, compared to 86% of the Korean merchants who believed their customers took advantage of them in these ways. However, despite the differing percentages, both groups listed "theft" as their number one business problem and leading cause of concern.

The second greatest area of concern for Korean merchants was verbal abuse from their customers, with 60% of them citing it as a major concern. Twenty-two percent of the African American owners shared the same concern. For both groups, a problem with customers lying about product exchanges was listed as the third highest area of concern. Forty-two percent of Korean merchants expressed this as a problem, compared to 25% of African American owners.

Significantly, both groups of business people considered the potential for verbal abuse from their customers to be an ongoing concern. However, a very high percentage of Koreans—nearly half—considered such incidents to be problematic. Since only a quarter of the African American business people experienced the same level of concern, they either weren't receiving as much verbal abuse as their Korean counterparts, or they were ignoring more of it.

Of Friendliness and Business Relationships

When asked to evaluate the relationship between the Korean American businessmen and the African American community, the two groups display different perceptions of the relationship. Only 11% of the African American businessmen consider this relationship to be friendly, while 20% of the Korean American businessmen believe this to be so. Twenty-six percent of the African American businessmen say that the relationship is unfriendly, but none of the Korean American businessmen say that is the case. However, a large 41% of the Koreans say that this relationship is in constant conflict (compared to 5% of the African Americans), obviously drawing the line between an "unfriendly relationship" and a relationship of "constant conflict."

Thus, to Koreans, an unfriendly relationship means a hostile relationship, highly tinged with threat and danger. On the other hand, a relationship of "constant conflict" simply means a turbulent relationship, not necessarily an unfriendly one. One thing is certain: Korean American business owners underestimate the level of unfriendliness African Americans perceive in their interactions.

When these responses are linked to the earlier ones about verbal abuse, a pattern emerges showing sharply differing reactions to the exchanges with their customers. Perhaps African Americans see verbal exchanges with their customers as just that, while Korean Americans think that verbal unpleasantness will lead to violence.

Business in the Neighborhood: Motivation and Image

Business relationships and interactions form the crucial intersections at which these two communities form interpersonal connections, and these are very limited. Still, such encounters underscore the economic dimensions that characterize the complex parameters of relationships between them.

Thirty-nine percent of the African American businessmen and 11% of Korean American businessmen believe that the Korean American business people "*definitely* take economic advantage" of the African American customers. However, when respondents were asked, in a less adamant way, if they thought Korean businesses took advantage of African American customers in "some way," 26% of the African Americans and 49% of the Koreans agreed. Only 14% of the African American businessmen believe that Korean American businessmen "do not *necessarily* take advantage" of the African American community, while over twice as many Korean Americans (29%) share this same sentiment. Still, it is significant that a majority of both groups agree that Korean American businessmen take economic advantage of the African American community to *some* degree.

Not one Korean American respondent thought that their businesses did the community any harm; however, all five of the African American business people who said that the Koreans "definitely take economic advantage" of the African American community also asserted that the Korean American business people have "done more harm than good."

MEDIA HABITS AND MEDIA IMAGES

When asked what media they regularly follow, 61% of the African Americans reported that they most frequently used television for news, compared to 41% of the Korean respondents. Many of the Korean Americans pointedly stated that they "did not have time" to watch television. Instead, 40% of them read English-language daily newspapers, with 88% of them reading *The Dallas Morning News*. Other papers specifically mentioned included *USA Today* and *The Wall Street Journal*. Equal percentages—10—stated that they regularly followed radio programs and magazines.

By contrast, a higher percentage of African Americans—92%—read daily newspapers of some kind, 76% mentioned *The Dallas Morning News* specifically, as well as other papers such as *The Fort Worth Star-Telegram* and *USA Today*. Thirty-three percent regularly follow radio programs, and 23% regularly follow magazines. However, although a high percentage mentioned that they read newspapers, only 6% reported a regular, or daily, newspaper regimen.

Interestingly, the importance the two groups placed upon the medium varied greatly when they were asked to select a "specific medium as the best source of information about American society." A high 86% of the Koreans surveyed picked television as the "best medium," while only 57% of the African Americans believed television to be the "best source" of information about American society. Only 12% of the Korean American respondents picked a newspaper as the best, compared to 20% of the African Americans who selected newspapers.

No Korean picked radio as an important medium. However, 11% of the African Americans surveyed cited radio as the second most important source of information about American society. Finally, magazines received comparable ratings by the two groups as "the best source," with 2% of African Americans and 1% of the Koreans singling out this medium.

Still, while African Americans did not report reading newspapers on a "regular" basis, a higher percentage of them follow daily newspapers and hold this medium to be an important source of information. Koreans may read newspapers more often, but a clear majority (86%) report that they regard television to be the best medium to know about American society.

Television's visual impact appears to be more appealing and informative to Koreans more than other media—like newspapers, magazines, and radio—which require a greater competence in English. At the same time, while African Americans follow television more consistently, they don't "trust" the medium to the same high degree as they do other media that may offer more context and reflection, especially upon issues important to them.

One thing both groups have in common is an amazingly high distrust of the majority media.

SEEING THEMSELVES THROUGH THE MEDIA'S EYES

As to the media's coverage of the tensions between the two communities, only 7% of the African American respondents and 2% of the Koreans believed that the media were "objective and accurate in their coverage."

TABLE 17.1
Media Coverage of Tensions between the
Two Communities is Objective and Accurate

African Americans	7%
Korean Americans	2%

Although 26% of the African American respondents believed that the media are biased against them, not one Korean respondent believed the media was anti–African American. Yet, when asked to evaluate the media coverage of both communities, 23% of the Korean American respondents believed that the media were favorable to the African American community, but only 9% of the African American respondents said that was the case. On the other hand, 15% of the African American respondents said that the media were pro-Korean but only 2% of the Korean Americans agreed with that evaluation.

Neither group thinks that the media are favorable to "both" their communities. Less than 1% of the Korean American respondents saw "any" favorable treatment of the two communities in the media and only 13% of the African Americans thought the media coverage of the two communities was positive.

Which ethnic group got the most favorable media coverage? Both groups unequivocally answered that they perceived the media to be "pro-Anglo." Ninety-eight percent of the Korean respondents and 82% of the African American respondents selected Anglos as the group receiving the most favorable coverage. Only 9% of the Koreans believed that African Americans were portrayed positively, while not one African American believed that his or her group received a positive portrayal. Similarly, 70% of the Koreans and 64% of the African Americans surveyed felt that the media portrayed African Americans in a negative light.

Significantly, despite this high percentage of Korean Americans who believed the news reported about African Americans was negative (70%), not one of these respondents saw such reportage as inherently biased, suggesting strongly that Koreans find such negative portrayals of African Americans credible.

Given the perceptions by both groups that the media coverage about them is inherently negative, respondents were asked to comment on any kind of discernible effects they perceived resulting from such coverage. Both African Americans (60%) and Koreans Americans (73%) believed that the media coverage of conflict between their two communities does not help. In fact, 64% of the Korean respondents and 33% of the African Americans accused the mainstream media of "sensationalizing" coverage of issues relating to both of them.

The two groups agreed that the media do not give adequate coverage of issues relating to the two communities. Only 17% of the Korean Americans and 21% of the African Americans thought that the media gave adequate or enough coverage to the issues relating to the two communities, while 58% of the Korean Americans and 49% of the African Americans believed that the media coverage of the issues was insufficient.

As to the role of the media in improving the relations between the two communities, the majority of both groups do not believe that the media play a role in that respect. Fifty-eight percent of the Korean-Americans and 48% of the African Americans did not think that the media coverage of the tensions between the two communities helped to improve their relationships. Just 11% of the Korean Americans and 15% of the African Americans thought that the media could offer any help improve the relations between the two groups.

The negative attitude of both groups toward the role of the press may be due to their doubt about the media's coverage of conflict between their two communities. Although Korean Americans (64%)

TABLE 17.2
Media Coverage of Tensions Adversely Affects
Attitudes of Customers Against Koreans

African Americans	14%
Korean Americans	76%

and African Americans (33%) believed that the media's coverage of the conflict between them was sensational, 26% of the Korean Americans, however, said that the media were "constructive and balanced" in their coverage of such issues, with 43% of the African Americans in agreement.

Overall, the Korean Americans appear to be more critical of the media's coverage of the tensions between the two communities and to be more doubtful about the role of the media in improving the relations between the two. The suspicion that both groups have of the media's coverage of the other group seems to indicate that the two ethnic groups consider themselves victims of negative coverage by the media, which they consider to be favorable to the Anglo Americans.

This lack of enthusiasm for the media's help in improving the relationships between the two communities indicates that the two groups have less confidence in the media's role as interpreter of their cultures. Such an attitude also illustrates that in the view of these two communities, the media have failed to play any positive role in bridging the gap between the two.

When the respondents evaluated the coverage given to *any kind of news* relating to African Americans and Koreans, as opposed to coverage about their intercommunity tensions, both groups show nearly equal levels of dissatisfaction. Sixty percent of the African Americans and 59% of the Koreans felt that the media gave either too little, or no coverage at all, to issues involving their communities outside of stories concerning interracial conflict.

Media and Money

Finally, despite their ambivalence about the reliability of information about themselves in the mainstream media, both communities are very comfortable with their uses of such media for advertising. Both groups agree that the use of mainstream media in advertising helps their business, with 79% of African Americans and 78% of the Korean respondents concurring.

At the same time, Korean businesses situated in Black neighborhoods are much more dependent upon clients in those environs. Yet, while only a small portion (25%) used media targeted for African Americans, an almost equal amount (20%) advertised in Korean American media. Not only do these messages miss their primary audience, they are directed to an audience that may not ever have occasion to patronize their stores. In light of the fact that these merchants do business with predominately African American clients, it is difficult to understand why Koreans do not advertise more aggressively with the African American media. These practices seem to underscore the Koreans' lack of understanding about how to establish reciprocal business relationships with African Americans, or a fundamental lack of sophisticated knowledge about the nature of marketing and advertising in this country.

CONCLUSIONS AND RECOMMENDATIONS

Relationships between African Americans and Korean Americans as seen through the eyes of business people from both communities are fractured and comprise mostly fragile accommodations. Though geographically close in urban, predominately African American neighborhoods, these businessmen and women recognize unresolved tensions between their two communities.

However, their perceptions of the reasons for these tensions vary significantly, and reveal how much mistaken perceptions and inadequate, direct communication between these two communities contribute to these tensions. African Americans identify a major element of economic exploitation underlying the Korean presence in their neighborhoods. However, Koreans, perceiving themselves to be simple, good business people, feel impeded by customers outside their cultural group who the owners feel are predatory and want to exploit them.

Both groups rely heavily upon the majority media and feel the media are good outlets for advertising. However, both are dismayed by the coverage given to both their communities, feeling that the amount is negligible and the content is negative. Both groups overwhelmingly agree that, while coverage of Korean Americans isn't great, the media focus upon African Americans is nearly always negative. Unfortunately, since Korean Americans surveyed did not detect a "bias" in the media overall, they are inclined to find the negative portrayals of African Americans believable. These may actually "frame" their expectations of African American behavior and motives, coupled with any negative, though limited, experiences they may encounter with their African American customers.

However, both groups can bridge these differences with their own cultural media, which both communities rely upon heavily. In fact, it is within this powerful arena of community-controlled discourse where these two groups have the greatest potential to propel social negotiations in the "contact zone" from strained to successful.

Korean American merchants, especially, need to develop some relationships with the African American media in order to enhance their business and civic profiles in these communities. Both African Americans and Koreans need to explore more interpersonal ways of getting to know each other, instead of relying upon the majority media. As both groups agree, the mainstream media do more to impede relationships between their communities, than they do to offer constructive ways of ameliorating and understanding the complex issues facing them.

REFERENCES

Davidson, J. (1995, March). Grabbing Black dollars: When foreigners own the corner store. *Emerge,* 26–30.

Entman, R. M. (1994). Representation and reality in the portrayal of Blacks on network television news. *Journalism Quarterly, 71,* 509–520.

Gandy Jr., O. H. (1994). From bad to worse—The media's framing of race and risk. *Media Studies Journals, 8*(3), 39–48.

Hacker, A. (1994). Are the media really 'white'? *Media Studies Journal, 8*(3), 81–88.

Mydans, S. (1994, June 2). Punitive damages denied in beating of Rodney King. *The New York Times,* p. A-16.

Pratt, M. (1991). Arts of the contact zone. *Profession 91,* 33–40.

Showalter, L. (1995). Dallas area statistics: General population. In U.S. Census Bureau, Population Division.

Stewart, E. (1993). Communication between African Americans and Korean Americans: Before and after the Los Angeles riots. *Amerasia Journal, 19*(2), 23–53.

van Dijk, T. A. (Ed.). (1985). *Discourse analysis in society.* London: Academic Press.

Wong, W. (1994). Covering the invisible "model minority." *Media Studies Journal, 8*(3), 49–60.

CHAPTER 18

Reporting Hantavirus: The Impact of Cultural Diversity in Environmental and Health News

JoAnn M. Valenti

In recognition of the 50th anniversary of the National Congress of American Indians, the U. S. Commerce Department released a report based on 1990 census data from over 300 tribes in the United States. The American Indian population increased over 30% during the last decade. The study identified nearly 450,000 families in the population of 1.9 million; in four of the ten largest tribes, more than 10% have college degrees; and the Navajo have the highest proportion (48.8%) of people living in poverty ("Survey," 1994). To help media accurately report on Indian issues and write articles involving tribal lifestyles, the Bureau of Indian Affairs encourages reporters to call for correct terminology or phrasing, and handbooks have been developed (e.g., *The American Indian and the Media* published by the National Council on Christian and Jews). Others have advocated the value of cultural journalism, an effort to encourage diversity among those who actually report and write the news (Creed, 1994).

In their article "Beyond the Culture Wars: An Agenda for Research on Communication and Culture," Davis and Jasinski (1993) warn against assumptions about the social world and advise us that "long-suppressed ethnic cultures are gaining strength" (p. 141). Most American journalists and communication researchers have been trained in educational and institutional environments founded on the preeminence of modern civilization. However, challenges to modernism and concerns raised by negligence in the dominant social order have become more evident (e.g., Habermas 1979, 1989). Signs of a developing consciousness, a sensitivity to diverse voices, have emerged slowly in mainstream media and mainstream communication research. Another underlying premise, however, recognizes journalistic standards and norms as fairly potent contaminates for any culture. Journalism considered as a learned "new" culture may be capable of taking precedence, overwhelming existing mores.

Deference to cultural rationalities, perhaps unscientific in the technical view, opens environmental journalism and the health risk dialogue to a wider range of voices, inclusive of those who see themselves as victims. Efforts by media to be more inclusive acknowledges the complexity and richness of the media audience. Questions arise, however, when reporters, not as advocates, but in the effort to follow the fuller story must understand diverse voices without framing news in a manner damaging to a culture. The case reported here examines whether barriers inherent in the journalistic process exist in addition to the personal history of any individual journalist.

Accepted mass communication theory suggests that regional media coverage is more likely to be balanced; proximity deters reliance on limited sources or overreliance on sources representative of only a partial point of view. Reporting in regional newspapers should also more often be the work of staff journalists rather than copy provided over national wire services. In the absence of cultural journalism, it is assumed that reporters rely on journalistic standards; cultural insights or privilege do not intrude on expected norms.

A cultural approach to environmental communication assumes "lay" experiential evidence and reasoning that constitute cultural rationality are as legitimate as the "expert" scientific evidence and technical rationality that normally dominate the risk debate (Krimsky & Plough, 1988). The problem, when compounded by cultural differences, becomes one of knowledge and possibly prejudice. The focus of this study was the production and negotiation of meaning for mass media audiences in the reporting and health communications surrounding the emergence of a new strain of hantavirus. The discovery of any disease in a new environment clearly presents a newsworthy health risk event. This research examines media portrayal of Navajo culture in reporting the hantavirus outbreak in 1993, the role of the journalistic process and cultural ignorance in the hantavirus coverage, and intent (meaning) sources for the hantavirus information that the media professionals themselves brought to the story.

COMMUNICATING ENVIRONMENTAL AND HEALTH RISK IN THE MASS MEDIA

The role of the mass media in public knowledge, perceptions, and attitudes, especially when information is new, has been widely studied. The media have been charged with activating apprehensions and myths. Consistent with general media role findings, in a study of British television coverage of environmental issues, Cottle (1993) found unopen and unequal access to the range of voices. He found news forums restricted to "outside" voices, but saw encouragement in "live" programming where more opportunities for discursive engagement occurred. Studio-based interviews, for example, offered the possibility of developing other, nontraditional points of view. He called for increased sensitivity to cultural expressions of environmental portrayals of news.

Waiting for journalists who promise by nature or birth to be more sensitive to nondominant cultures to report environmental and health risk stories proves frustrating, and may, as this researcher suspects, fail to alter the product. Figures on diversity among America's news professionals show improvement at a snail's pace (Lieberman, 1994). According to a recent survey from the American Society of Newspaper Editors (ASNE), minorities overall account for 10.5% of the total population of close to 54,000 newsroom professionals. At only .3%, Native Americans are the least represented.

Those who watchdog the watchdogs are concerned about what journalists bring to their reporting. Dunwoody and Griffin (1993) studied how reporters covered Superfund sites in differing communities and found predictable factors influencing journalistic strategies. In addition to reaffirming that journalists are event driven, for example, they report that journalists "simply adopt the frames of references of the bureaucracies that they cover; a dimension of an issue will be deemed newsworthy because officials have defined that piece of the process as important" (p. 46). But they also find that sources of all kinds are able to drive story themes, and that occupational or organizational norms and resources can influence story frames. However, prevailing power structures tend to build environmental coverage frames. Those media frames then influence both societal risk judgments and personal risk judgment (Coleman, 1993).

As one might expect, the amount of media coverage given to environmental or health risks is related to people's estimates of principal causes of death (Kasperson et al., 1988). The media are "highly selective, often sensationalized, and sometimes inaccurate" when reporting environmental and health risks and recommended actions (Wilkins & Patterson, 1987, p. 19). Rarity is a more compelling story than commonality; ratings and newspaper sales are assumed to be driven by dramatic events, not in-depth analysis of important emerging issues. Not surprisingly, public understanding and involvement in environmental issues has been hindered by the quality of information provided (McCallum, Hammond, & Covello, 1991).

Media attention appears unrelated to the number of deaths or injuries, but closely related to newness, rarity, or perceived drama. Singer and Endreny (1987) also found that media offer no or inadequate information about the likelihood of the occurrence of a risk, often leaving inaccurate public perception and unnecessary or misguided anxiety. Slovic (1986), who has researched public perception of risks extensively, finds memorability and the ability to imagine a risk culpable in distorted public risk perceptions. Anything that causes a risk to be more memorable increases the perceived likelihood of occurrence (Ryan, Dunwoody, & Tankard, 1991).

Of additional note is the text-audience relationship, framed not only by the media writer but also by the reader, listener, or viewer. Frameworks of interpretation involve personal experience or predisposition, political and environmental concern filters, assessment of evidentiary contributions (how an argument or narrative, image or statistic is added to knowledge), and judgment of balance or fairness (Corner & Richardson, 1993). Meaning and interpretation of news are contingent on influences beyond the mediated message.

THE HANTAVIRUS STORY

Although hantaviruses are distributed worldwide (Stone, 1993), when the emergence of a new strain of hantavirus in the United States hit the mass media agenda in 1993, charges of media stereotyping and environmental racism came in tandem. The initial storytelling was accused of being laden with negative images of a Native American culture and generalities that leapt from scientific uncertainty to labels associating the disease in error with a particular minority group of people and their culture. From the onset, Navajo spokespersons attempted to respond to what they saw as a crisis in the public sphere and to correct misperceptions, as well as to defend themselves in the face of ethnocentrism from both the media and health communities. Within weeks of the discovery of yet another strain of hantavirus, a National Public Radio (NPR) report (June 9, 1993) broadcasted interviews with Navajo spokespersons, who already resented the insensitivity of journalists covering the story and linking the disease to the tribe. A reversal of the more respectful trend in the treatment and understanding of Native American cultures seemed likely as hantavirus reports recreated a fearful image of an entire region of the country and a culture. The Navajo people were left to confront a host of hostile publics.

Unfortunately, this story may never end. As naturalist Terry Tempest Williams (1987, 1994) might explain, in her efforts to help audiences become more sensitive to Navajo culture, the coyote is everywhere. A study by state, federal, and Indian groups indicates rodents throughout the state of Montana also carry the hantavirus disease, and an ominous recent headline in the *Salt Lake Tribune* read, "Hantavirus Returns to Strike Navajos" (Becenti, 1996).

Within one year of reporting of the outbreak in the Four Corners region in the western states, 40 people had died in 17 states. The disease was tagged as "an Indian ailment" because the new viral strain was discovered on a Navajo reservation covering parts of Utah, Arizona, Colorado, and New Mexico. *USA Today* may have been first to use the tag "the Navajo flu," although a representative from the National Center for Infectious Diseases (CID), an M.D. who authored the original formal notices announcing the news viral strain, claims a headline in the *Albuquerque Tribune* first used the label "Navajo Flu." *Albuquerque Tribune* science reporter Lawrence Spohn equated this to calling AIDS "the gay disease" (Richard, 1993). *The Arizona Republic* used the label "the Navajo epidemic," and NBC News made reference to "the Navajo disease."

The public information director for the Navajo Nation, told one *Inquiry* writer that while the spread of the disease might end, "the false image of Navajo life as impoverished and unsanitary may persist in the minds of many Americans" (Richard, 1993, pp. 2–3).

The Centers for Disease Control (CDC) based in Atlanta, Georgia, became a key government source for the story, although the CDC makes an effort to refer media to state and local health departments. CDC press officer Bob Howard labeled the problem a "data dump," referring to the estimated 25,000 media calls he receives each year. In hindsight, CDC spokespersons describe the case of the hantavirus outbreak, as an example of "dueling amateurs," the amateurs being a CDC investigator trained in epidemiology and a non-specialist reporter.

ANALYSIS OF MEDIA COVERAGE

Although the original time frame for analysis was set for April 1993 (the "crisis" story actually broke in major national media in late May 1993) through May 1994, headlines and wire stories continued for months to herald the Navajo/hantavirus story, first as the tribal government objected to the originally recommended name for the "deadly" virus discovered in the Four Corners area, and later as more victims were identified.

The first name proposed for the strain of hantavirus, Muerto Canyon virus (MCV), in use in the scientific literature (*Science*, 1994), was derived from Canyon del Muerte (canyon of death), a site on the

Navajo reservation. Traditionally, new viruses are named after where they are discovered, but to avoid offending local people, CDC called this new strain Pulmonary Syndrome Hantavirus (Marshall, 1993; Hughes et al., 1993). "The hantavirus was all over the United States," Navajo Nation Council member Genevieve Jackson told an Associated Press reporter. "We resent the fact that it is named after a canyon here. . . . CDC should have a little more respect and consideration for the Navajo people" ("Navajo," 1994). The name finally accepted for the new strain, "Sin Nombre," introduces an interesting sidestep (meaning "without a name") from the cultural versus scientific tradition conflict.

Continuing stories reported new cases of the disease with some fatalities, and analyzed long-term economic woes created as fearful tourists canceled plans to visit the Four Corners area (Becenti, 1994). In a related turn of events, the CDC announced a "war" on diseases, comparing "virulent cholera ravaging India" to "hantavirus killing Americans" ("CDC," 1994). In the 3 years since the outbreak on the 25,000–square-mile reservation, over 100 cases of hantavirus have been reported in 23 states with 55 deaths recorded.

FINDINGS

An analysis of 67 news stories in three regional newspapers (*The Phoenix Gazette*, *The Arizona Republic*, and *The Salt Lake Tribune*), and a small sampling of coverage from television news (ABC and CNN) during the period from late May 1993 through April 1994, found support for early criticism of media's performance as this story broke. Press articles selected using NEXIS, CARS, and home delivery service were coded as either local (staff) written or from wire services. In the three regional newspapers analyzed, 60% of stories originated from wire services, while 40% were reported by local staff (see Figure 18.1). The

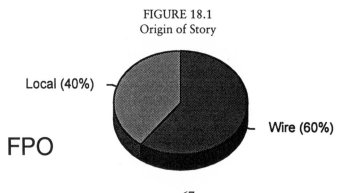

FIGURE 18.1
Origin of Story

Local (40%)

Wire (60%)

FPO

n = 67

number of mentions of "Navajo" were counted and each was evaluated in context as negative, neutral, or positive. Coders judged each mention of "Navajo" in reference to modifying or other specific words also appearing in the same sentence or paragraph, and general tone based on context.

The number of sources used in each story was then recorded and each quote or attribution categorized as Navajo, Government, Business/Industry, Citizen/Member of General Public, or Other (with notation of expertise or affiliation if evident). A random recode resulted in a reliability of 82%.

As Figure 18.2 shows, of the total number of references (n = 302) to Navajo, 35% were judged to be negative. Some 39% of references to Navajo were neutral; 26% were positive. However, it appears that specific mention of Navajos or contextual references derogatory to the Navajo or Native American culture declined as the story unfolded. Reports of the virus and specific mention of the Four Corners region as a Navajo reservation appear to give way to increased attention to science and medical information, although general geographic mention of the southwest or Four Corners area continued.

Some 1 to 11 sources were used in each of the stories examined (n = 251). Of these, 34% were clearly identifiable as Navajo or Indian/Native American (see Figure 18.3). Government sources, usually the CDC or state Health Department officials, accounted for 45%, while business or industry represented 6% of those quoted. The "Other" cat-

FIGURE 18.2
Reference to "Navajo" (Regional Dailies)

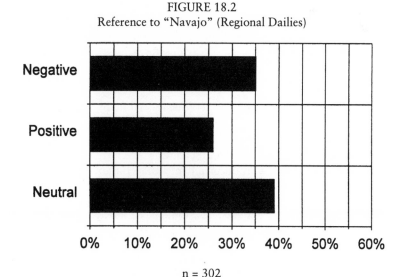

n = 302

FIGURE 18.3
Sources (Regional Dailies)

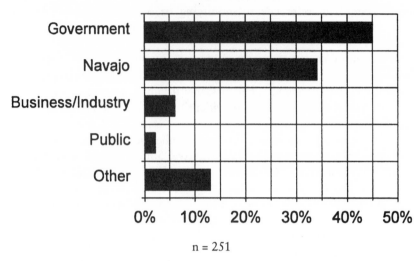

n = 251

egory provided 13% of sourcing; these were generally university scientists or medical professionals in the private sector, and occasionally quotes from other media sources. Only some 2% of sources used to tell the story were voices from the general public, usually tourists.

Examples of quotes from Navajo Tribal Council spokespersons and from government sources demonstrate the unraveling conflict:

- Zah [president of the Navajo Nation], at a press conference here said, "Navajos are finding themselves shunned in public places and business establishments. . . . Navajos have been made to feel like plague bearers or lepers whose touch is to be feared." (*Arizona Republic*, June 18, 1993, p. A1)

- "I believe it behooves you as an educational institution to learn the known facts about this illness before resorting to actions that discriminate against our students," [Marshall] Plummer [vice president of the Navajo Nation responding to the University of Colorado and New Mexico State's announcements that Indian students would need a medical screening] said. "Be assured that this illness is not Navajo specific. The illness has struck non-Indians and people who live far away from Navajo lands. This is not a racial illness, but a regional one." (*Phoenix Gazette*, June 15, 1993, p. B1)

- "People who have been personally affected by this, by friends and relatives, in some cases because of the publicity and the presence of the media are reluctant to talk to our investigators," said Dr. C. Mack Sewell, New Mexico's chief epidemiologist. (*Phoenix Gazette*, June 3, 1993, p. A2)

For this study, only three sample transcripts from television news (ABC News and CNN) were examined. Again, analysis for negative, neutral, or positive association between the disease and the culture, and frequency of sources representing diverse cultures, suggests a similar pattern as exemplified in the following excerpts:

- "An army of health care workers has descended on the U.S. Southwest—its mission, to identify a mysterious illness that has killed 13 people, mostly Navajo Indians. The professionals have all the tools of modern medical investigation, but tribal traditions and taboos are complicating their probe." (Natalie Allen, CNN anchor, lead-in to report from correspondent Robert Vito, June 3, 1993)
- "Navajo children from Arizona were headed home today after being told they could not visit with their pen pals at a Los Angeles school. The principal of the California school and her students were worried they might catch the disease from the Navajo children." (ABC News reporter Gary Shepard, June 2, 1993)

Electronic media's references or associational tagging, however, followed print's lead and became less negative in later coverage.

COVERAGE IN *THE NAVAJO TIMES*

To explore the possible effects of cultural journalism on this same coverage, articles about hantavirus appearing in the Navajo Tribal Council newspaper, *The Navajo Times*, during the peak months of the breaking story (June and July) were also coded. Two coders independently analyzed the 20 identified stories noting placement and coding the number and categories of sources and evaluating references to "Navajo" as positive, negative, or neutral. Intercoder reliability was measured at 87%.

Almost all coverage during the studied period appeared as front page stories, and either carried staff bylines or ran with writer/reporter unidentified. Although the majority of references to "Navajo" were found to be "neutral" (60%), even in this tribe-sponsored periodical, nearly one third (32%) of all references to the Indian name were coded as "negative." And, as Figure 18.4 shows, of the total 100 direct references to the term, only 8% were judged to be "positive."

FIGURE 18.4
Reference to "Navajo" (Navajo Times)

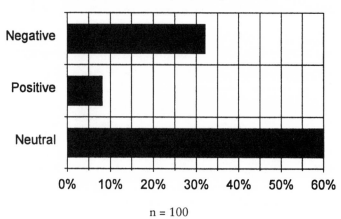

n = 100

FIGURE 18.5
Sources (Navajo Times)

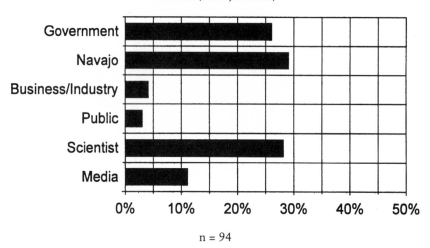

n = 94

In the analyzed articles, with attribution to a range from 1 to 13 sources, the most often cited source was not a government spokesperson or report. As Figure 18.5 shows, 26% of the 94 identified sources were categorized as "government," while Navajo sources, the anticipated primary source for this publication, comprised slightly more (29%) of the sources used in this reporting. Other media were quoted or paraphrased in 11% of the *Navajo Times* coverage, but unlike the reporting in the regional dailies studied, journalists writing for this tribal newspaper went to the science community for 28% of the attributed information. Business and industry sources accounted for 4% of the coverage, and members of the public (not identified as Navajo) made up the remaining 3% of voices contributing to this coverage.

SUMMARY AND CONCLUSIONS

This analysis of a small sample of local media directly involved with the coverage of the hantavirus outbreak confirms some criticism of media, but it is not clear what lasting impact, if any, such media coverage has on those who read or see such reporting, nor is it clear what problems result from negative reinforcement of existing stereotypes. And, indeed, an effort to balance the usual government and expert sources with attention to Navajo perspectives is evident in this study. But, as has been pointed out in reference to poor media coverage of religion, "prejudice is a minor problem compared with apathy and ignorance," (Mattingly, 1993, p. 12).

What this study suggests is that cultural sensitivity alone may not override deeply rooted journalistic training and processes. As one reporter covering this story pointed out, "Everybody that had an Indian on the staff sent them." And although a total population of only .3% seems not to offer a large pool of Native American journalists, peak news events during this story often looked like "a convention of the Native American Journalists Association," according to one NAJA member.

Even though an unexpected number of the journalists who covered this story extensively for mainstream print and electronic media were Native American, the differences in coverage that minority reporters brought to the story suggest only an initial "better understanding" and easier access to some sources. Barriers to unbiased intercultural journalism are strong. Conroy Chino, a reporter for an Albuquerque television station and an American Indian, says he understands the criticism of how media performed in covering the hantavirus story. "There is some legitimacy to those complaints," Chino told Bob Gassaway in an article for *Quill.* "We came with satellite trucks, flashing cameras, and probing questions," he said. "We pounced on this story because of its impact, its intriguing quality." Navajos chased Chino away from a funeral for one victim on the reservation. In Navajo culture, not only are burial ceremonies considered private, but that person's name goes unspoken for a year after his or her death. Most journalists covering the story were ignorant of many Navajo traditions, customs, and the privacy of spiritual rituals.

Another reporter, who is Navajo and filed numerous lengthy stories for one of the studied regional newspapers, said, "I have to put my Navajo-ness in the back seat and go on." To this reporter's advantage, she spoke the Navajo language, and on more than one occasion was able to get to stories and Navajo sources others missed. However, she added that when the story was over, she planned to see her medicine man to conduct a traditional ceremony for restoring her harmony with the universe.

Of additional importance, although minority reporters were involved in the regional coverage, their input is hardly exclusive. At one major newspaper where a correspondent who is Navajo contributed much of the reporting on the hantavirus story, wire stories were also run, often with such leads as: "Three months after a mysterious, life-threatening malady struck around the Navajo reservation . . ." and ended with a death count. Headlines for wire service coverage typically read, "Hantavirus Scare Has Slowed N.M. Tourism" (*Salt Lake Tribune*, 1993). Interestingly, the assignment editor during this coverage at one of the studied regional newspapers is Native American and in an interview with this researcher discussed personal involvement in the story. A relative living on the Navajo reservation had actually contracted the disease. As Hahn (1994) reminds us in *The Politics of Caring*, "The biases of reporters, editors, and publishers and the influence of advertisers surely have an effect, if only in subtle and not completely conscious ways" (p. 198). What Hahn fails to address is the influence on individual bias not only from the journalistic process, but inherent in journalistic norms. The long-term impact of media's initial framing of a new issue may be too deeply embedded in the public sphere for media, even when they "correct" their interpretation, to undo misperceptions. Considering the role of CDC and other public health investigators in this story, and the equally harsh criticism of their "cultural insensitivity" during this virus outbreak, future research should include attention to the effect of sources as well as media. If the content of point source information changes to better reflect a sensitivity and understanding of all cultures, it may curtail waiting for the ASNE survey data on diversity in hiring to improve, or the advent of approval for cultural journalism. What this case study suggests is that shooting the messenger, *or* making assumptions about the messenger, may conjure only more stereotyping and is unlikely to resolve the environmental or cultural justice issue in the long run if the difficulty lies within the process standards and norms. Attention to training in cultural sensitivity within our own national boundaries, and more importantly, thought to insensitivities built into our media processes offer more promise in the effort to remove the existing barriers to accurate and fair coverage.

REFERENCES

Becenti, D. (April 20, 1994). Reservation businesses hurt by hantavirus coverage. *The Salt Lake Tribune*, p. D4.

Becenti, D. (March 16, 1996). Hantavirus returns to strike Navajos. *The Salt Lake Tribune*, p. A7.

CDC finds new strain of hantavirus. (1994, Feb. 25). *Science, 262*, 1079

CDC starts early-warning system in war on disease. (1994, April 24). *The Salt Lake Tribune*, p. A7.

Coleman, C. (1993). The influence of mass media and interpersonal communication on societal and personal risk judgments. *Communication Research, 20*, 611–628.

Corner, J., & Richardson, K. (1993). Environmental communications and the contingency of meaning: A research note. In A. Hanson (Ed.), *The mass media and environmental issues* (pp. 222–233). Leicester, UK: Leicester University Press.

Cottle, S. (1993). Mediating the environment: Modalities of TV news. In A. Hanson, A. (Ed.), *The mass media and environmental issues* (pp. 107–133). Leicester, UK: Leicester University Press.

Creed, J. (1994). The value of cultural journalism to diversity in the mainline press. *Journalism Educator, 49*, 64–71.

Davis, D. K., & Jasinski, J. (1993). Beyond the culture wars: An agenda for research on communication and culture. *Journal of Communication, 3*, 141–149.

Dunwoody, S., & Griffin, R. J. (1993). Journalistic strategies for reporting long-term environmental issues: A case study of three Superfund sites. In A. Hanson (Ed.), *The mass media and environmental issues* (pp. 22–50). Leicester, UK: Leicester University Press.

Gassaway, B. M. (1993, Nov./Dec.). Press virus strikes Navajos. *Quill*, pp. 25–25.

Habermas, J. (1979). *Communication and the evolution of society*. London: Heinemann.

Habermas, J. (1989). *The structural transformation of the public sphere*. Cambridge, MA: MIT Press.

Hahn, A. J. (1994). *The politics of caring*. Boulder, CO: Westview Press.

Hantavirus scare has slowed N.M. tourism. (1993, Sept. 15). *Salt Lake Tribune*, p. A10. (Rpt. from *Dallas Morning News*)

Hughes, J. M., Peters, C. J., Cohen, M. L., & Mahy, B. W. (1993). Hantavirus pulmonary syndrome: An emerging infectious disease. *Science, 262*, 850–851.

Kasperson, R. E., Renn, O., Slovic, P. Brown, H. S., Emel, J. Goble, R., Kasperson, J. X., & Ratick, S. (1988). The social amplification of risk: A conceptual framework. *Risk Analysis, 8*, 177–187.

Krimsky, S., & Plough, A. (1988). *Environmental hazards: Communicating risks as a social process*. Dover, MA: Auburn House.

Lieberman. D. (1994, April 15) Newspaper diversity: Slow progress. *USA Today*, p. B48.

Marshall, E. (1993). Hantavirus outbreak yields to PCR. *Science, 262,* 832–836.

Mattingly, T. (1993, July/Aug.). Religion in the news. *Quill,* pp. 12–13.

McCallum, D. B., Hammond, S. L., & Covello, V. T. (1991). Communication about environmental risks: How the public uses and perceives information sources. *Health Education Quarterly, 18*(3), 349–361.

Navajo council hears objection to disease name. (1994, April 19). *The Salt Lake Tribune,* p. A8.

Richard, D. (1993). Navajo, press cultures at odds. *Inquiry, 7*(2), 1–3.

Ryan, M., Dunwoody, S., & Tankard, J. (1991). Risk information for public consumption: Media coverage of two risky situations. *Health Education Quarterly, 18*(3), 375–390.

Singer, E., & Endreny, P. (1987). Reporting hazards: Their benefits and costs. *Journal of Communication, 6*(3), 10–26.

Slovic, P. (1986). Informing and educating the public about risk. *Risk Analysis, 6,* 403–415.

Stone, R. (1993). A rogues' gallery of hantaviruses. *Science, 262,* 835.

Survey Reviews American Indian lifestyles. The Associated Press, Nov. 18, 1994.

Wilkins, L., & Patterson, P. (1987). Risk analysis and the construction of news. *Journal of Communication, 37*(3), 80–92.

Williams, T. T. (1987). *Pieces of white shell: A journey to Navajoland.* Albuquerque: University of New Mexico Press.

Williams, T. T. (1994). In cahoots with coyote. In *An unspoken hunger: Stories from the field.* New York: Pantheon.

PART IV

Mass Media and Education

CHAPTER 19

The (Mis)Representation of Ethnicity and the Omission of Racism in the K–12 Cultural Diversity Curriculum

Christy Hammer

Messages are sent to consumers both explicitly and more subliminally through the media and other mass-marketed material, such as curricula and writings in educational trade magazines designed for classroom teachers. Here I highlight some of the messages about cultural, racial, and ethnic diversity found in a content analysis of instructional materials such as teacher's guides, activity books, and curricula, all ostensibly on topics of cultural diversity. My intention was to confirm my hunch, based on my casual use of cultural diversity materials in civil rights training with teachers, that racism was often avoided and that ethnic stereotyping existed.

This content analysis was part of the research for my doctoral dissertation in sociology, "The Manifestation of Multiculturalism in the Public Schools" (1994, University of New Hampshire). It was obvious that many of the writings ostensibly on cultural, racial, or ethnic diversity did not actually discuss issues of race or ethnicity directly. Furthermore, in cultural diversity materials, while there are many examples of excellent curriculum, there exist numerous cases of inaccuracy or inappropriate characterization, including belittling caricatures.

THE CURRICULA

To understand multicultural education is to understand how it is practiced. Curriculum materials reviewed are on cultural diversity and related topics such as racism and race relations, themes of the melting pot in the United States, and on the New History (which studies family genealogy and the history of the common folk rather than focusing almost entirely on the history of the White Male Warrior and the White Male Inventor). In my civil rights work, many educators are not that comfortable using curriculum materials that focus on race. The materials that are most borrowed by teachers are those that blur and soften the racial grounding of multicultural education materials in favor of more loosely defined conceptions and goals of "respect for all," "tolerance for cultural diversity," and knowledge of the American melting-pot mosaic.

I will review cultural diversity curricula that appear to be the most well known and most widely used by teachers in the classroom in my state. Most of these curricula attempt to infuse multicultural concepts into everyday instruction through the use of structured activities.

The curricula to be reviewed include:

1. *America's Civil Rights Movement: Complete Teaching Package in Text and Video*, by the Teaching Tolerance Project (Klanwatch, Southern Poverty Law Center, Atlanta, Georgia, 1991)

2. *Fair Play in the Gym: Race and Sex Equity in Physical Education*, by Judith Placek and Pat Griffin (Women's Equity Program, University of Massachusetts, 1983)

3. *The Multicultural Catepillar: Children's Activities in Cultural Awareness*, by Ana Consuelo Matiella. (Network Publications, Santa Cruz, 1990)

4. *The United States: A Cultural Mosaic: Teacher Handbook for the Primary-Grade Multidiscipline, Multicultural Program* by Jimmie Martinez et al. (The Anti-Defamation League of B'nai B'rith, New York, 1989)

5. *America's Women of Color: Integrating Cultural Diversity Into Non-Sex-Biased Curricula*, Elementary Curriculum Guide by Gloria L. Kumagai (Women's Educational Equity Act Program, U.S. Department of Education, Washington D.C., 1990)

6. *America's Women of Color: Integrating Cultural Diversity Into NonSex-Biased Curricula*, Secondary Curriculum Guide by Gloria L. Kumagai (Women's Educational Equity Act Program, U.S. Department of Education, Washington D.C., 1990)

7. *The Culture Puzzle: Cross-Cultural Communication for English as a Second Language*, by Deena Levine et al. (Prentice Hall Regents, New Jersey, 1987)

8. *Americans All* for intermediate grades, published by Instructional Fair, Inc. (Social Studies Series, Instructional Fair, Inc., Grand Rapids, MI, 1978)

9. *Anti-Bias Curriculum: Tools for Empowering Young Children,* by Louise Derman-Sparks (A.B.C. Task Force, National Association of the Education of Young Children, Washington, D.C., 1989)

10. *My Backyard History Book,* by David Weitzman (Brown Paper School Series, Little, Brown and Company, Boston, 1985)

11. *Open Minds to Equality: A Sourcebook of Learning Activities to Promote Race, Sex, Class and Age Equity,* by Nancy Schniedewind and Ellen Davidson (Prentice Hall, New Jersey, 1983)

The first curriculum selected to review is called *America's Civil Rights Movement: Complete Teaching Package in Text and Video.* This is produced and distributed free of charge by the Teaching Tolerance Project of Klanwatch, an organization based at the Center for Democratic Renewal to serve as a watchdog for organized racist activities. This curriculum is rare in that it is distributed free of charge to any school on request, and includes a video, a 108-page text for students, and a teacher's guide complete with daily lesson plans. The video chronicles the civil rights movement as remembered by participants today with a great deal of historical footage provided as background over the reminiscing voices.

The learning objectives, as outlined in the teacher's guide, include students' knowing what were the goals of the movement and what were the strategies of movement participants (including knowing in what ways nonviolent resistance, or civil disobedience, was particularly successful in gaining sympathy for the movement). Students are also expected to know why the movement succeeded and what the spectrum of views are of both Whites and Blacks about the legacy of the movement and the existence of continued racial discrimination.

The second curriculum reviewed is called *Fair Play in the Gym: Race and Sex Equity in Physical Education,* by Judith Placek and Pat Griffin, developed through a U.S. Department of Education's Women's Educational Equity Act (WEEA) grant in 1983. The curriculum comes out of the University of Massachusetts's Project TEAM, which designed and taught the first experimental undergraduate equity class. Most of the activities in the curriculum have been field tested through in-service work with Massachusetts teachers.

It is the only curriculum of its kind of which I am aware that focuses on race and sex equity issues solely in physical education classes and interscholastic athletics. Some of the questions that provided the impetus for writing *Fair Play in the Gym* are included in the introduction. They include: what a physical education teacher can do when boys won't pass the ball to girls in a class basketball game; how a coach should respond to racial name-calling and a potential fistfight in the lockerroom, and, what strategies can help a physical education teacher meet the diverse needs of a class that includes highly skilled athletes and reluctant beginners.

The activities in *Fair Play in the Gym* include physical games that are generally noncompetitive and focus on form and technique rather than on the potential raw power in a physical move or athletic ability. The activities tend to avoid pitting individuals against each other, but rather structure opportunities to assess your own ability in a physical activity or a sport and compete against yourself, in a sense, by trying to continually improve no matter what your ability level might be. The second focus is on brainstorming and other exercises that are designed to help the inservice or preservice physical education teachers examine and reduce their own racism and sexism.

The missing piece to *Fair Play* is any discussion of institutional or societal racism and discrimination. The tone of the curriculum implied that racism was mostly personal and could be overcome by teaching the physical education teacher to "move towards the goal of the color-blind society."

The third curriculum is one for primary grades called *The Multicultural Caterpillar*. Written in 1990, it focuses on the Three Fs of cultural diversity: Food, Fun, and Festival. Instead of providing substantive information about ethnic and cultural difference, it focuses on recipes and scenarios for acting out holidays and customs from around the world. A disturbing series of pictures throughout the book illustrates White children playing with darker-colored caterpillars. Also, as one moves through the curriculum, the incidence of pictures of darker-skin (both human and animal) noticably decrease to the point that the brief descriptions of Brazilian maracas and Squanto's cornballs are surrounded by picture of White children only.

The fourth curriculum is called *The United States: A Cultural Mosaic*, a "multicultural program for primary grades" that is distributed by the AntiDefamation League of B'nai B'rith. The introduction notes that while "most research indicates attitudes are formed at a very early age and that many attitudes may be well-established by the time the child completes the primary grades," the available multicultural curricula were targeted for upper elementary and secondary school children.

A stated objective in this curriculum is to move away from examining diversity through "heroes and holidays" exclusively (such as with the previous curriculum) toward a "larger" framework of human similarities and differences. The author's foreword warns teachers that they must find a balance between the "whitewashing" of cultural differences with the rhetoric of "we're all the same" and the portrayal of homogeneous cultural difference, as when educators have well-meaning programs on Native Americans that ignore substantial differences among Native American tribes and individuals. This curriculum also benefits from a focus on classroom climate issues rather than compiling a set of classroom exercises for teachers to do with their students without examining the attitude toward cultural difference in the school and classroom climate. There are many excellent student exercises and projects in the Anti-Defamation League's curriculum, although it lacks more structured lesson plans.

The fifth and sixth curricula I had reviewed are the elementary and secondary versions (with accompanying teacher training guides) of *America's Women of Color: Integrating Cultural Diversity Into Non-Sex-Biased Curricula*. Like *Fair Play in the Gym*, the curriculum was developed through a Department of Education grant from the Women's Educational Act Program. For both the elementary and secondary versions, the contents are split into three categories: Similarities and Differences, Stereotyping, and Discrimination.

The section entitled Similarities and Differences in the elementary curriculum, for example, has subsections that review how White American females are both alike and different from Asian, Black, and American Indian females. An example from the section on Black American females is a short story called *Sunflower for Tina*, which describes the events of one day in the life of an African American female. The story is followed by questions to be asked of the students. The questions that are intended to emphasize similarities include: Do all Black girls enjoy planting a garden? Do you enjoy planting a garden? Do all Black girls daydream? Do you daydream? Questions that help to explore differences include items like: How is Tina's daily life different from your own?

The evaluation procedure is about the same for the sections on Asian American, Black American, and American Indian females. A main learning objective in each section is for students to demonstrate increased knowledge of the similarities and differences by listing three ways in which she/he is similar to and different from females of color. There are also more general exercises that do not explore culturally different artifacts and habits of daily life but focus on understanding prejudice and the harm that can occur from stereotyping as well as ways to avoid stereotyping.

The secondary curriculum is very similar to the elementary one. It, too, relies mostly on age-appropriate short stories followed by a series of discussion questions for each story that explore similarities and differences. The secondary curriculum also explores prejudice and stereotyping, but at greater length and in more detail. One lesson plan involves stereotyping in television programs. The first day, students are led through a discussion on why we stereotype, of the harm of stereotyping, and a brainstorming session on what the most common stereotypes are for Asian, Black, and American Indian women.

Next, the homework assignment given for the next week is to evaluate three television programs and ten television commercials using a guide that is provided to students as part of the curriculum. The guide has blank spaces to note how many males and how many females were in the program or commercial, in what activities the males and the females were engaged, and whether the main character was a male or female. This was followed with questions on how many Black, Asian, Native American, and Hispanic males and females were in each show. (I am unable to explain why, but it is interesting that Hispanics are occasionally included in particular activities but that they did not warrant their own subsection in either curriculum.)

The final activity is a post-test in which students define stereotyping, list three ways stereotyping can be harmful, list two stereotypes for both males and females of different race/ethnic groups, and lists harmful effects of television stereotyping. Activities similar to the activity just described are also interspersed throughout the curriculum and include analyses of textbooks, novels, and newspapers.

The seventh curriculum is *The Culture Puzzle: Cross-Cultural Communication for English as a Second Language*, by Deena Levine et al. This curriculum focuses on classroom strategies and exercises that foster positive self-esteem for Limited English Proficient (LEP) students as well as encouraging tolerance and understanding among all students working in a classroom environment with LEP students. There is a teacher's guide to using the curriculum. The curriculum covers topics such as cross-cultural communication, including how interpersonal interactions, complimenting, gift-giving, and expressing emotions are often culture-bound and vary widely between cultures. The intent is to supply examples of real, plausible situations where one might offend another person from another culture unintentionally because one is not aware of cultural differences. On some level, this curriculum seem to serve as a "survival guide" for new immigrant children and adults to the United States.

The Culture Puzzle has a second section on interacting in English that covers the cross-cultural dimensions of the acts of showing that you understand someone, giving feedback and interrupting, and guiding the conversation and holding your turn. A third section explores the cross-cultural dimensions of making contact in another culture, including the protocol for greetings and farewells, on avoiding certain topics and discussing common topics, on extending invitations and visiting. The last section of *The Culture Puzzle* focuses on cultural learning with units on how to learn from miscommunication, on observing cultural behavior, on asking without judging, and on examining your own experiences.

The Culture Puzzle is interspersed with "Cross-cultural Notes" in small boxes. One, for example, notes that Vietnamese people often use special forms of address. Thus, when someone calls his older brother or sister, instead of using a proper name this sibling is called "older brother" or "older sister." Another box notes the common Japanese perception that Americans give so many compliments that it seems insincere. They quote a Japanese woman saying she gives one compliment a week while an American woman says she gives at least one compliment a day.

Another of these boxes noted a conversational difference between Saudi Arabians and Americans. The American thought the person from Saudi Arabia always took too long to get to the point of the conversation because they started the interaction with a litany of polite questions such as "How is your spouse?" "How are your children?" "How are your parents?" etc. It is noted that people need to work hard not to get upset at cultural differences and realize that there are different standards of proper behavior and politeness.

Of particular value for the new immigrant, I would imagine, is the section on inappropriate and appropriate topics of conservation for many Americans. Among the topics that many may consider to be too personal are money, age (particularly for older people), religion, and physical appearance. (Another "cross-cultural note" box here says that among some Chinese it is a sign of interest and respect to ask one how much they weigh!) There is a discussion about how Americans like to make "small talk," followed by a list of the "safe" or common topics of conservation including the weather, sports, possessions, your job, school, weekend and vacation activities. There are amusing anecdotes about how bewildered some cultural groups are to hear how much Americans talk about the weather.

This curriculum avoids the obvious sandtrap of overgeneralizing cultural differences. The text makes clear that everybody is different and not all people belonging to a cultural group—including all-purpose Americans—are going to act and react in the same way. This message is consistently integrated into the activities.

The eighth curriculum is *Americans All*, which is designed for intermediate grades, published by Instructional Fair, Inc. *Americans All* uses a cultural pluralism model (as the name suggests) to "help students understand the richness of the ethnic heritage of their country, the areas from where the early immigrants came and why they came." The student-led activities in this book are self-contained and can thus be used to reinforce basic reading comprehension skills.

The difference in *Americans All* is that the contents are much more focused on the "White ethnics" and other European nationalities than any other multicultural curriculum I have seen. Various cultures of the Pacific Islands, the Middle East, and Central and South America are covered, but the bulk of cultures addressed are European: Scandinavians, Hungarians, Czechs, Poles, Greeks, Italians, Irish, French, English, and German. Each of these nationalities has its own section that describes some of the assimilation experiences for these immigrants in American. This curriculum carefully avoids, in my estimation, any smack of radicalism or critical thought about the immigrant experience. The section on American Blacks or African immigrants is extremely short compared to the others and somewhat odd in that it is embedded in the midst of various European immigrants and separated from other cultures of people of color.

Before the sections specific to cultural groups, there are activities (mostly worksheets with blanks for written answers) that work with vocabulary and definitions. Among the vocabulary words to learn are "alien," "emigrant" and "immigrant," "ethnic," "race," "assimilate," "descendant," and "citizen." This section is followed by other worksheets on topics such as "What Nationality Are You?," "Borrowed Words," and "What's Cooking?"

One example of a worksheet for students in the intermediate grades is called "Italians in America." This used a crossword puzzle with words describing Italian cuisine, and shows a drawing of an Italian male with a long, black mustache and big, white chef hat serving what appears to be spaghetti to two Anglos. The text credits Christopher Columbus with discovering America and notes that "one could say if it were not for the Italians there might not be an America." The flagrant racism here—the belittling and the caricature—makes the page shocking to look at.

Another example of prejudice from this curriculum is in a worksheet entitled "Arab Americans." This worksheet has a map of the Middle East and Northern Africa with the names of the countries "scrambled." Students are asked to unscramble the names of the countries then list them under three geographic categories: Middle East, Arabian Peninsula, and Northern Africa. The two paragraph text states that "The term Arab-American is a cultural one. . . . Most Arab-Americans are third and fourth generation Americans and are *free of the old world customs*. It is difficult for Arabs to enter the United States now because the number allowed is small. This is because not many immigrants had come from Arab-speaking countries before quotas, based on previous numbers of immigrants, were set by the United States Government [my emphasis]." I was struck by the implication that Arab Americans are "free" from the presumably barbarian customs of the "old world." The discussion on immigration restrictions—like other discussions about other cultural groups—is pointedly apolitical.

The statement concerning quotas shows a profound ignorance of American history let alone incredible small-mindedness. The 1924 Immigration Act was based on a quota system, designed to keep non–Western Europeans and non-Protestants (Catholics, Jews, etc.) out of the United States. This curriculum was produced almost 15 years after the abolition of that quota system in 1965. Since 1965, there is no specifically fixed quota or restriction on Arabs or anyone else wishing to come to the United States. The numbers "allowed" are not "small," since under new immigration policy, 20,000 people can immigrate to the United States from any given country per year. Hence, it is difficult to justify the curriculum writers' need to single out Arabs in this regard.

The small amount of attention to African Americans comes in the form of a timeline (from 1492 to 1967) that noted different historical events involving African Americans. Students read the timeline, then use it to answer true or false to a series of questions that simply verify the information in the timeline. Much has been written the last few decades on the annoying and limiting way that race/ethnic groups like African Americans are described by those who were "firsts": the first Black graduating from Harvard, the first Black to sing with the Metropolitan Opera, and so on. Of the 14 events listed in the timeline, 7 of them were describing some of these "firsts."

The ninth curriculum is *Anti-Bias Curriculum: Tools for Empowering Young Children*, by Louise Derman-Sparks of the National Association of the Education of Young Children. This curriculum is one often seen on display at civil rights and multicultural conferences. It has the corner on the market among those few curricula devoted to primary grades because *Anti-Bias Curriculum* begins with activities for 2-year-olds. It makes sense to develop multicultural activities that promote understanding of differences at such a young age as that is when much of our concept formation is occurring and children are already deciding that the White doll is the "good and pretty" doll and the Black doll is the "bad and dirty" one.

The *Anti-Bias Curriculum* begins by justifying the need for such a curriculum and discusses how to create an anti-bias environment focusing on the visual and aesthetic effect and messages in an environment and the toys and educational materials that one selects for children. It also has a section on teachers working with parents on anti-bias issues, which is unusual in a educator's curriculum. Other sections include "Activism with Young Children," "Learning About Racial Differences and Similarities," "Learning about Gender Identity," and "Learning to Resist Stereotyping and Discriminatory Behavior."

In the section on advice and strategies for teachers in the *Anti-Bias Curriculum*, the author provides a three-page piece entitled "Ten Quick Ways to Analyze Children's Books for Sexism and Racism," reprinted from materials produced by the now defunct Council on Interracial Books for Children. The 10 tips for analyzing children's books include methods for looking for stereotypes, looking for tokenism, looking for who is doing what ("Do the illustrations depict minorities in subservient and passive roles or in leadership and action roles? Are males the active "doers" and females the inactive observers?"), and determining the standard for success ("Does it take 'White' behavior standards for a minority person to 'get ahead'?"). Other suggestions include checking out the author's perspective ("No author can be entirely objective. All authors write from a cultural as well as form a personal context.") and trying to consider the effects a particular book might have on a child's self-image. This book focuses on issues of oppression and racism directly, and avoids any overgeneralizations about cultural or ethnic difference. In addition, it also warns to "avoid exaggerating the histories of people of color in the same way European history has been written." This is a common sentiment among teachers I work with—the concern that multicultural education is "going too far."

The ninth curriculum is *My Backyard History Book*, by David Weitzman for the Brown Paper School series, is part of a new breed of K–12 tools to teach the "new social history;" history that focuses on the Everyperson and the contributions to history made by ordinary people rather than just the warring and ruling history made by White Males. Two of my favorite activities to share with teachers are from this curriculum, and both of them share the goal of encouraging children to explore their own family histories. These exercises, I believe, are of upmost importance for multicultural education in relatively homogeneous (e.g., White) areas of the country. Exercises like "Families Come in All Shapes and Sizes" and "A Test!" encourages White students who are largely ignorant of their cultural background to explore issues of "White ethnicity." If students realize that most all White ethnic immigrants experienced discrimination, including their own ancestors, then perhaps it will be harder for them to buy into the beliefs of White supremacy groups.

"Families Come in All Shapes and Sizes," which is age-appropriate for upper elementary school students, presses into service the standard anthropological symbols for kin "trees" and encourages students to draw their own kinship charts using circles for females and triangles for males. There are also spaces to write in known anecdotes or "stories" about particular relatives and their country of origin. "Families Come in All Shapes and Sizes" and "A Test!" are both valuable because they encourage students to talk to their parents, grandparents, and any other relatives or friends of the family to find out cultural and personal details. This richer knowledge of cultural background will hopefully go some distance to dampen the harmful misperception of the monolithic and generic White society.

"A Test!" starts out by stating that this is the students "very own personal history test. See how much you know about your own past!" It is written in a light-hearted and comical style with funny drawings and places to fill in the answers to questions such as "From which country did your father's family come originally? (Unless you are an Native American, they came from somewhere else!)," and "When did your ancestors (on both sides) first come to this country?" Under this question there is a picture of a child with a balloon caption answering "Oh, about 12 o'clock."

My Backyard History Book also has structured activities to begin to get students interested in their own genealogy and to build a family archive. There are many interesting old photographs of many different types of people coming from many different countries throughout the book that serve to encourage the learners to explore their own cultural history.

The eleventh and last curriculum is *Open Minds to Equality: A Sourcebook of Learning Activities to Promote Race, Sex, Class and Age Equity*, by Nancy Schniedewind and Ellen Davidson. *Open Minds to Equality* focuses on the social-psychological and interpersonal dimensions of multicultural education. Topics include learning creative cooperative skills, building trust and open communication between individuals and as part of group process, the "isms" and prejudice and stereotypes, recognizing roadblocks to equal education and empathy and understanding toward others' situations as a way to broaden one's own perspectives.

Open Minds is structured so that a teacher can choose learning activities appropriate for the age of their students within the sequential chapters and with varying subject matter. Overall, the activities in *Open Minds to Equality* focus on the processing of experiences rather than on learning factual information. I was impressed by the length of the list of discussion questions after each activity which the authors claim are crucial for the processing and integrating of the lessons learned into one's psyche and sense of the world. Again, however, there is much talk of "accepting differences" but little of race and ethnic differences, much less discussion of racism or oppression.

DISCUSSION

The major themes and topics found in materials and writings for educators on cultural diversity were: (1) prejudice and discrimination; (2) minority demographics and immigration, with their relationship to multicultural education often left out; (3) images of the "shrinking global village" as a justification for multiculturalism, and (4) assertions that multiculturalism was "righting the record" and has presented a healthier, fuller worldview to students.

A theme in some instructional materials is the concern that multicultural education can replace one biased view with another. The concept of ethnocentricism has come to be generally thought of as relating to Eurocentricism, yet pundits on the Right use it to complain about what we might call reverse ethnocentrism. The concept of "centricism" implies a relationship of power whereby one group has the authority of creating history for all other groups. There is currently a belief in the United States that "reverse" discrimination is even worse than discrimination itself. This idea of "reverse" discrimination—applied to the notion that the canon needs to be changed from a Eurocentric perspective to a more inclusive one—is what I call *reverse ethnocentrism*. Therefore it is odd to cast Afrocentrism as a movement legitimized by social power. This is similar to the thinking involved in claims of "reverse discrimination."

The ten curriculum packages I reviewed were all generally favorable toward multicultural education, although some were more favorable than others. *America's Civil Rights Movement* from Klanwatch, *Fair Play in the Gym*, the *Anti-Bias Curriculum*, and *Open Minds to Equality* all presented strong social justifications and historical background in making the case for the need of that particular curriculum. Other curricula launched right in to activities and suggested lesson plans without background or justification. An example of this type is *The Culture Puzzle*. This curriculum focuses on English as a Second Language (ESL), so perhaps the authors felt explanation and historical background were not necessary since ESL teachers would already know the importance of multicultural education. Another example of this type is *My Backyard History Book*, whose excellent exercises for classroom use seem to beg for a context in which reasons are given why this is important and useful, what effect such self-examination and cultural examination has on child development, and so on.

Still others focused extensively on a criticism of how multicultural education is practiced currently and then suggested new approaches. *The United States: A Cultural Mosaic* spends almost as much time criticizing current approaches focusing on "food, fun, and festival" as it does providing alternatives. This too, however, has a place, particularly for those teachers who have been using multicultural approaches and wish to evaluate their classroom teaching and learning. However, this curriculum does present some of the best activities to use with students to increase cultural awareness and sensitivity.

The two curricula on *America's Women of Color* symbolized precisely that for which other curricula (like *A Cultural Mosaic*) criticized multicultural education: overgeneralization and a teaching *of* the stereotypes instead of teaching to break down the stereotypes. These curricula made repeated blanket statements about how "Black women are . . ." and "Asian women are . . ." Indeed, the goal of many of the exercises simply seemed to be to confirm stereotypes.

The curriculum *Americans All* is also not entirely favorable to multicultural education, or at least that part of multicultural education concerned with celebrating cultural differences. Instead, histories of White ethnics and racial minority groups are given with an eye toward celebrating their amalgamation into all-purpose Americans. In addition, this curriculum has a share of insults, such as saying with some relief that modern Arab Americans are "free of the old world customs." To be fair, *Americans All* was the oldest curriculum of all of the 10 I reviewed, published in 1978. Reading it makes me realize how far multicultural education has come just in the last decade.

CONCLUSION

Overall, what is most striking is how the curriculums largely avoided centering directly on any of the structural dimensions of power related to the facts of oppression and prejudice. The direct dealing with issues of racism and systemic oppression is avoided. This avoidance shows how difficult it is for many people—educators included—to handle the emotionally and politically laden issues of race in a school setting and the desire to confront race issues with watered-down "feel-good" curriculum that focuses on "everybody getting along" and "valuing differences" and "celebrating diversity." Instructional materials on cultural diversity are mostly generalized and stripped of most the most profound political and social significance. Class issues are noticeably absent from any discussions or portrayal of cultural diversity in this curricula. Although low in incidence, it is disturbing that extreme stereotyping does exist in contemporary materials that the well-meaning but uninformed classroom teacher has to use.

The marketing of materials on cultural diversity is a "hot" field right now, particularly those designed for primary grade teachers. With the increasing commodification of cultural diversity materials, educators need to be aware that not all will be accurate or appropriate. Having reviewed such materials, I cannot underestimate the importance of sharing cultural diversity writings and instructional materials with individuals of the cultural or ethnic group specified and ask them to critique such materials for accuracy and appropriateness.

CHAPTER 20

Representing Arabs: Reliance on the Past

Greta D. Little

In 1984 Jack G. Shaheen published *The TV Arab*, documenting the negative dehumanizing stereotype that dominated American television programming of the 1970s and 1980s. He argued that while the civil rights movement of the 1960s had helped to create more even-handed television treatment of African Americans and other ethnic minorities, the treatment of Arabs remained tainted by inaccurate myths and stereotypes. The media had not extended a second look to Arabs, who continued to be portrayed as wealthy, hedonistic princes; warlike, anti-American fanatics; or barbaric and repressive polygamists engaged in White slavery. The film industry followed suit with "depictions of Arabs as Muslims, fabulously wealthy, barbaric, uncultured, backward, terrorists, murderers, oil sheiks, Bedouins, desert dwellers, and sex maniacs with harems and a penchant for Western women" (Hashem, 1995, p. 156).

We are still waiting for the second, objective look at Arabs. The accepted stereotype persists. News magazines report "attacks, crises, invasions, kidnappings, killings, peace treaties, and wars (Hashem, 1995, p. 154). The predominant picture is that of the fanatical terrorists, driven by maniacal devotion to irrational causes. That image is underwritten by U.S. State Department profiles to protect American diplomats and airline passengers. The immediate aftermath of the Oklahoma City bombing, in fact, underscored the extent to which that stereotype has been embraced. The first assumption was that Arab terrorists were responsible. Even when it became clear that the terrorists were homegrown, suspicions were not dispelled. Demonized images of the Arab pervade the public media—television, movies, newspapers, magazines, and the Internet.

Books convey similar messages about Arabs and the Arab world. Such stereotypes are prevalent in books for children. Impressions formed in early childhood, the result of what Robert Schrag calls "first story" (cited in Schrag & Javidi, 1995, p. 214), "become unchallenged building blocks for subsequent epistemological assumptions" (p. 217). Because of their comparative lack of experience, children cannot be expected to dispute the stereotypes they encounter. The children accept these stereotypes from those early first stories as fact even when later faced with counterevidence. In this context, authors and publishers of children's books are especially culpable for the widespread representation of Arabs as unfathomable "other"—unfriendly, incompetent, and inferior—often dishonest, irrational, and violent. Consequently, the primary focus of this essay will be books—both fiction and nonfiction—written for children and young people that contain negative representations of Arabs.

The impact on children was one of the reasons Shaheen chose to examine stereotypical portrayals of Arabs on television: " [Children] are quickly captivated by its images and quickly absorb the notions of life that the medium serves up for better or worse" (p. 21). The examples he cites are taken from special programs for children (animated cartoons, *Hardy Boys Electric Company*, etc.) as well as more general family programs (*Fantasy Island, Bionic Woman, Hart to Hart*, and others). He concludes: "Ask a child to define Arab. The response will best summarize the problems. . . . To a child the world is simple, not complex. Good versus Evil. Superman versus Arabs" (p. 38). Adult programs, especially news programs and documentaries, reinforce this simplistic depiction. Although Shaheen focuses the major part of his book on television, he neither ignores nor absolves the other media. He quotes Helen Loukas, compiler of a 1977 U.S. Civil Rights Commission report on women and minorities on television. Spreading the responsibility to other media as well as television, Loukas asserts that stereotypes diminish our ability to deal realistically with other human beings: "At an early age we get a germ of an idea of what people are like. That idea exists for a long periods of time and it can become so basic, so deeply felt, that it eventually becomes accepted as truth" (pp. 114–115). Fighting this "cultural assassination" (p. 115) requires an examination of the origins of theses stereotypes.

In his *Orientalism*, Edward Said (1978) examines how writers though the ages have approached the Orient (and specifically, the Arab world) and argues that the very act of representing, speaking for another, is divorced from reality and truth. Further, he claims that these representations are more concerned with Western culture and audience than with the Orient itself:

I believe it needs to made clear about cultural discourse and exchange within a culture that what is commonly circulated by it is not "truth" but representations. . . . The value, efficacy, strength, apparent veracity of a written statement about the Orient therefore relies very little, and cannot instrumentally depend, on the Orient as such. (p. 21)

Thus the view of Eastern culture is constructed by Western observers and translated by them to Western readers. Further, Said argues that past representations continue to shape the view that is found in most contemporary studies of the East. The region remains enigmatic, in need of "Western attention, reconstruction, even redemption" (p. 206). Our stereotypes have evolved out of a tradition in which Arabs are seen as an undifferentiated group, set in opposition to "us" in the West, and consequently inferior.

The traditional picture of the Orient found in children's books is circumscribed by Western views and values. In the nineteenth century, most of the literature depicting Arabs and the Arab world was to be found in versions of *Arabian Nights* or books concerning history, travel, or religion. Political correctness was unheard of; the cultural superiority of Western civilization was an accepted reality; and Christian hegemony was unchallenged. Children's books reflected these values.

The imaginative tales of the *Arabian Nights* were seen as indicative of Eastern life. In his preface to an 1878 edition, Joseph von Hammer-Purgstall attributes the popularity of *Arabian Nights* to

the expression of the genius of the East, which breathes throughout this inimitable work, and to the faithful picture it offers of the manners and customs of the Arabs. Here we find the truest representation of the mind, the character, the civil life and domestic habits of a people once powerful enough to carry its civilization and its conquests into three of the great divisions of the globe. These tales exhibit to us in his own light the Arab under the tent in the desert, and at the court of caliph; in his commercial relations, and amid the wandering caravan; in the usual intercourse of society, and in the seclusion of the harem. (Dulcken, p. v)

Thus the exotic, sensual and superstitious tenets of Orientalism became key components of every child's perception of the Arab world. In the twentieth century, some still see the tales as aids to understanding. Amabel Williams-Ellis, whose version of *Arabian Nights* appeared in 1957, thought they should be revised somewhat to meet current tastes, but she believed the stories could help readers come to understand "what members of the Moslem brotherhood feel about the dominance of 'unbelievers'" (pp. 332–333). And that they could experience "vicariously . . . the power of a variety of absolute and highly unreliable Eastern monarchs"

(p. 333). No such claims have been made for Disney's very popular movie version of *Aladdin,* however. It has been soundly criticized for its Western perspective and stereotypical Arab villains.

Travel books for both adults and children form the basis for most of the early published images of the Arab. The most common narrative technique for establishing authority in children's books is to have a young male tell or write to his family about his observations and personal experiences as he traveled through North Africa, Egypt, the Holy Lands, and occasionally in Turkey, Persia, or the Arabian peninsula. Like the nonfiction accounts from which these books for children were drawn, authors give scant attention to consistent or accurate designations of ethnicity or nationality. The natives are referred to as Arabs, Bedouins, Berbers, Moors, Turks, Mohammedans. To these early authors, it scarcely mattered what people called themselves; they shared the same features, character, and customs. And they were different from "us."

In their representations, authors repeated again and again these characteristics throughout the literature both for adults and children. Each repetition became support for the validity of the generalization. As Said (1978) pointed out, truth was less relevant than Western perceptions and beliefs. Whether true or false, these constructed realities became received knowledge. They fall into roughly five patterns. Each is demonstrated below with typical examples.

1. *Arabs are dirty and lazy.* First and foremost, Arabs were different—"The people are as strange as the animals" (Carpenter, 1905, p. 17). When Alfred Campbell looked at Cairo, "he could see nothing but filthy, miserable streets, houses with shattered windows, rooms covered with cobwebs at the top, and filth of every kind below" (Hofland, 1826, p. 31). An adult traveler claimed Egyptians are "a very indolent people who delight in sitting still and hearing tales; indeed . . . more fit for a quiet, than an active life" (*World Displayed,* 13, 1760–61, p. 17). They are "an ill-looking people. . . . They are very dirty and slovenly" (*World Displayed,* 13, 1760–61, p. 21). Another generalized, "Arabs of Africa are dark from continual exposure to the sun, as well as from want of personal cleanliness" (Aspin, 1827, p. 267). Experienced hands warned newcomers, "Arabs are a lazy race of people; even Yusuf, who tries hard to do right, likes better to sit and suck sugar cane than to work" (Hunt, 1880, p. 228).

2. *Arabs are ignorant, superstitious and silly.* Although travelers writing of the East acknowledged long-past achievements, they asserted that "the knowledge of medicine, of philosophy and the mathematics . . . are now so lost that there are scarcely any traces of them remaining" (*World Displayed,* 18, 1760–61, pp. 53–54). Arabs are said to have

no interest in education, having lost the scientific knowledge they once had (Mitchell, 1840, p. 424). A school reader includes a selection on Moors declares that they are "ignorant of any pleasure that is derived from the exercise of the intelligence," that they despise knowledge while accepting "the most puerile superstitions" (Rupert, 1894, pp. 340–341). In one account for young people, the parents say of Egyptians: "They are a very childish set of people . . . and how superstitious they are! what absurd tales they believe! what charms they wear!" (Hunt, 1880, p. 109). On hearing the story of Mohammed's going to paradise, two boys visiting Jerusalem immediately express their disbelief. When asked why, the reply is, "Because it is not reasonable" (Eddy, 1868, p. 83). Islam is presented as a false religion, nothing more than superstition.

3. *Arabs are irrational, cruel, and violent.* A late-19th-century reader proclaims the character of the moors: "A race of vipers and foxes—false, pusillanimous, cringing to the powerful, insolent to the weak, gnawed by avarice, devoured by egotism and burning with the basest passion of which the human heart is capable" (Rupert, 1894, p. 340). A well-traveled, young protagonist says, "Thieving, lying and cheating in bargains are vices so common amongst this people, that they may be said to be almost universal" (Wakefield, 1814, p. 108). The explanation for an early-19th-century board game also tell readers of the dangers. At one landing a caravan is attacked by Arabs, and the book advises, "Plundering Arabs cannot resist the temptation, but, . . . attacking the straggling parties of the cavalcade, carry off vast quantities of their treasures." The explanation continues telling of a 1757 ambush in which "these barbarous Arabs attacked no less than 60,000 pilgrims; many were destroyed by the sword, the women reduced to slavery, and immense riches lost" (*An Explanation*, 1822, pp. 54–55).

4. *Arabs mistreat women.* Alfred Campbell's father explains the state of women to him: A woman is considered inferior to a man, "her judgment, wishes, and feelings are never consulted, and even in cases where she is treated with indulgence and distinction, it is on account of her relationship to a man, never from a sense of individual merit" (Hofland, 1825, p. 45). His friend later asserts they are "mere beasts of burden; they . . . bring the water and wood, cook, and in short do all the drudgery; whilst the men sit down and smoke the whole day" (Hofland, 1825, p. 173). The Clifford family reaches a similar conclusion: "They are made perfect drudges to their husbands: . . . must walk behind their liege lords . . . and if there is any burden to be carried, the woman is always the one on whose shoulders it is placed" (Hunt, 1880, pp. 124–125). Moorish women are said to be "not infrequently bought and sold like slaves" and "immured in the harems" (Aspin, 1827, p. 266). Women are portrayed as having a very low place in society; their

"lives are narrow, loveless, full of intrigue and deceit" (Hume-Griffith, n.d., p. 155).

5. *Arabs hate Christians and engage in the slave trade.* A geography textbook from 1810 asserts, "Nothing can be more vile to Muslims than Christians" (Parish, p. 337). One story tells of a man having to drink from cow trough because Moors would not drink after a Christian (Taylor, 1821, p. 38). These books and others create and feed Western fears: "Christians of the town live in a state of fear and horror; for they are always afraid lest, when the Mohammedans become excited and furious, they will rise and massacre them" (Hume-Griffith, n.d., p. 125). When he returns to the East, a now-experienced Alfred warns his companion: "The land . . . to which we hasten will place us decidedly amongst enemies to our faith, and therefore despisers of our persons" (Hofland, 1826, pp. 18–19). Arthur Middleton of *The Traveller in Africa* shares Alfred's concerns, writing to his brothers and sisters, "The Moors are Mahometans, are bigoted to their own faith, and regard those of a different religion, Christians especially, with detestation and contempt" (Wakefield, 1814, p. 8). Alfred is later taken enslaved until he is freed by a sultan fond of the British. Particularly books about Barbary pirates include accounts of foreign vessels plundered, taken to Algiers, Tripoli, or Tunis "where they were condemned as prizes and their crews sold into slavery" (Knox, 1893, p. 67). Countries are ruled by "cruel despots, [who are the] most ruthless persecutors of the Christians and terrible slave-owners" (Cobb, 1868, p. 239). "The Algerines . . . are a race of pirates and love to be at war with all the weaker nations, to capture their ships, and make slaves of all the people" (Taylor, 1821, p. 9).

These negative representations of Arabs have persisted. Fiction books have continued to tell of adventures entailing violent encounters with ferocious, greedy pirates or slavers: "They surveyed us as if we were cows or pigs. . . . [S]lave-drivers with their whips . . . made life well nigh unbearable" (Kauffman, 1929, p. 135). Even stories that sympathetic Arab characters perpetuate the stereotypes established earlier. In *The Lance of Kanana*, a Bedouin boy is unwilling to accept the ways of his people—"to drop all menial labor" and live "by a warfare that was simply murder and robbery" (French, 1932, pp. 14–15). Textbooks and readers also maintained the picture. Bedouins are described as unfriendly, gypsy-like bands of robbers who "live a lazy life with their goats and camels and dogs" (Mirick, 1918, pp. 61–62). There were fewer direct mentions of Christianity, but the area was seen as unfriendly to Westerners: "The Arabs do not welcome visitors to mysterious Arabia" (Smith, 1933, p. 26). Islam, still referred to as "Mohammedanism," was contrasted to Christianity as a "religion of war rather than a religion of peace" (Rogers, Adams, & Brown, 1936, p. 205).

The myths and stereotypes found in television in the 1970s by Shaheen (1984), in the news media by Hashem (1995), and in films by Fuller (1995) differ only slightly from those identified above. The importance of oil in the modern world has reversed the image of the Arab as poor. Nevertheless, not all Arab lands are rich in oil and poverty persists. Alongside the wealthy prince stands a ragged, dirty peasant whose life may make less interesting television fare, but continues to be prominent in books for children. Writers charge Arabs of lacking ambition and repeatedly show the men gathered in cafes smoking their waterpipes. Arab adults are often portrayed as less resourceful and less intelligent than their children (who have profited from contact with the West). Presentations and representations of Islam as a religion reduce it to rote recitation and unfounded superstition. The violence and irrationality are now centered in acts of terrorism. Muslim women, especially those in the Arab world, are depicted as victims of neglect or exploitation with no meaningful role in life. Arab hatred for Christians is now a more general antipathy to the West, targeting Israel and its allies especially. They no longer trade in slaves; they now deal in hostages. Yet for the most part, studies of American perceptions of Arabs turn up remarkably similar results. They are seen as an uniformly anti-Christian, cunning, unfriendly, warlike (Fuller, 1995; Nasir, 1979; Shaheen, 1984; Suleiman, 1989). Even when presented with evidence that contradicts prior beliefs, the overall impressions persevere. Arabs can be both filthy rich and filthy poor; they can be cowards and fanatical fighters at the same time.

Where other studies reveal the inadequacy of prevailing Arab stereotypes, my purpose is to give historical context to these images, to show that they are as deeply ingrained in Western teachings as mistrust of the West is a part of the typical Arab worldview. The images I discuss have been updated, dressed in the fashion of the time, directed at children, yet deliver the same negative message. Two aspects of that vision are directly relevant to current events—Arab hatred for the West, especially Israel, and their fanatical violence.

In "The Children of Hagar and Sarah," Rita Kissen (1991) focused her attention on the picture of Palestinians in books for young people. She found that "juvenile readers have absorbed a version of the story that recapitulates in modern dress the myth of Isaac and Ishmael, reinforced by American attitudes toward people of color and non-Western cultures. Both in the media and the classroom, American children have been presented with an image of Arabs and Palestinians as stupid and lazy at best, or terrorists and rapists at worst" (1991, p. 112). In the books she examined, Arabs were sometimes good, often bad, but "always subordinate and inferior to their European cousins" (p. 112). Kissen cites a number of books that feature cross-cultural friendships between Palestinians and Israelis, especially before the 1967 war. These friendships foreshadow the ultimate possibility of peace in the area. Kissen, however, points out that these relationships operate on Israeli terms and affirm Western values. Furthermore, even in books with examples of successful coexistence, Arabs are often depicted "as brutal terrorists (in contrast to the human and 'rational' Israelis)" (p. 116).

Arab response to Zionism is crucial to Lynne Reid Banks's two novels set in Israel 25 years apart. The first book, *One More River* (1973), tells the story of a young Canadian immigrant who settles on a kibbutz across the river from a small village in Jordan. As Lesley adjusts to her new life as an Israeli, she makes contact with Mustapha, a young Palestinian from the village. Although their interaction is limited, they trust one another and through them hope for eventual peace seems possible; however, the force of political division is too strong:

> It came down to him and her. If they could not make peace then . . .
> "But you wouldn't kill me?"
> "I don't know," he said. "Perhaps. If I fight your village and you are killed, I am sorry. But you are just one person. I am just one person. We are not important." (1973, p. 235)

After a chance encounter, Lesley feels "a hollow sense of loss. It was more than the loss of a friend, or the exchange of a friend for an enemy. It was something like the loss of hope" (p. 236). In the final pages, however, Banks brings back that hope, when Mustapha states that he does indeed believe that he and Lesley are the two most important people in the world.

In the sequel, *Broken Bridge* (Banks, 1994), 25 years later, Lesley's daughter, Nili, and her nephew have been the target of a senseless Palestinian attack on the streets of Jerusalem. The nephew is killed, but Nili is mysteriously spared by one of the terrorists. As she and her extended family try to comprehend what happened to her and to accept her decision not to identify the man who spared her, readers learn more about the complexities of political issues dividing Israelis and Palestinians. This book ends with Mustapha's death. The second book differs significantly from the first in its portrayal of the situation. The Israelis no longer share a utopian picture of the future on the kibbutz. Their soldiers have committed their own atrocities. Although Banks tries to give readers a better sense of the Arab perspective, she accomplishes this by having some Israeli characters project themselves into the Palestinian situation and comment on it. The Arab characters themselves are not rounded and are developed only in connection with the murder and its aftermath. They live in poverty and filth, kill without provocation, and betray their own families. Their commitment to the liberation movement is unquestioning and absolute. Mustapha and his nephew are very like their forefathers in the books of the 19th century. Banks's rhetoric, however, is more subtle, yet the patterns of representation are remarkably similar to those found in earlier writing. For example, where earlier books discoursed at length on the status and treatment of women, Banks conveys the message by briefly revealing that Mustapha's father has abandoned his wife and young daughters at the outbreak of war in 1967.

The plot device of terrorist action is not uncommon in young adult fiction. A number set in the Middle East have appeared in recent years. Some feature well-meaning protagonists who are lost in the swirl of events around them. *Call Back Yesterday* (Forman, 1984) is a story of nuclear disaster brought about by Saudi terrorists who attack the U.S. embassy and take all personnel hostage. Once again there is a personal relationship established between the young people, Cindy and Salim. Salim and the other Arabs fit the stereotype. Cindy's father says of the Saudis: "A bigger problem is an aversion to physical toil. I'm not talking about laziness, but a religious conviction that manual labor is demeaning" (p. 52). Salim's response after the rebels execute one of the Americans is "We Arabs, our hearts do the work of our brains" (p. 128). The Bedouin National Guard is described as sinister, and the opposition are fanatics opposed to Western reforms. Women are veiled and sequestered. Salim rejects the philosophy of his rebel colleagues and ultimately sacrifices himself to save Cindy. But again the forces of world politics and national pride are too strong; world conflict is the outcome.

Even books that are relatively kind to Arab characters accept the wisdom of the 19th century and portray Arabs as unable to solve their own problems without the assistance of Western civilization. *Captives in a Foreign Land* (Rardin, 1984) is a hostage tale set in North Africa. Six American children are being held by a group of Arabs seeking to promote nuclear disarmament. During the course of their captivity, the children learn about their captors, Islam, and about themselves. The Arab characters are more developed as individuals than is usually found in the genre, and the result is an unusually sympathetic portrait of the Arab. However, power and authority continue to rest with the West. The terrorists themselves accept Western hegemony; their only goal is to influence U.S. nuclear policy.

The United States has taken the place of Christianity and the colonial powers as guardian and guide to Arab peoples and states. In earlier books, travelers saw the absence of Christianity as responsible for their complaints. On their arrival back in Europe, Alfred Campbell and his companion congratulate themselves that they come from a Christian country where good can exist. (Hofland, 1826, p. 205). Poverty and lack of development are attributed to religion; improvements are the result of contact with the West. Carpenter's reader, *Africa,* asserts that Algeria is "prospering under the protection of the French . . . advancing in civilization and wealth" (1905, p. 39). He goes on to remark: "We . . . cannot help contrasting the excellent condition of Algeria under the French with the barbarism of Morocco as ruled by the Sultan" (p. 47). Agricultural productivity is tied to the influence of colonial powers, whose abilities are so great that "even the Sahara desert may one day be fertile and productive" (Willard, 1914, p. 68). In modern books, Western education and technology provide the basis of prospects for peace between Palestinians and Israelis and for economic advancement elsewhere.

These neocolonialist attitudes in the West inhibit our ability to move beyond stereotypical perceptions of the past. The images of Arabs in children's books are symptomatic of the problem and also contribute to its perpetuation. Our children read books that convey images conceived during the colonial expansions of the 19th century. Those images now wear subtler, more fashionable dress, but they nonetheless promote the same fears and apprehensions.

REFERENCES

Aspin, J. (1827). *Cosmorama: A view of the costumes and peculiarities of all nations.* London: John Harris.

Banks, L. R. (1973). *One more river.* New York: Avon Books.

Banks, L. R. (1994). *Broken bridge.* New York: Avon Books.

Carpenter, F. G. (1905). *Africa.* New York: American Book Co.

Cobb, J. (1868). A peep at Algeria and the Arabs. *Chatterbox, 24,* 186–187.

Dulcken, H. W. (1878). *Dalziels' illustrated Arabian nights' entertainments.* London: Ward, Lock, & Co.

Eddy, D. C. (1868). *Walter's tour in the East.* New York: Thomas Y. Crowell & Co.

An explanation of, or key to, the noble game of the elephant and castle; or, travelling in Asia. (1822). London: William Darton.

Forman. J. D. (1981). *Call back yesterday.* New York: Scribner's Sons.

French, H. W. (1932). *The lance of Kanana.* New York: Junior Literary Guild.

Fuller, L. K. (1995). Hollywood holding us hostage: Or, why are terrorists in the movies Middle Easterners? In Y. R. Kamalipour (Ed.), *The U.S. media and the Middle East: Image and perception* (pp. 151–162). Westport, CT: Greenwood Press, pp. 187–197.

Hashem, M. (1995). Coverage of Arabs in two leading U.S. newsmagazines: *Time* and *Newsweek*. In Y. R. Kamalipour (ed.). *The U.S. media and the Middle East: Image and perception,* pp. 151–162. Westport, CT: Greenwood Press.

Hofland, Mrs. B. (1825). *Alfred Campbell, the young pilgrim.* London: John Harris.

Hofland, Mrs. B. (1826). *The young pilgrim, or Alfred Campbell's return to the East.* London: John Harris.

Hume-Griffith, M. E. (Ed.). *Tales of the Arabs.* London: The Religious Tract Society.

Hunt, S. K. (1880). *On the Nile: A story of family and adventure in the land of Egypt.* London: T. Nelson & Sons.

Kauffman, R. W. (1929). *Barbary Bo: A story of the Barbary pirates.* New York: Hampton Publishing.

Kissen, R. (1991). The children of Hagar and Sarah. *Children's Literature in Education, 22,* 111–119.

Knox, T. W. (1893). *John Boyd's adventures: Merchant sailor, man-of-war's-man, privateersman, pirate, and Algerine slave.* London: Sampson, Low Marston & Company.

Mirick, G. A. (1918). *Home life around the world.* Boston: Houghton Mifflin.

Mitchell, S. A. (1840). *Geographical reader: A system of modern geography.* Philadelphia: Thomas, Cowperthwait & Co.

Nasir, S. J. (1979). *The Arabs and the English* (2nd ed.). London: Longman.

Parish, E. (1810). *A new system of modern geography.* Newburyport, MA: Thomas & Whipple.

Rardin, S. L. (1984). *Captives in a foreign land.* Boston: Houghton Mifflin.

Rogers, L., Adams, F., & Brown, B. (1936). *Story of nations.* New York: Henry Holt & Co.

Rupert, W. (1894). *A geographical reader, or pen-pictures in geography.* Boston: Leach, Shewell, & Sanborn.

Said, E. (1978). *Orientalism.* New York: Vintage Books.

Schrag, R. L., & Javidi. M. N. (1995). Through a glass darkly: American media images of Middle Eastern cultures and their potential impact on young children." In Y. R. Kamalipour (Ed.), *The U.S. Media and the Middle East: Image and perception* (pp. 212–221). Westport, CT: Greenwood Press.

Shaheen, J. G. (1984). *The TV Arab.* Bowling Green, OH: Bowling Green State University Press.

Smith, J. R. (1933). *Foreign lands and peoples.* Philadelphia: John C. Winston.

Suleiman, M. (1989). America and the Arabs: Negative images and the feasibility of dialogue. *Arab Studies Quarterly, 11,* 251–269.

Taylor, I. (1821). *Scenes all the world over, for the amusement and instruction of little tarry-at-home travellers. Vol. II, Africa and America.* London: Harris & Son.

Wakefield, P. (1814). *The traveller in Africa.* London: Darton, Harvey & Darton.

Willard, M. F. (1914). *Along Mediterranean shores*. Boston: Silver, Burdett & Co.

Williams-Ellis, A. (1957). *The Arabian nights*. London: Blackie.

The world displayed; or, a curious collection of voyages and travels, selected from the writers of all nations. Vol. 20 (1760–61). London: J. Newbery.

CHAPTER 21

Using C-SPAN to Evaluate Sensitivity Toward Cultural Diversity: The Case of Ross Perot's 1992 Presidential Campaign

Jim Schnell

This report will describe how C-SPAN (Cable-Satellite Public Affairs Network) has been used to evaluate a public figure's sensitivity toward cultural diversity. Such analysis highlights findings from the study, outlines a method for the study, and illustrates how other public figures can be studied using this method. That is, even though Ross Perot is the focus of this report, other prominent individuals, who have periodically been broadcast on C-SPAN, can also be analyzed.

Ross Perot, a Texas businessman, appeared on the Larry King Show in the spring of 1992 and indicated an interest in being president of the United States. During the next 6 months he rose from relative obscurity and received 19% of the popular vote in the 1992 presidential election. Perot's primary strength was his emphasis on the U.S. economy and his intention to promote job growth. A weakness for Perot was the public perception that he was insensitive to diversity issues in America. A logical approach for studying this perceived insensitivity is to analyze Perot's public presentations.

It is hypothesized that Perot's presentations will contain statements conveying insensitivity toward diversity issues. The formulation of this hypothesis is based primarily on newspaper reports of Perot's June 11, 1992 speech to the NAACP (National Association for the Advancement of Colored People) convention. The *Washington Post* reported "Perot drew a cool reception from the group when he referred to Blacks as 'you people' and 'your people'" (*Washington Post*, July 12, 1992). The *Chicago Tribune* referred to Perot's use of "'you people' and 'your people' as a gaffe in his speech that offended some in the audience as racially insensitive" (*Chicago Tribune*, July 12, 1992).

"'The expressions are something you do not use with African Americans. Never,' said Lacy Steele . . . a member of the NAACP's national board from Washington D.C. . . . Many African Americans find the words offensive when coming from a White speaker" (*Chicago Tribune*, July 12, 1992). Perot's use of "you people" and "your people," as reported by the *Washington Post*, is included in the statement "I don't have to tell you who gets hurt when this sort of thing [economic crunch] happens—you people do. Your people do" (*Washington Post*, 1992). This speech is significant in that Perot withdrew from the presidential race within 5 days of his NAACP speech, perhaps partially due to negative press reports on the NAACP speech.

The method for this inquiry is analysis of videotapes of Perot's appearances. The videotapes, recorded by C-SPAN, were obtained from the Public Affairs Video Archives (located at Purdue University). The archives provided an index listing of all Perot's presentations delivered during the presidential campaign period (January–November 1992) that were covered by C-SPAN. A total of 55 presentations are available on videotape. Fourteen of these videotapes that are representative of Perot's presentations (in content, context, and formats) were selected for analysis. The content and context of his speeches were studied to see if there is evidence to support the claim made by Perot critics that Perot is insensitive toward diversity issues.

The following is a list of the selected videotapes. Title, date, format, and length are listed for each presentation.

1. Life & Career of Ross Perot (3/18/92)
   American Profile Interview (1:03)

2. Perot Candidacy: American Newspaper Publishers Association (5/5/92)
   Speech (:34)

3. University of Oklahoma Commencement Address (5/9/92)
   Speech (:21)

4. Perot Campaign Speech: NAACP Annual Convention (7/11/92)
   Speech (:35)

5. Perot Withdrawal (7/16/92)
   News Conference (:20)

6. Perot Campaign Commercial (10/6/92)
   Broadcast (:29)

7. Presidential Candidates Debate (10/11/92)
   Debate (1:36)

8. Presidential Candidates Debate (10/15/92)
   Debate (1:32)

9. Perot Campaign Commercial (10/15/92)
   Broadcast (:30)

10. Presidential Candidates Debate (10/19/92)
    Debate (1:38)

11. Perot Campaign Commercial (10/20/92)
    Speech (:31)

12. Perot Campaign Commercial (10/26/92)
    Broadcast (:31)

13. Perot Campaign Commercial (10/28/92)
    Political Event (:28)

14. Perot Campaign Commercial (10/30/92)
    Broadcast (:29)

There is no widely accepted paradigm for analyzing a speaker's sensitivity toward diversity issues, so this inquiry poses unique challenges. What connotes sensitivity? What connotes insensitivity? Use of C-SPAN tapes to study the aforementioned subject is particularly relevant in that the C-SPAN index helps define the sample to be studied, and the tapes provide literal verbal meanings, indirect nonverbal meanings, and context for speeches. Transcripts provide literal statements, but the tapes frame the literal statements. Perot was criticized after his July 11, 1992 speech to the NAACP convention, according to the Public Affairs Video Archives index abstract, for his "apparent paternalistic nature" toward minorities. Analysis of this type of criticism rests on *what* is said and of equal importance on *how* it is said.

Data relevant to the research question of this inquiry regarding Perot's sensitivity/insensitivity toward minority issues, was studied by viewing all the aforementioned videotapes. This data includes 10 hours and 37 minutes of videotape. The data clearly disproves the hypothesis of this study (that Perot's presentations would contain statements conveying insensitivity toward diversity issues). Perot's statements consistently convey sensitivity toward diversity issues.

The videotapes were observed for any references to diversity in America. All of Perot's references to diversity, whether be direct statements or indirect responses to questions, reflected sensitivity toward diversity issues. Each of these references (to diversity) will be described to show the consistency in Perot's perspective.

On March 18, 1992, C-SPAN broadcast an American Profile Interview entitled the "Life and Career of Ross Perot" (Perot, 3/18/92). During the interview, Perot mentioned that his father's support of African Americans influenced his perspective and that one of his first philanthropic gifts was to an experimental school for disadvantaged (mainly minority) youth. Interviewer Brian Lamb asked what his response would be if the public, via an electronic town hall, wanted racial segregation rather than integration. Perot responded "It's not constitutional. . . . We're not gonna turn the clock back. Segregating would hurt the economy."

Perot spoke to the American Newspaper Publishers Association on May 5, 1992. During this speech, he stated "If you hate other people I don't want your vote. . . . If you don't mind living in a society where one out of eight women are raped I don't want your vote" (Perot, 5/5/92).

Perot's speech to an NAACP convention on July 11, 1992, contained numerous statements related to diversity in America. "You have made tremendous progress but there's more to be done. . . . You people do, your people do [regarding who is most affected during an economic crunch]. . . . Our diversity is our strength not a weakness. . . . [W]e ought to love one another, at least get along. . . . Divided teams lose, united teams win. . . . If you hate people I don't want your vote. . . . Drugs are devastating you and your people. . . . Our country will not be great until we are all united and equal. . . . I cannot be free until we are all free" (Perot, 7/11/92). He also described how his mother and father raised him to be sensitive to the plight of Blacks and the disadvantaged (Perot, 7/11/92).

During the Presidential Candidates Debate on October 11, 1992, Perot restated many of his views from his NAACP convention speech. Perot stated "We shouldn't appeal to the differences between us. . . . We should love one another. . . . Our diversity is our strength, we've turned it into a weakness. . . . Divided teams lose, united teams win. . . . If you hate people I don't want your vote" (Perot, 10/11/92).

Perot was asked during the October 15, 1992, Presidential Candidates Debate when either political party will have a Black or woman on its ticket. He responded that Colin Powell could be on either party's ticket in 4 years (Perot, 10/15/92).

A reporter asked Perot, "Why aren't women and ethnic minorities better represented in upper levels of government?" during the October 19, 1992 Presidential Candidates Debate. Perot answered the inquiry acknowledging women that have done very well in the computer industry (based on Perot's own business background) and women are part of his team (Perot 10/19/92).

In a Perot Campaign Commercial broadcast October 20, 1992, he again spoke of his philanthropic efforts with the Dunbar School in 1968. The Dunbar School was a school for disadvantaged youth (including Blacks and Hispanics) to help them prepare for the first grade (Perot, 10/20/92).

The only speech containing comments perceived as offensive is the 7/11/92 speech to the NAACP convention. In this speech Perot's referral to the Black audience as "you people" and "your people" was perceived by some to be racially insensitive. However, the NAACP is a self-defined organization comprised of African Americans. To refer to such a group as a distinctive entity, which the organization does with its name and objective, does not substantiate that Perot is insensitive to diversity issues. The aforementioned Perot quotations clearly establish his sensitivity toward American diversity.

Perot continues to be a controversial player in U.S. politics. Scholars will no doubt be defining Perot's future in reference to his past. Findings from a media analysis study, contrasting a person's words against his/her public image, help to reinforce accurate observations and to correct misconceptions. This phenomenon can obviously be studied by analyzing other public figures in a similar manner.

REFERENCES

Chicago Tribune. July 12, 1992, p. 6.

Perot, R. (3/18/92). Life and career of Ross Perot. C-SPAN American profile interview. West Lafayette, IN: Purdue University Public Affairs Video Archives.

Perot, R. (5/5/92). Perot candidacy: American Newspaper Publishers Association. C-SPAN recorded speech. West Lafayette, IN: Purdue University Public Affairs Video Archives.

Perot, R. (7/11/92). Perot campaign speech: NAACP Annual Convention. C-SPAN recorded speech. West Lafayette, IN: Purdue University Public Affairs Video Archives.

Perot, R. (10/11/92). Presidential candidates debate. C-SPAN recorded debate. West Lafayette, IN: Purdue University Public Affairs Video Archives.

Perot, R. (10/15/92). Presidential candidates debate. C-SPAN recorded debate. West Lafayette, IN: Purdue University Public Affairs Video Archives.

Perot, R. (10/19/92). Presidential candidates debate. C-SPAN recorded debate. West Lafayette, IN: Purdue University Public Affairs Video Archives.

Perot, R. (10/20/92). Perot campaign commercial. C-SPAN recorded speech. West Lafayette, IN: Purdue University Public Affairs Video Archives.

Washington Post. July 12, 1992, pp. 1 & A-10.

CHAPTER 22

Distortion of *"Islam"* and *"Muslims"* in American Academic Discourse: Some Observations on the Sociology of Vested Enmity

Bud B. Khleif

During the Gulf War crisis (1990–1991) and thereafter, I took detailed field notes at a number of teach-ins about the Middle East, as well as at colloquia and public lectures that were manned and womanned by American academic "experts" with their audiences. A prevalent theme seemed to dominate, specially during the question-and-answer part of these public occasions—a theme of negativism often rooted in stereotypes and prejudices against the Middle East, its ethnic groups, customs, languages, and the region's predominant religion, Islam. As part of my interest in the sociology of language (see Khleif, 1980a, 1980b, 1982, 1992), I decided to construct a typology of the distortions I had heard and attempt to interpret them within a sociocultural framework.

The purpose of this paper is not merely to present an analysis of the categories of cultural disfigurement regarding a seemingly unknowable "Other," but to advance some hypotheses about the geopolitical interests underlying such stereotypes, their cultivation by the mass media, and their anchoring in certain aspects of American culture itself, a culture that in its postindustrial stage appears to thrive on manufacturing endless enemies (see Kwitny, 1987; Keen, 1991). This is an exploratory study: analysis of data is preceded by some overarching considerations.

ISLAM AND MUSLIMS: THE "ORIENTALIZED OTHER"

What factors seem to nurture and reproduce enmity toward the Middle East? It can be said that American national culture—in the sense of some typical tendencies we associate with it—consists of three general components: (1) European pre-Columbian and colonial culture; (2) frontierism in the New World; and (3) post-1945 American superpowerism.

For more than 800 years, first the Arabs, then the Turks controlled the trade routes between the Far East and Europe, the Eastern Mediterranean being closed off to European expansionism. The Crusades (A.D. 1096–1291) were the first European colonial wars against the people of the region now known as the Middle East, a commercial and religious conflict that has left a hostile legacy in modern Euro-American attitudes toward the region.

In addition, the culture of the United States itself is historically that of a settler-regime (cf. Sontag, 1969, p. 195), that is, imbued with the importance of violence in human affairs (Jacobs et al., 1971, p. xxxv), with dreams of "manifest destiny" (Gossett, 1965, pp. 314–318), with heroes proudly termed "Indian fighters" (for example, Andrew Jackson): No wonder the rest of the world may at times be regarded by some Americans as "Indian territory" (a label actually heard during the Gulf War).

In 1945, the United States inherited the imperial mantle of Great Britain, France, the Netherlands, and Belgium, becoming the leader of the "Free World" (Western Europe and other "friendly" allied countries). The post-1989, post–Berlin Wall era, and the post-1991 Gulf War era—that is, after the collapse of the U.S.S.R. and its "satellites" as a bloc capable of defiance and countermeasures—marked the further consolidation of U.S. hegemony into a "New World Order," which means one and only superpower, one and only one political-economic camp, an unprecedented singularity. The United States, even more than before, has recognized the importance of controlling Middle Eastern oil for the benefit particularly of industrially advanced allies, for worldwide strategic planning toward that end, for keeping the price of oil within tolerable bounds (as a form of hidden subsidy to the Western economies), for encouraging the flow of petrodollars into Euro-American corporate and governmental endeavors, for maintaining the political status quo in the region (not democracy—secular, representative, and civic, American style—but, if necessary, making the world safe for medieval monarchs, princelings, sheiks, dictators). It is no wonder that the Persian Gulf, from a global viewpoint, is merely the Gulf-of-Mexico East.

As Habermas (1975) maintains, the modern nation-state has become a decisive corporate actor, influencing markets globally, but facing a problem of legitimation. In mobilization of the populace, such agencies of legitimation as the schools and the mass media are important marketers of ideology, of answers supplied and questions omitted; in short, for control of consciousness (see Khleif, 1986). As Baudillard (1975, 145) has opined, nowadays meanings are *consumed*: "Power consists in the monopoly of the spoken word." It can be said that he who controls the "domain assumptions" of a culture, its interpretive vocabulary, especially through the mass media and through "experts," tends, to some extent, to control the hearts and minds of some segments of the population, to condition them to think about the world in certain preset ways.

What does all of the above mean in relation to Islam and Muslims? It means that both are seen through the thick haze of "orientalism," a Euro-American cultural industry bent on *negation of the other*, on belittling non-Europeans, an industry with an ideology of racism and denigration toward the East, the "Orient" (see Said, 1978). Orientalism is a discourse of exclusion and Eurocentric attitudes in which Islam appears as a "list of deficiencies," a series of gaps (see Turner, 1991; Shohat & Stam, 1994).

Overall, Orientalism in contemporary American academic discourse (of "experts" and audience, and questions and answers) at times takes the form of mild or moderate contempt, derision, dehumanization, demonization, that is, of treating the "Other" as ignorable, punishable, having no right to live ("low life"); in a word, if necessary, a candidate for genocide. This *Indianization* of the world is noticeable in American life (for example, in Robert Bly's poem, "Hatred of Men with Black Hair").

The discourse of derogation belittles the Islamic "other." Now that communism is no longer the enemy of choice, Islam may be a substitute, particularly an Islam that may be associated with *nationalism*, the real enemy of American economic and security interests in the Middle East. Nationalism offers a threat of potential unity in the region, where the Arabs, for example, could get to control their natural resources, using them for their own, not Western, interests. For the past several decades, the Middle East has supplied, and continues to supply, a succession of enemies who are thought to stand in the way of increased Western hegemony, from Nassar of Egypt onwards.

Where the United States and the Middle East meet not only concerns Islam and Muslims but also what may be regarded as the central problem of the region, the Palestine-Israel problem in all its post-1947 facets. Here, global, regional, and domestic considerations become interlinked. Discussion of the Palestine-Israel question in the American media and in American academic circles is often linked with anti-Arab and anti-

Islamic sentiments, vested enmity for Middle Eastern cultures, and news management (Flapan, 1987; Shlaim, 1994).

Another issue at which global U.S. interests, regional happenings outside the United States, and domestic American considerations meet is the treatment of Arab Americans within the United States. The way in which the U.S. government treats a country or countries from which a segment of its population has historically emigrated is mirrored domestically in matters of ethnic bashing or interethnic tension (see Khleif, 1984, 1990). Arab Americans and their heritage are often targets of hostility for the media and politicians (*ADC Times*, 1990–1995).

DISTORTION AND DEROGATION
OF "ISLAM" AND "MUSLIMS"

What do the data show? What have American academic experts and their audience emphasized? Perpetuation of stereotypes and distortions about Islam and Muslims often take the following forms:

The Dichotomy of West versus East

(a) An attitude of arrogance based on a false dichotomy: the so-called "Western" man is, above all, *rational* and *pragmatic*, whereas non-Western man, at times referred to as the "Oriental Mind" is "emotional" and "volatile" (meaning untrustworthy—accusations in American life also hurled at Italians and women among others).

(b) Only one term of the dichotomy of "us and them" is at times mentioned, "the West's respect for human life" (this is usually said with finality, as if it was an heirloom or monopoly). If Islam has supposedly been "spread by the sword," is "the West's respect for human life" spread in brilliant, little, colonial wars by "smart bombs" or "dumb" ones?

(c) Another term of the dichotomy, which when mentioned implies its opposite for speaker and audience, is that Muslims are "irrational," "wild-eyed," "violent," "fanatic," that is, menacing apparitions, capable of inflicting untold harm to society. The speaker, whether student or faculty member, usually forgets he/she lives in a culture with the highest crime rate in the world and the highest ratio of prison inmates, where fanaticism and violence are familiar patterns.

The "Inscrutable East"

(a) Another emphasis in academic discourse is that the Middle East defies understanding. One way to perpetuate such a cliché is for professors who teach history or political science, for example, to resort to a discussion of the Islamic schools of jurisprudence and minute technical differences among them—Hanbalites, Shafiites, what not—matters of no consequence to the average Muslim in his/her daily life, let alone to the average American, who has no reason even to know the difference between Methodists and Baptists! Muslim life has not been frozen at the classical juridical level. This focus only makes Muslims "sound weird," as a young undergraduate once put it.

(b) "Muslims pray five times a day, facing Mecca." How many times do Christians pray, and do they ever face anything when they do so?

(c) "How can people who invented algebra and Arabic numerals be the same as people we see in movies and on TV—very backward?" This statement points to the two separate compartments into which Muslims are put in some students' and faculty members' thinking in the United States.

Sociolingusitic Distortion

A third category of distortion is of a sociolinguistic nature, as outlined below:

(a) "Islam" is mispronounced as "*Izzlem*" (ratherthan "Iss-laam")—as if the speaker had a speech impediment or wanted to convey the message that it doesn't matter how you pronounce any word related to "that religion" because it is not worthy of being taken seriously.

(b) "Islam" is called "Mohammedanism" by some people—not only an inaccuracy, but considered by Muslims to be a religious slur.

(c) "Islam" has recently been called by a doctoral student—in all seriousness—"the Arabic Religion . . . you know what I mean" (sic). Is Protestantism, then, "the English Religion"?

(d) Often academic speakers assert knowingly that "Islam" means "submission." This, of course, may be one of the dictionary definitions, but it is formalistic, and noncommunicative. For speakers of Arabic (whether Christian, Muslim, Druze, or Sephardic Jews), "Islam" simply means "obedience to God," that is, equivalent to "serving the Lord." To translate "Islam" as "submission," particularly in the context of an American culture that glorifies assertiveness, makes "Muslims" appear as submissive. Are Muslims, then, those who submit, while Christians are those who fight?

(e) "They worship their own god, Allah," that is, they have a rather peculiar deity, unrelated to "our" God. The word "Allah" simply means God, the same God of the three Abrahamic faiths: Judaism, Christianity, and Islam. In the interest of accuracy and good will, the word "Allah" should always be rendered in English as "God"; otherwise, should we, then, in an equalizing fashion call the God of the French "Dieu" and of the Germans "Mein Gott"?

(f) Academicians and TV "experts" usually have a fieldday with the word "Jihad," giving it the connotation of primordial menace, a sort of cosmic attack on *Westernhood* (equivalent to "woman-hood" in its implicit call for protectiveness). They usually want it to mean a "holy war" of unsurpassed fanaticism and irrationality, a word with which they could, *tout de suite*, dismiss as unworthy the whole Middle East, if not the whole Islamic world. The word, "jihad," as it is used daily in Arabic, in its full-fledged, overwhelm-ing denotation, means simply "striving," "exertion of effort," "struggle"; it is used in the context of trying to do well in school, in scholarship, in working hard. "Jihad" is also linked with a sense of justice, with the struggle for justice, with efforts to create a moral community. Don't we need an internal "Jihad" (exertion of effort) against the Willie-Hortonizing of American politics?

(g) "They use a battlecry, 'God Is Great' . . ." Actually "*Allahu Akbar,*" a Koranic phrase, is used daily by speakers of Arabic—whether Muslim or Christian. In its daily usage, it connotes surprise, per-plexity, astonishment, adulation, wonder, "Praise be to God." An equivalent English phrase, "In God We Trust," is not an American battlecry, is it?

The Amalgamation of Arab and Muslim

(a) Often, there is confusion in the academic speaker's mind and his/her audience's between "Arabs" and "Muslims" (akin to confusing Americans with Southern Baptists). "Arabs" means Arabic-lan-guage speakers, those of Arab heritage and customs; it does not mean "Muslims." The confusion at times seems to be fostered a bit deliberately, either because the academic lecturer or his/her audi-ence are not being serious enough about the subject to be accurate, or because they do not want to explore the link of Christianity between the Arabs and the West (Christianity was an older religion among the Arabs than Islam; Christian Arabs of the Middle East were Christian centuries before Europeans had been "Christian-ized"—see Trimingham, 1979; Hitti, 1970). When it comes to reli-gious affiliation, those who call themselves "Arab" or "of Arab her-itage" may be Christian, Muslim, Druze, or what is still known in the Middle East and even within Israel itself, as Arabized Jews or

"Yehoud Arab" (see Halsell, 1981, on "Arab Jews"). The confusion between "Arabs" and "Muslims" in American academic discourse is akin to the confusion between "Jews" and "Zionists" in the discussion of the Palestine-Israel problem. Not all Muslims are Arabs, and not all Arabs are Muslim: The largest Islamic country in the world is Indonesia, not an Arab country.

(b) "Arabs come from Saudi Arabia and such sand-dunes as Kuwait, which we liberated" (said by a student—equivalent to saying, "Americans come from Mississippi and Tennessee," or is it "Cape Hatteras" or the "Everglades"?). Actually, Arabs come from Lebanon, Syria, Jordan, Iraq, the Emirates, Qatar, Oman, Yemen, Israel, the West Bank and Gaza, Egypt, Libya, Tunisia, Algeria, Morocco, and outlying regions. There are also Arabic-speaking minorities in Southern Turkey, Western Iran, Western China, North and South America, Australia, and New Zealand. Not all Americans come from Mississippi, Arkansas, or California; by the same token, Arabs come from many countries and regions.

(c) Asked an inquiring student, "Does the holy book, the Koran, always have to be chanted?" The answer is: "Do you always chant your Bible? . . . The answer: You can simply read it, if you wish."

Misleading Terminology

(a) At times, there is a sort of mystification in the title of talks, for example, "Islam: From Revolution to Normalcy," when the bulk of the talk is about Iraq's dictator, his blunders and miscalculations during and after the Gulf crisis. "Islam" in the title of academic lectures is often used to mean the Arab countries of the Middle East (imagine yourself, through substituting new terms, using "Protestantism" to mean Canada and the United States).

(b) "What do you mean the Iranians are not Arabs; of course, they are!"—protested a faculty member to a colleague (that is like saying New Englanders and Quebec Canadians are the same). No, the Iranians, called Persians until the 1920s, and Parthians in Roman times, speak Persian (Farsi): they are Muslims, not Arabs!

(c) "In Lebanon, the Maronite-Moslems are the largest population" (heard during a question-answer, postlecture period). You can call them "Moslem," rather than "Muslim," if you wish, but Maronites are an old, 9th-century Christian sect, Eastern-rite, but now part of the Middle Eastern Christian sects who joined with Rome (called "Uniates"); they certainly are not Muslim, and Muslims certainly are not Maronite!

(d) Lectures on Islam or the Middle East in general, seem to treat Islam or the region as if it were a self-contained entity, not part of global politics or military and economic alliances and interventions. Academic discourse about the Middle East at times treats the United States and Israel as if they were innocent bystanders there! To focus on "Islam and its problems in the modern world" (title of a lecture) in isolation from political and economic trends, is like earlier anthropological studies that focused on preliterate societies as if such societies were never part of, or influenced by, European colonial administrations.

Misrepresentations of the Arabic Language

The Arabic language is sometimes portrayed in academic presentations as "emotional," "flowery," "ornate," "more fit for poetry than 20th-century technology"—the speaker forgetting that prior to the Latin of early modern Europe, Arabic was the *lingua franca* of science, astronomy, math, and medicine from India to the British Isles (see Hayes, 1983). A favorite illustration of what is supposed to indicate the unfitness of Arabic for "rationality" or "communication" is misunderstanding of the stock phrase used universally in vernacular Arabic to start a narrative, an absorbing tale for an audience. The phrase in Arabic is "Kaan, ya ma kaan," which means "the events took place a long, long time ago; lots of things happened then." (The adverbial "ma" in this case means "abundantly" or "galore," denoting the relentless passage of time—compare "of time and tide" in English, in which "tide" is an obsolete word for time, for example, "noontide" does not refer to the tides of the ocean). Those who have a superficial knowledge of classical or spoken Arabic tend to interpret "ma" grammatically as a negative article in "Kaan ya ma Kaan," that is mistakenly as "The events took place, did *not* take place," a clear logical contradiction. In other words, Arabic cannot make up its mind, so to speak, to say anything clearly. The misinterpreted "ma" is another "ma" altogether, requiring different verb endings. Denigration of the language of others, of Arabic in this instance, is similar to denigration of Welsh by the English (see Khleif, 1980b, 34–80).

The Black Beast (or Bête Noir) of Fundamentalism

La pièce de résistance, so-to-speak, in attacking "Islam" and "Muslims," is the word of choice, *fundamentalism*, as in "Islamic fundamentalism." The word is supposed to conjure up unmitigated evil, boundless threat, even worldwide in its scope. To quote an academic speaker: "The Muslim republics of central Asia, part of the former Soviet Union, may become *fundamentalist* and anti-Western, posing a threat to U.S. interests." Academic speakers and "experts," it seems, often forget that the very word itself, "fundamentalism," was originally coined in 1910 to refer to an *American* phenomenon, to single out those opposed to liberal Protestantism (Crim, 1989, 268; cf. Halsell, 1986). But what about American fundamentalism and its political linkage with elections and commercial linkage with electronic evangelism? Isn't there a saying in the Bible about "talking the beam out of thine eye before thou notice the mote in thy brother's"?

Prejudices Against Muslim Women

One of the most noticeable "orientalizations" in American culture, with distinct manifestations in academic culture, is the subject of women, "Islamic" or "Muslim" women. Here the prejudices tend to be plentiful, the ignorance, boundless. Examples of statements that are supposed to be universally true, regardless of social class, degree of urbanization, regional location, historical tradition, dialect, subtlety, or sophistication follow:

(a) "Moslem men eat before their wives and children; wives eat last" (stated by a woman professor as if she had discovered a law of nature). What Muslim households have you been to, Professor? On what continent?

(b) "Muslim women do not shake hands with a man; they don't want bare skin to touch bare skin" (said smilingly by a male lecturer). Very Orthodox women, Muslim or Jewish, do not particularly like to shake hands with men who are not part of their immediate families. By the same token, the Japanese like to bow rather than shake hands. Even some White, Protestant, American women do not like to shake hands at all—for example, Southern women:

> The battle between Southern gentility and modernism continues. . . . In the mid-1980s, as a guest in a governor's mansion in the South, I thoughtlessly extended my hand to a woman guest who laughed nervously and extended her fingertips. Seeing my embarrassment, another woman came over and told me, "I know men and women shake hands in business in the North, but *a properly raised Southern lady* just doesn't shake hands with a strange gentleman." (Hagstrom, *Beyond Reagan*, 1989, 200, emphasis added)

Should we blame Southern women for "not wanting bare skin to touch bare skin"? Or just Muslim women?

(c) "Moslem women are subservient to men; they lead a sheltered life. . . . [T]hey are subordinate . . . victims of patriarchy" (stated by a woman lecturer). Usually, stereotypes and fantasies associated with such statements also include reference to two Western obsessions about Muslims, Arabs, inhabitants of the "Orient": the "veil" and the "harem." The "veil" was originally a Persian and Turkish custom, used by town dwellers: obviously, women today who do agricultural work, or any work in a public place, beyond the home, cannot be veiled. "Harems" are not an integral part of the 20th century; very few Muslim men can afford, or are permitted, to have another wife. Because of the emphasis on the family, on the integrity of the kinship structure, women in the Middle East—for example, Muslim, Christian, Jewish—are among the most competent in the world in managing their households; managing their husbands, children, relatives, and kinship-work. They have enviable autonomy and a sense of security in this regard. Are men and women actually equal in the United States today?

(d) "Islamic women have a reputation of being totally submissive to the men in their lives, whether it be the husband or father. They are treated harshly since they are considered property, really not sharing an equality with men. . . . In Christianity, women are equal to men in the eyes of God" (stated by a female lecturer). Note first of all how "Islamic" in "Islamic women" is used as a code for the Eastern world: Shall we from now on begin to call European women "Christian women"? Obviously, there is an undercurrent of superiority in making "Islamic" the opposite of "Western," and triply so when "Islamic women" are thought to be uniformly "submissive" and "considered property." The enemy, then, has no internal differentiations, no differences whatever linked to social class or region.

(e) Discussion of women, harems, and veils, usually supplies mirth for academic audiences, at times, an undercurrent of "soft porn," almost an expectation of titillation or promise of orgies. For here "orientalism" brings to the fore the construction of women as providers of sensual pleasure, and of men as hyperviolent exploiters of women. Muslims, or Arabs in general, become, then, merely actors in a drama meant essentially for men and women in the United States, the drama of the social construct of American masculinity as the embodiment of violence, and of American femininity as weakness and subordination (see Norton, 1991).

(f) At times, the fantasies about treatment of women in Islamic cultures seem to get out of hand, prompting especially young undergraduates to accuse Muslim societies of being "primitive." But even then, other undergraduates rush to object to such sweeping accusations and to say, among other things, that such societies have no "serial killers," no attacks on children or rape of women as a routine occurrence, practically no unsafe streets. In short, who is "primitive" and "who is telling what to whom?"

DISCUSSION

We have seemingly emphasized that American national culture—with noticeable trends inherited from its European and colonial background, settler-regime frontierism with a credo of "manifest destiny," together with the post-1945 and the post-1989 sense of superpowerism—places a premium on negation, rather than affirmation, of the other, the *seemingly unknowable other!* In short, it possesses a constant hunger for an enemy (a quasi–"last Mohican") to concentrate its thinking, and such an "Indianizable" nest of potentially usable enemies nowadays seems to be located in the Middle East, which coincidentally is *where the oil is.*

In a multi-ethnic society composed of more than 200 ethnic groups and combinations thereof, there is always a modicum of hostility against the unfamiliar, a hostility encouraged by belief in possessive individualism, litigation, adversarial relations, confrontation. Invidious comparisons abound, particularly as measured against a faraway, unknown, and "non-Christian" enemy, Islam. Islam and Muslims serve as a target for displacement of frustration onto an allegedly menacing and evil "other." This image is especially prevalent during an economic or war-mobilization crisis. Particularly now that the Soviets are no longer a threat, the Third World and Muslims can serve the same cultural mobilization and integration purpose.

Historically, Islam served as the nonhuman "other" for Europeans and now for Euro-Americans: Arabs, Turks, Persians, whatever ethnicity or ethnolinguistics Islam dwells in. Witness the deep roots of such antipathy as expressed in an archaic, 16th-century Eastertide prayer, where the word "Turks" stands for all Muslims: "Have mercy upon all Jews, *Turks*, infidels, and heretics—*Collect for Good Friday*" (Trench, *Dictionary of Obsolete English*, 1958, 254, emphasis in the original). This prayer contrasts with Islamic countries at the time, in which Christians and Jews, considered by Muslims as "People of the Book," that is, of the Gospels and the Torah, were well treated, not singled out with special prayers as excludable entities.

Within the United States nowadays, particularly since the Kennedy era, institutional racism in America against Catholics, Jews, and Blacks has considerably diminished, particularly in the mass media. Many discriminatory laws have been struck down, and rightly so. There is, however, nowadays one ethnic group in the United States that consistently bears the brunt of media discrimination: Arab Americans. It seems that everyone can make pejorative remarks on TV and in newspapers against them and get away with it: They are now a focal point of, and a substitute for, prejudice and stereotyping that used to be directed against a number of other ethnic and ethnoreligious groups. This prejudice in part because of hostile U.S. relations with some Arab countries in the Middle East, because of the tumultuous, festering nature of the Palestine-Israel problem, and because Arab Americans are not noticeable in the "political process" or effectively organized as a lobby. Superficial knowledge of Arab culture and deep ignorance about the Middle East and its ethnic groups fuel Arab-bashing on American television, in American congressional attitudes, and in editorials and cartoons appearing in magazines and newspapers.

Anti-Arabism can be considered a form of anti-Semitism. Muslim Arabs in particular believe that they are, like Jews, descendants of Abraham. While the former are descended from Isaac, Abraham's and Sarah's son, the latter are descended from Ishmael, Abraham, and Hagar's son. In this context, then, we may think of two kinds of anti-Semitism: *anti-Isaackism*, directed against Jews, and *anti-Ishmaelism*, directed against Arabs.

With the success of the peace process in the Middle East and restabilization of the region, anti-Arab, anti-Jewish, and anti-Muslim sentiments may be somewhat lessened. American academic discourse may then perhaps be less distorted.

REFERENCES

Baudrillard, J. (1975). *The mirror of production*. St. Louis, MO: Telos Press.

Crim, K. (Ed.). (1989). *The perennial dictionary of world religions*. San Francisco: Harper & Row.

Flapan, S. (1987). *The birth of Israel: Myths and reality*. New York: Pantheon Books.

Gossett, T. F. (1965). *Race: The history of an idea in America*. New York: Schocken.

Habermas, J. (1975). *Legitimation crisis*. Boston: Beacon Press.

Hagstrom, J. (1989). *Beyond Reagan: The new landscape of American politics*. New York: Penguin.

Halsell, G. (1981). *Journey to Jerusalem*. New York: Macmillan.

Halsell, G. (1986). *Prophecy and politics*. Chicago: Lawrence Hill.

Hayes, J. R. (Ed.). (1983). *The Genius of Arab civilization: Source of renaissance*. Cambridge, MA: The MIT Press.

Hitti, P. K. (1970). *History of the Arabs* (10th ed.). New York: St. Martin's Press.

Jacobs, P. et al. (Eds.). (1971). *To serve the devil.* 2 vols. New York: Vintage.

Keen, S. (1991). *Faces of the enemy: Reflections of the hostile imagination.* New York: Harper.

Khleif, B. B. (1980a). Insiders, outsiders, and renegades: Towards a classification of ethno-linguistic labels. In H. Giles and B. St. Jaques (Eds.), *Language and ethnic relations* (pp. 159–172). Oxford: Pergamon Press.

Khleif, B. B. (1980b). *Language, ethnicity, and education in Wales.* The Hague, Netherlands: Mouton de Gruyter.

Khleif, B. B. (1982). Ethnicity and language with reference to the Frisian case: Issues of schooling, work, and identity. In Zondag, K. (Ed.), *Bilingualism in Friesland* (pp. 175–203). Franeker, Friesland, Netherlands: T. Weber Publishers.

Khleif, B. B. (1984, Spring). The ethnic crisis in Lebanon: Towards a sociocultural analysis. *Sociologus, 34*(2), 121–139.

Khleif, B. B. (1986, Autumn). The nation-state and the control of consciousness: Towards a sociology of schooling, language, and colonialism. *Sociologia Internationalis, 24*(2), 219–244.

Khleif, B. B. (1990, Spring). Ethnicity as a social movement: The case of Arab Americans. *Sociologus, 40*(1), 19–38.

Khleif, B. B. (1992, March 28). *Corporate culture: Japanese vs. American codes.* Paper read at the annual meeting of the Society for Applied Anthropology, Memphis, TN.

Kwitny, J. (1987). *Endless enemies: The making of an unfriendly world.* New York: Penguin.

Norton, A. (1991, November-December). Gender, sexuality, and the Iraq of our imagination. *Middle-East Report, 173,* 26–28.

Said, E. W. (1978) *Orientalism.* New York: Pantheon.

Shlaim, A. (1994). *War and peace in the Middle East: A critique of American policy.* New York: Viking.

Shohat, E., & Stam, R. (1994). *Unthinking Eurocentrism: Multiculturalism and the media.* New York: Routledge.

Sontag, S. (1969). What is happening in America. In *Styles of radical will* (pp. 193–204). New York: Farrar, Straus and Giroux.

Trench, M. C. (1958). *Dictionary of obsolete English.* Wisdom Library Series No. 38. New York: Philosophical Library.

Trimingham, J. S. (1979). *Christianity among the Arabs in Pre-Islamic times.* New York: Longman.

SELECTED BIBLIOGRAPHY

Bell, E., Haas, L., & Sells, L. (Eds.). (1995). *From mouse to mermaid: The politics of film, gender, and culture.* Bloomington: Indiana University Press.

Berumen, F. J. G. (1995). *The Chicano/Hispanic image in American film.* New York: Vantage.

Bogle, D. (1992). *Toms, coons, mulattoes, mammies and bucks: An interpretive history of Blacks in American films.* New York: Continuum Publishing.

Bona, M. J., & Tamburri, A. J. (Eds.). (1996). *Through the looking glass: Italian and Italian/American images in the media: Selected essays from the 27th annual conference of the American Italian Historical Association.* Staten Island: American Italian Historical Association.

Campbell, C. P. (1995). *Race, myth, and the news.* Thousand Oaks, CA: Sage.

Dennis, E. E., & Pease, E. C. (Eds.). (1996). *The media in black and white.* New Brunswick, NJ: Transaction.

Dines, G., & Humez, J. M. (Eds.). (1995). *Gender, race, and class in media: A text reader.* Thousand Oaks, CA: Sage.

Friedman, L. (1982). *Hollywood's image of the Jew.* New York: Ungar.

Friedman, L. (Ed.). (1991). *Unspeakable images: Ethnicity and the American cinema.* Urbana: University of Illinois Press.

Ghareeb, E. (Ed.). (1983). *Split vision: The portrayal of Arabs in the American media.* Washington, DC: American-Arab Affairs Council.

Gray, H. (1995). *Watching race: Television and the struggle for "blackness."* Minneapolis: University of Minnesota Press.

Hudson, M., & Wolfe, R. (Eds.). (1980). *The American media and the Arabs.* Washington, DC: Georgetown University Press.

Hunter, J. D. (1991). *Culture wars: The struggle to define America.* New York: Basic Books.

Kamalipour, Y. R. (Ed.). (1995). *The U.S. media and the Middle East: Image and perception.* Westport, CT: Greenwood.

Lichter, R. S., & Amundson, D. R. (Eds.). (1994). *Distorted reality: Hispanic characters in TV entertainment.* Washington, DC: Center for Media and Public Affairs.

Lichter, R. S. (1996). *Don't blink: Hispanics in television entertainment.* Washington, DC: National Council of La Raza.

List, C. (1996). *Chicano images: Refiguring ethnicity in mainstream film.* New York: Garland.

Naficy, H. (Ed.). (1993). *Otherness and the media: The ethnography of the imagined and the imaged.* Langhorne, PA: Harwood Academic Publishers.

Navarrete, L., & Kamasaki, C. (Eds.). (1994). *Out of the picture. Hispanics in the media: State of Hispanic America.* Washington, DC: National Council of La Raza.

Philipsen, G. (1992). *Speaking culturally: Explorations in social communication.* Albany, NY: State University of New York Press.

Reyes, L., & Rubie, P. (Eds.). (1994). *Hispanics in Hollywood: An encyclopedia of film and television.* New York: Garland.

Riggins, S. H. (Ed.). (1992). *Ethnic minority media: An international perspective.* Newbury Park, CA: Sage.

Ross, K. (1996). *Black and White media: Black images in popular film and television.* Cambridge, MA: Polity Press.

Shohat, E. (1994). *Unthinking Eurocentrism: Multiculturalism and the media.* New York: Routledge.

Sowell, T. (1994). Race and culture: A world view. New York: Basic Books.

Storey, J. (Ed.). (1996). *What is cultural studies: A reader.* New York: St. Martin's Press.

Toplin, R. B. (Ed.). (1993). *Hollywood as mirror: Changing views of "outsiders" and "enemies" in American movies.* Westport, CT: Greenwood.

Turner, P. A. (1994). *Ceramic uncles and celluloid mammies: Black images and their influence on culture.* Desplaines, IL: Bantam-Doubleday-Dell.

Valdivia, A. N. (Ed.). (1995). *Feminism, multiculturalism, and the media: Global diversities.* Thousand Oaks, CA: Sage.

van Dijk, T. A. (1987). *Communicating racism: Ethnic prejudice in thought and talk.* Newbury Park, CA: Sage.

Wilson, C. C. (1995). *Race, multiculturalism, and the media: From mass to class communication.* Thousand Oaks, CA: Sage.

Winokur, M. (1995). *American laughter: Immigrants, ethnicity and 1930's Hollywood film comedy.* Basingtoke: Macmillan.

Woll, A. L. (1987). *Ethnic and racial images in American film and television.* New York: Garland.

ABOUT THE EDITORS

Yahya R. Kamalipour (Ph.D., University of Missouri–Columbia) is Professor of Mass Communications and director of graduate studies at the Department of Communication and Creative Arts, Purdue University Calumet, Hammond, IN. He has taught university courses at Oxford, England, and Tehran, Iran. He is editor of *The U.S. Media and the Middle East: Image and Perception* (1995), and *Mass Media in the Middle East: A Comprehensive Handbook* (with Hamid Mowlana, 1994), and is a board member of the Cultural Environment Movement. A recipient of several significant awards, including Speech Communication Association's Distinguished Scholarship Award in International and Intercultural Communication (1966), his articles on media effects, broadcast education, image and perception, and international communication have appeared in professional and mainstream publications in the United States and abroad.

Theresa Carilli (Ph.D., Southern Illinois University) is an associate professor of Communication and Creative Arts at Purdue University Calumet. Her work explores the connection between culture and the creative process. She has published a book of plays, *Women As Lovers: Two Plays* (Guernica Editions, 1996). Her work appears in *Performance Studies: The Next Millenium* (NCA Press, 1998), *Beginnings* (Alyson, 1998), *Italian American Women Writers* (Women's Press of Canada, 1998), *Fuori* (Bordighera, 1996), and *Performance Studies: The Interpretation of Aesthetic Texts* (St. Martin's Press, 1992). She has a forthcoming book of plays which explores the Italian American experience and is currently guest editing an upcoming theater issue of *Voices in Italian Americana*.

ABOUT THE CONTRIBUTORS

B. Lee Artz is assistant professor and chair of the Social Justice Task Force in the Department of Communication at Loyola University, Chicago. A former union steelworker and machinist, he has served on committees for affirmative action. His research interests include cultural studies, participatory communication, and communication and social change.

Jeffrey E. Brand is assistant professor of communication and media studies, Bond University, Queensland, Australia. His research interests include effects of media on gender and race, and on children and adolescent audiences.

Christopher P. Campbell is assistant professor of communications, Department of Communication, Xavier University, New Orleans. He is the author of *Race, Myth and the News* (1995).

Meta G. Carstarphen is assistant professor of journalism at the University of North Texas, Denton. Her research interests include race, rhetoric, and the media.

Fernando Delgado is assistant professor of communication studies at Arizona State University West, Phoenix. His areas of research include rhetoric and politics, Mexican American popular culture, cultural identity, and film. His work is published in *Communication Quarterly, Howard Journal of Communication*, and *International Journal of Intercultural Relations*.

James A. Donowski is assistant professor of communication at the University of Illinois, Chicago. His research interests include statistical analysis of large textual and speech corpora, textual effects on audience cognitive/emotional response, user information retrieval behavior, mathematical modeling of optimal persuasive messages, and network analysis.

Bradley S. Greenberg is distinguished professor of communication and telecommunication, Michigan State University, East Lansing. He is immediate past president and fellow of the International Communication Association. An accomplished scholar, his research focuses on the media socialization of young people in different countries.

Beth Haller is assistant professor of communications, Department of Speech and Mass Communication, Towson State University, Towson, Maryland. Her research interests include quantitative and qualitative content analysis of news media, particularly coverage of the disability community.

Christy Hammer is a Civil Rights–funded teacher trainer in educational equity issues and race and sex discrimination for the New Hampshire Department of Education, Concord. She is also an adjunct instructor in sociology and women's studies at the University of New Hampshire. She has written on the politics of multicultural education and on the gender equity implications of sex differences in brain research in such journals as *Brain and Behavior Science*.

Marouf Hasian, Jr. is assistant professor of communications, Department of Communication, Arizona State University, Tempe. His areas of research include ethnicity and the mass media, law and rhetoric, and postcolonial discourse. He is the author of *The Rhetoric of Eugenics* (1996).

Darnell Montez Hunt is assistant professor of sociology at the University of Southern California, Los Angeles. Prior to pursuing his studies in sociology, he worked at a Washington, DC, local television station. He is the author of *Screening the Los Angeles "Riots": Race, Seeing, and Resistance*. His areas of research include sociological studies of mass media and race.

Mee-Eun Kang is a teaching assistant in the Department of Communication, the University of Michigan, Ann Arbor. A former newspaper reporter for *Kyung-Hyang Daily* in Korea, her research areas include public opinion formation processes under social influence, international communication, and effects of advertising.

Bud B. Khleif is professor of sociology in the Department of Sociology and Anthropology, University of New Hampshire, Durham. His research interests include ethnic studies, cross-cultural communication, and identity. He has published numerous articles in professional journals in the United States and abroad.

Tae Guk Kim is associate professor of journalism at the University of North Texas, Denton. His research interests include Asian ethnic press in the United States and the media.

Rebecca Ann Lind is assistant professor of communication at the University of Illinois, Chicago. Her research interests include audience studies, evaluations of media performance, journalism, media ethics, and race and gender issues in media.

Greta D. Little is associate professor of children and adolescent literature, English Department, University of South Carolina, Columbia. Her interests in Arabs and their portrayal in children's books grew out of her teaching experience, as a Fulbright lecturer, in Morocco in 1993. She has published several articles on children's literature, including an edition of Christopher Pearse Cranch's fiction for children.

Scott McLean director of Warm Springs Healthy Nations, a joint project of the Robert Wood Johnson Foundation and the Federated Tribes of Warm Springs, Oregon. His research interests include intercultural communication, native language preservation, computer-assisted language learning, and comics.

Richard Morris is associate professor of communication, Department of Communication, Northern Illinois University, DeKalb. He has authored and edited several books and articles on culture and communication, including *Sinners, Lovers, and Heroes: An Essay on Memorializing in Three American Cultures*, and *Devouring Savages: The Cannibalization of Native America* (with Mary E. Stuckey, in progress).

Angela M. S. Nelson is assistant professor in the Department of Popular Culture at Bowling Green State University (Ohio) where she teaches courses on Black popular culture, popular music, television studies, and television situation comedy.

Mark P. Orbe is assistant professor of communications, Department of Communication, Indiana University Southwest, New Albany. His research interests include exploring the relationship between culture and communication in a variety of contexts.

Jim Schnell is associate professor of communication at Ohio Dominican College. His research focuses on cross-cultural communication, specifically U.S.-China relations. He has traveled to China six times, and has lectured at Northern Jiaotong University in Beijing. He is also a major in the Air Force Intelligence Agency, as a reservist.

Ruth Seymour is a lecturer in journalism, Department of Communication, Wayne State University, Detroit, Michigan. Her research interests include intercultural communication via mass media.

Alan J. Spector is professor of sociology, Department of Behavioral Science, Purdue University Calumet, Hammond, IN. He is co-author (with

P. Knapp) of *Crisis and Change: Basic Questions of Marxist Sociology* (1991), recipient of the Distinguished Scholarship Award from the Section on Marxist Sociology in the American Sociological Association. He is active in antiracist community groups and has served on the boards of several journals. He is also the founder/editor of REVS, an Internet List that studies racial/religious/ethnic violence.

Mary E. Stuckey is associate professor of political science, Department of Political Science, University of Mississippi, Oxford. She has authored several books and articles on presidential and political communication, including *The President as Interpreter-in-Chief*, and *Devouring Savages: The Cannibalization of Native America* (with Richard Morris, in progress).

Alice A. Tait is associate professor of communication at the Department of Journalism, Central Michigan University, Mt. Pleasant. She has received several academic awards, including a Teaching Excellence Award, and a Teaching Fellowship Award. An active scholar in several professional organizations, her research interests include journalism, mass media research, public communication, and African American studies.

JoAnn M. Valenti is professor of communications at Brigham Young University, Provo, Utah. Her research areas include natural resources, environmental issues, journalism, and mass media. She serves on the board of the Society of Environmental Journalists.

Marsha Woodbury is director of Information Technology for the Graduate School of Library and Information Science at the University of Illinois, Urbana-Champaign. Prior to her current position, from 1971 to 1989, she and her husband lived in New Zealand where they farmed and worked. Her research interests include computer-aided instruction, journalism, and information technologies.

INDEX